CW01506924

Investigating Murder

CLARENDON STUDIES IN CRIMINOLOGY

Published under the auspices of the Institute of Criminology,
University of Cambridge, the Mannheim Centre, London School of
Economics, and the Centre for Criminological Research, University of Oxford.

GENERAL EDITOR: PER-OLOF WIKSTRÖM *(University of Cambridge)*

EDITORS: ALISON LIEBLING AND MANUEL EISNER
(University of Cambridge)

DAVID DOWNES AND PAUL ROCK
(London School of Economics)

ROGER HOOD, LUCIA ZEDNER, AND RICHARD YOUNG
(University of Oxford)

Recent titles in this series:

Investigating Murder

Detective Work and the Police Response
to Criminal Homicide

Martin Innes

OXFORD
UNIVERSITY PRESS

OXFORD
UNIVERSITY PRESS

Great Clarendon Street, Oxford OX2 6DP

Oxford University Press is a department of the University of Oxford.
It furthers the University's objective of excellence in research, scholarship,
and education by publishing worldwide in

Oxford New York

Auckland Bangkok Buenos Aires Cape Town Chennai
Dar es Salaam Delhi Hong Kong Istanbul Karachi Kolkata
Kuala Lumpur Madrid Melbourne Mexico City Mumbai Nairobi
São Paulo Shanghai Taipei Tokyo Toronto

Oxford is a registered trade mark of Oxford University Press
in the UK and in certain other countries

Published in the United States
by Oxford University Press Inc., New York

British Library Cataloguing in Publication Data

Data available

Library of Congress Cataloging in Publication Data

Innes, Martin.
Investigating murder: detective work and the police
response to criminal homicide / Martin Innes
p. cm. – (Clarendon studies in criminology)
Includes bibliographical references and index.
1. Murder–Investigation. 2. Detectives. I. Title. II. Series.
HV8079.H6 156 2003   363.25'9523–dc21   2002192599
ISBN 0–19–925942–9
1 3 5 7 9 10 8 6 4 2

Typeset by Kolam Information Service Pvt Ltd
Printed in Great Britain
on acid-free paper by
T.J. International Ltd., Padstow, Cornwall

For Bernard and Jennifer Innes

General Editor's Introduction

The *Clarendon Studies in Criminology* was inaugurated in 1994 under the auspices of the centres of criminology at the Universities of Cambridge and Oxford and the London School of Economics. It was the successor to *Cambridge Studies in Criminology*, founded by Sir Leon Radzinowicz and J.W.C. Turner almost sixty years ago.

Criminology is a field of study that covers everything from research into the causes of crime to the politics of the operations of the criminal justice system. Researchers in different social and behavioural sciences, criminal justice and law, all make important contributions to our understanding of the phenomena of crime. The *Clarendon Studies in Criminology* series tries to reflect this diversity by publishing high quality theory and research monographs by established scholars as well as by young scholars of great promise from all different kinds of academic backgrounds.

Few things catch the public's imagination as much as cases of murder and their investigations. Numerous are the media accounts that follow police and forensic work of high profile crime cases. But what do we really know about the investigative process? In *'Investigating Murder: Detective Work and the Police Response to Criminal Homicide'*, Martin Innes gives us insights into the inner workings of the criminal investigations of homicides. He describes and analyses in detail the investigative process through an explorative qualitative study of an English police force. He also offers us a tentative theoretical framework for understanding the process of investigation. Innes sees the work of the homicide investigators as 'concerned with the social construction of meaning' which 'allows both the police and other socio-legal actors to act as if they know how and why the victim died, and who was responsible.' He also argues for an 'important symbolic dimension' of police investigations of murder as they relate to 'the maintenance and reproduction of the moral, social and cultural order.'

This book should be an interesting read for all those involved in criminal investigations, and more broadly in the criminal justice system. Innes' book is also likely to engage those who want to develop a more academic understanding of criminal justice. The ideas and interpretations put forward by Innes are thought provoking and at times challenging. They will most likely create debate. They will force practitioners and academics alike to reflect upon their own perspective on the criminal investigation process and its role in society. And that cannot be a bad thing.

Per-Olof H. Wikström,
University of Cambridge &
Centre for Advanced Studies in the Social and
Behavioral Sciences, Stanford, (2002–03)
December 2002

Preface and Acknowledgements

In writing this book my aim has been to throw light on the subject of police murder investigations. At first glance this seems to be something of an ironic objective, in that few areas of policing are subject to as much scrutiny as the work that is conducted on major crime enquiries. Stories on television, in the press, and in literature serve as an almost constant reminder that the investigation of unlawful deaths remains a key component of the police function. But although these stories frequently offer glimpsed descriptions of what it is that the police do, for the most part they do not provide a detailed analysis of the nature of the investigative work performed.

In what follows my aims remain modest. I see this book as an exploratory study that seeks to understand the practices, processes, and procedures utilized by detectives, together with the problems that they encounter, when investigating homicides. In focusing upon this topic I touch on a wide range of issues drawn from the disciplines of sociology, criminology, and law in an attempt to provide a comprehensive account of detective work. Throughout the book I have sought to integrate an empirically grounded approach with ways of seeing informed by themes drawn from wider debates in social theory, the purpose being not just to describe the work performed, but to provide genuine insight into how and why it is performed in particular ways. In addition then to the detailed descriptions and analyses of the work of detectives, underpinning the discussion is a concern to better understand aspects of the relationship between beliefs and actions. Reduced to its basics, stripped of context and detail, detective work is about establishing and fixing a set of beliefs about how and why a particular crime happened. The production of these beliefs is the outcome of particular investigative actions, which are themselves informed by a wider belief system. It was never a stated intention of mine when starting this research to examine this aspect of social life, rather this theme of the interplay and inter-working of belief and action emerged in a number of permutations from the data.

I hope that the approach adopted will assist the book in finding an audience among both academics and practitioners. For those with academic interests in policing, the sociology of deviance, criminology, and law, this book is intended as a contribution to our collective knowledge of one of the mechanisms by which social control is enacted and social order produced in contemporary society; whilst for police officers and others working in the criminal justice system, I would hope that the study provides greater depth of understanding in terms of the work that is conducted.

In working on this book I have accrued many, many debts. The present book started life as a doctoral thesis at the London School of Economics. And although, in the intervening years, I have substantially reworked and developed some of the ideas, it still owes much to my supervisors who got me through the Ph.D. process. I would therefore like to say a special thank you to Professors Bridget Hutter and Robert Reiner, for their support, kindness, and intellectual guidance during my time at LSE and since. I owe you both an enormous amount. Thanks also to Paul Rock, David Downes, and Stan Cohen for sharing their thoughts and ideas, and in the process showing me what it means to be a scholar. Since leaving the LSE, in developing my ideas I have benefited from debates and discussions with my colleagues at the University of Surrey, including Nigel Fielding, Alan Clarke, Geoff Cooper, and Roger Tarling. Thanks also to Ian Robertson, Graham Hill, Dave Gee, Nina Cope, Andy Wilson, and Ian Loader whose kindness has helped me at different stages in working on this project. The study was made possible in the first place by the remarkable assistance provided to me by the police force with whom I conducted the fieldwork and although I cannot name the force concerned, or any of the officers who assisted me in various ways, I would like to record my gratitude to them for all the help they provided. Some of the ideas included in the book were originally presented in papers published in the *British Journal of Criminology* and the *British Journal of Sociology*, and I am grateful to the editors and referees for their comments and criticisms. John Louth and Oxford University Press were extremely patient with me during the publication process and have helped to improve the presentation of my work.

Finally, the biggest thank-you to my family, Mum, Dad, Joanne, and Helen, who have been a source of strength and support, and made the effort worthwhile.

Contents

List of Figures

List of Tables

PART I
Setting the Scene

PART I

Setting the Scene

1

Detective Work

The body of the victim was discovered on a winter morning, on a remote piece of land near to a small river. The police were called, and due to the extent and nature of the victim's injuries a murder investigation was launched. A Home Office pathologist attended the scene and later at the post-mortem examination he confirmed that the young woman had been subjected to a violent assault before being strangled to death.

In the meantime, the police enquiries into the victim's death had begun to make progress. A significant proportion of murders are solved for the police because a suspect is still at the scene of the offence when they arrive. Where, as in this case, there is no obvious suspect, then the first tasks to be undertaken are to collect the evidence from the scene and to identify the victim. The preliminary investigation quickly identified the young woman and a number of significant pieces of forensic evidence were located at the scene. Following on from this, the unpleasant task of breaking the bad news to the victim's family was undertaken. As is usual in murder cases, the family were to act as an important source of information for the police. Through interviews with them and several friends of the deceased, the police began to build up a picture of the victim's life. They collected details on the victim's habits, her likes and dislikes, who she was friends with, and her movements leading up to the time when it was estimated that she had been attacked. Interestingly for the police, the information collected suggested that for several months the victim had been associating with a group of people who were not her usual type of friends.

As a result of this information the police elected to carry out a line of enquiry to examine the potential links between the victim, the crime, and her 'friends'. Background checks on these 'friends' revealed that they were 'known' to the police and a decision was taken to follow up this lead. The three individuals were interviewed separately by police and they all confirmed that they had last seen the victim two days before the body was found, when they had spent the evening with her. The two men in the group made a statement to police saying that at the end of the evening, as usual, they had walked the victim to the railway station and she had left, safe and well. For the police this was the last confirmed sighting of the victim alive. Appeals through the local media for sightings of the victim prior to the assault had been made, but little information of any value had been forthcoming.

Whilst all this was going on, further enquiries had been carried out to explore the possible connections between the three suspects and the crime. The detectives carrying out these enquiries un-covered strong substantive evidence which linked the suspects to the murder. The suspects were confronted with the new evidence in further interviews. The two men continued to try and deny any involvement despite the highly incriminating evidence against them. However, the third member of the group, the wife of one of the men, when confronted with the evidence, was persuaded to incriminate both her husband and the other man in the killing, whilst denying any involvement on her part. Combined with the physical evidence and other information collected by the police enquiries, the wife's statements provided the police with a strong case against the two men. After consultations with members of the Crown Prosecution Service, the two men were charged with murder. Further enquiries were conducted by detectives in order to substantiate the case and a bloodstain that was found on a piece of clothing of one of the suspects was shown to match the blood type of the victim. Nine months later the jury at the Crown Court returned a unanimous verdict that the two defendants were guilty of murder.

The above is an outline of a real case, involving real people, in real situations. It is something that very few of us will ever experi-ence first-hand and yet as a story it is very familiar. These are the sorts of event that are discussed on a daily basis in our newspapers and on our televisions. News presentations relay these types of narrative to us from the outside world, but death and violence of these kinds are also a staple ingredient of what we consume as entertainment. There is a general level of awareness within our culture about murder, murderers, and murder investigations, which is perhaps striking only in relation to how few of us are ever involved in such events in real life.

However, the actual processes through which the facts of such cases are established, the sorts of details that I provided at the start of this book, have not been subjected to rigorous, detailed, and methodologically informed academic analysis. Whilst there has been a large growth in the industry of police studies over the past twenty years, a development which has greatly expanded our knowledge of many of the social and technical aspects of the police and policing, there remains a large gap in our knowledge in terms of how the police respond to one of the most serious types of crime, murder.

Home Office statistics record that approximately 90% of all the 700 or so criminal homicides that occur each year in England and Wales are 'cleared' by police. This high clearance rate, combined with the low levels of incidence compared with other crimes, have helped to discourage researchers from looking at this aspect of police work. However, a 'clearance' as defined by the Home Office Counting Rules is not equivalent to a successful prosecution. In addition to the 10% of homicides that remain long-term unsolved, in a further 25% of all cases recorded as homicide between 1989 and 1999 all suspects have been acquitted by the courts. Additionally, in a number of cases where the suspect or suspects are charged with murder, they are convicted of a substantively 'lesser crime' in court. Added to this, there are a small but increasing number of cases where the conviction has been overturned by the Court of Appeal, as a result of problems with the original investigation being identified. It is also worth noting that police often experience problems and difficulties in relation to those crimes that they do solve. Furthermore, recent research by Her Majesty's Inspectorate of Constabulary (2000) has suggested that different police forces in England and Wales appear to have different levels of investigative performance in terms of responding to major crimes. This combination of factors establishes murder investigation as a legitimate object for research.

This study is presented as a step along the path to an increased awareness of the social reality of investigating crimes of murder.[1] It seeks to open up 'the black box' of murder investigations to examine how detectives investigate these crimes and why they do it in this way. The book provides a conceptually informed, empirical examination of the practices, processes, and problems of homicide investigation. The data on which the study is based were collected via a multi-method strategy, combining ethnographic observation of five investigations in progress, semi-structured interviews with detectives of different ranks and roles who have experience of investigating homicides, and ethnographic content analysis of police case files.[2]

In this study, investigative work is understood as being more constructive than descriptive. Detectives investigating a crime do not simply compile the facts of the case from a range of sources, rather they make interpretations and inferences, which contribute to how the 'facts' of a case are assembled and established. Consequently, investigative work can be conceptualized as being involved in the social construction of meaning.

Investigation and the Construction of Meaning

A murder does not possess some pre-existent ontological status. An act becomes classified as a murder, or some other form of homicide, as a result of the interpretative and definitional work that is performed by detectives and other actors within the criminal justice process. Similarly, the fact that we are able to label individuals as murderers also depends upon such processes. Drawing upon a form of interpretative sociology, this study argues that the fact that the public and other agencies of the criminal justice system understand and react to particular incidents as murders, with certain actions and roles being accepted as constitutive of the event concerned, is an outcome largely attributable to the interpretative, definitional, and classificatory work performed by detectives.[3] As such, the investigative function can be identified as being concerned with 'making crime' (Ericson, 1993) and 'constructing the case for the prosecution' (McConville et al., 1991), through the interpretation and application of specific labels and understandings which establish crimes as situationally embedded artefacts of the legal process (Becker, 1963).

Although informed by previous studies of detectives, this study also seeks to overcome a number of limitations that can be identified in the case of earlier research in this area. In particular, whilst McConville, Sanders, and Leng (1991) and Ericson (1993) respectively offer a number of important and penetrating insights into the social worlds of detectives, their accounts are problematic in several respects. Most significantly, they are both founded upon an implicit assumption that the sorts of processes and problems that they identify through studying fairly standard and routine forms of detective work are common to all investigations. Little sense is provided of how the characteristics of individual incidents and different crime types might invoke different investigative problematics and thereby shape the practices of detectives. Moreover, because they commence their analysis of crime investigation at the stage where a suspect 'enters the frame', McConville *et al.* miss a lot of the important work that precedes this point of an investigation.

Whilst obviously influenced by these works, I will also seek to overcome the limitations that they exhibit. In particular, my objective is to provide a more focused and nuanced examination of the logics, processes, and techniques that detectives employ when investigating a particular type of crime. Because I have restricted my focus to one particular type of investigation, I make no claim that the concepts, practices, and methods that I identify are to be found in other types of police enquiry, although I have a suspicion that they may be.

Developing the findings of the earlier studies of detective work, crime investigation can be conceptualized as a complex form of 'sense-making'. Detectives, through the investigative process, attempt to negotiate and assemble an account of what 'really' happened in the incident that explains who did what to whom and why. Notions that the account produced is 'true', 'real', or 'factual' are not then a reflection of some quality inherent in the incident itself, nor the evidence used as 'warrants' within the account. The 'facts' of the case are dialectical social accomplishments that result from the interpretative practices enacted by detectives situated within a process of enquiry. They are used by detectives to construct instruments for action informing subsequent lines of enquiry.[4] The attribution of the social meanings associated with murder to an incident is then dependent upon symbolically mediated, inter-subjective agreements, through which a sense of a stable 'reality' is actively negotiated and constructed.

Framed by the criminal justice process, in assembling their account of the incident, detectives routinely identify, interpret, and construct information, sometimes contested, at other times complementary, derived from an array of sources, thereby attributing particular legal and social meanings to the incident concerned. But key to understanding how such meanings are assembled and sustained are the dramaturgical qualities of the communications that are made as an integral part of the investigative process.[5] Particular aspects of the incident are selectively emphasized and focused upon by investigators (i.e. the actions of the suspect and victim), whilst other material that is viewed as having less influence upon how the act transpired is selectively ignored or downplayed. As such, the police identify what are and are not the key points of tension surrounding how aspects of the situation are to be defined and understood, thus shaping the work performed in subsequent stages of the criminal justice process.

Detectives and Crime Investigation

The approach to understanding homicide investigation work, as outlined above, builds upon and develops a number of themes established in the academic literature on policing. Empirical research has suggested that in the majority of cases, crime investigation is composed of a fairly routine and mundane set of activities. A number of studies have found that by far the most significant determinant of investigative success is the quantity and quality of information provided to the police by members of the public (Greenwood et al., 1977; Burrows and Tarling, 1987; Chatterton, 1976; Zander, 1979).[6] A recent study (Audit Commission, 1993) found that 55% of all arrests resulted from actions taken by uniform officers and identification evidence from witnesses and/or victims, and that approximately 40% of detections occurred within two days of the offence being reported. Overall, it has been suggested that only a small proportion of crimes cleared can be directly attributed to police investigative activity (Greenwood et al., 1977; Steer, 1980; Bottomley and Coleman, 1982). As Ericson (1993, p. ix) identifies, '. . . detectives are rarely able to proceed with an investigation that starts out "cold" and ends up with a chargeable suspect. Rather they are dependent on others to identify and produce suspects, and their main work is routine processing and preparing documents on suspects who have been produced by others.' However, we should not dismiss the importance of such work, because as the Audit Commission (1993) demonstrated, in 51%

of cases studied it was information collected in interviews conducted by detectives that led to a detection being recorded.

If we narrow our focus somewhat to concentrate upon those offences classified as 'violent crimes', a number of interesting trends emerge. In England in 1995, there were on average 5.14 violent crimes per 1,000 members of the population and the police detected 71.8% of these as primary detections. This compares with figures of 98.0 per 1,000 population and a primary detection rate of 21.8% for all crime types. The fact that the police consistently clear up a higher proportion of violent crimes than is the case for most other crime types can be explained by virtue of the fact that the inter-personal nature of violent crime means that there is often sufficient witness and physical evidence available to assist the police in their enquiries. Secondly, offences involving violence are often seen as being particularly serious, as a result of which they may receive more thorough and assiduous investigation.

The Dialectic of 'Craft' and 'Science' in Detective Work

The detectives studied understood the conduct of their work as founded upon a 'dialectical' synthesis of 'craft' skills blended with a 'scientific' style of rationality. They saw it as a mix of the rational and the intuitive, a synthesis of art and science. Good investigators were held to be possessed of a combination of fairly intuitive perceptual skills and 'technical' knowledge related to crime and its investigation.

The affinity between how police officers view their work and the 'craft' metaphor has been previously noted (Reiner, 1992) and there is a particularly strong association in this respect in terms of how detective work is conceptualized. At the heart of police notions of 'the good detective' was the sense that certain individuals had a particular flair for the work. The most valuable skills were held to be those developed through natural instinct and experience. Experience continues to be seen as central to becoming a good investigator and this is reflected in the ways that detectives continue to be selected and trained. It is held to be necessary to the development of the individual's 'recipe knowledge' that enables them to operate efficiently in order to solve crimes and expeditiously construct 'solid' cases. A form of 'streetwise' intelligence, and the ability to quickly interpret information and draw inferences from it, was particularly valued by detectives. This reflected their beliefs that investigators often had to be able to think creatively in obtaining evidence and be adroit at using and manipulating information, in order to identify and exploit even the smallest clue, lead, or inconsistency.

This echoes Hobbs's (1988) and Ericson's (1993) comments about the 'entrepreneurial' qualities of detective work, where investigators utilize a range of strategies to produce 'crime-relevant' information from their interactions with members of the public. A process that can, according to Willmer (1970), metaphorically be thought of as akin to an information game, in that the criminal is seeking to restrict the amount of information available to the police, whilst the police are looking to recover as much relevant information as possible (see also Sanders, 1977).

For more senior officers though, the creative skills of 'the case-maker' had to be tempered by a degree of integrity. They observed that 'wheelers and dealers' and 'rule-breakers' compound problems for the management of an investigation, in that as a supervisor you could never be sure of the accuracy of what they told you.

The craft metaphor and its application to investigative work is exemplified by notions used by detectives to describe their decision-making processes, such as 'playing a hunch'. Shorthand expressions such as this, which convey an almost instinctual, intuitive quality to investigative work, are replete with symbolic capital, reinforcing the conception of detectives as engaged in a craft. In actual fact, when detectives say they were 'playing a hunch', they were making decisions arrived at by the application of the tacit knowledge of policing, framed by the organizational structure. The processes that lead a detective to develop a 'hunch' that a particular line of enquiry is worth pursuing may be subtle and discreet, but that does not mean that they are not developed as a result of the particular skills possessed by that individual or their colleagues. This notion of the 'hunch' was linked to the sense that the detective should be able to empathize with and 'read' people. To understand the motivations that people may have for committing certain acts puts the detective in a position where they can exploit such knowledge to assist them in achieving their objectives.

But whilst this conception of investigative work as a 'craft' was a recurrent theme in the accounts provided by detectives, it was countered by an equally important emphasis upon a rational, logical, and systematic approach to the work. As Ericson (1993) has identified, much detective work is administrative in nature, based around 'accounting practices' that require detailed records of actions taken. Similarly, compliance with the rules of evidence and other legal criteria requires that detectives have a reasonable 'working knowledge' of the technical requirements of legal procedure. In addition, the ability to approach a problem in a systematic and orderly fashion, and to work it through accordingly, paying attention to the details, was perceived as an attribute for detectives.

Previous accounts of detectives and police identify a pervasive cynicism and suspicion that is seemingly endemic to their working personalities (Skolnick, 1994; Matza, 1969). My research suggests that such attitudes reflect the continual need for detectives to critically appraise the motives of the people and the quality of the information with which they have contact. Because of the nature of the work in which they are involved, detectives quickly become familiar with the fact that expecting the worst of people is a pragmatic strategy for coping with the uncertainties that surround the information provided to them. Not unreasonably, a steady stream of lies, purposely edited accounts, and half-truths induce a degree of caution in the police officer with even limited experience, about how people and information should be treated. To routinely act on 'bad' information would prove detrimental to the perceived competence of the individual officer amongst their peers and supervisors.

For the detectives themselves, successful and effective detective work required both individualized perceptual and interpretative faculties, together with a knowledge of legal procedure and regulations, and a systematic approach to solving particular investigative problems. It was obvious though from an examination of the activity logs on major enquiries that not all the detectives demonstrated these qualities all of the time. On a number of occasions officers were sent to re-check matters or re-interview witnesses, where it was felt that they had not collected sufficient detail or approached the activity with sufficient rigour.

The fact that there are established modes of practice and attitudes maintained by detectives, and that symbolic capital is attributed to their work, is the product of several connected and interacting social factors. These are: the historical legacy of how the detective function was developed and has evolved; the values

and norms of detective culture; the structurated relationship between the organization and its environment; the processes associated with becoming a detective; and an array of wider cultural
sensibilities. Therefore, although individual officers develop particular skills and attributes, the fundamental bases of detective
work can be seen to be socially produced and maintained.

The Development of the CID

Although in many respects detective work has become more technical and complex over recent years, and has been subject to a
range of reforms, the bases of many of the principal strategies
that continue to be routinely employed in the investigation of
crime can be traced back to the early development of the detective
role in policing. Furthermore, in terms of understanding the values
and orientations of detective culture, for many police officers, the
Criminal Investigation Department (CID) and the detective role
continue to represent 'real' police work, that is, crime-fighting,
action, and dealing with 'villains'. In part, this status attributed to
detective work is a reflection of wider cultural representations, but
it is also connected to the historical development of the detective
function at an organizational level.

Two detective inspectors and six detective sergeants, with a
specialist role to investigate crime, were first introduced into the
Metropolitan Police in 1842 as a response to a murder in that year
and the popular fear it provoked. Following on from these modest
beginnings and in spite of a number of high-level corruption scan-
dals, the detective branch of the service was progressively expanded
and in 1878 the CID was formed (Hobbs, 1988; Miller, 1979;
Klockars, 1985).

Although detective officers were given responsibility for the investigation of more serious crimes, the acquisition of professional
status for this specialist role was achieved only gradually. It was not
until the late nineteenth century and the early part of the twentieth
century that members of the CID began to enjoy the prestige and
status that are popularly associated with such work today. This
process of status enhancement was the outcome of both police and
state interventions to control crime being increasingly accepted by
the majority of the populace (Reiner, 1992; Garland, 1985). This
enhanced legitimacy was, in turn, buttressed through a degree of

'impression management', whereby the police undertook the 'strategic' prosecution of a number of 'high profile cases' (Hobbs, 1988). As part of this, the media co-operated in bringing the exploits of a number of 'celebrity detectives' to the attention of the public (Prothero, 1929).

The ways in which police detectives operated at this time served to further enhance the 'mythology' of the detective as an expert crime-solver. Prior to World War II only the Metropolitan Police was large enough to maintain a full-time CID. Consequently, the town and county forces had only limited capabilities in terms of responding to a small number of serious crimes when they occurred. In order to address this problem, an arrangement was set up by the Home Office, where any force could make a request for Scotland Yard to provide them with detective assistance if they were faced with a particularly difficult and serious crime. The assistance provided would consist of two experienced detectives with a rudimentary information management system, who would be despatched from London to aid the investigation. It was not until the Police Act of 1964 and the consequent reorganization of police jurisdictions and local government that all police forces could establish their own properly functioning CIDs. Up until this time though, the 'man from the Yard' mode of operation and its notion of the individual detective as an expert crime-solver contributed greatly to the status that detective work acquired, both within the police service and amongst the public.

From the police point of view, the status attributed to detective work is not simply a result of the historical legacy of detective working practices detailed previously. Detective work continues to be characterized by a greater degree of autonomy and a lower degree of visibility than patrol work (Ericson, 1993) and detectives are subject to much less direct supervision and are expected to work on and manage a fairly personal case-load (Irving and Dunnighan, 1993). In addition to this, the moral ambiguities of policing disputes located in diverse and factional communities which are characteristic of much uniform patrol activity (Waddington, 1994; Fielding, 1995; Fielding, 1991) are reduced when investigating crime and chasing 'bad guys' (Herbert, 1996). The status of detective work is further reinforced by the absence of a uniform, where plain clothes can be enacted by the detective as a source of 'negative identity' that sets them apart from the uniform officers (Manning, 1980).

Detectives are, however, subject to different kinds of pressures than uniform officers and even though the traditional individual-istic bias of CID working routines has been lessened in recent years, detectives are still expected to 'produce' an adequate number of detections. This leads to one of the central ironies of detective work, in that whilst culturally a premium is placed on 'good collars', or securing the conviction of 'hard-core villains', there is a feeling amongst many detectives that their individual competency and that of their department continues to be assessed through more quantitative criteria. Divisional detectives who spend too much time working on long, complex investigations which do not have any particular 'political' value, at the expense of maintaining a reasonable overall clear-up rate, risk the ire of both their colleagues and supervisors. They have to try and strike a balance in their active case-loads, between pursuing a few key 'villains' and continuing to contribute to the turnover of routine cases.

Detective Culture

These sorts of pressures are ameliorated by the presence of a strong occupational culture. A number of authors have identified that police culture, defined as a loosely coupled set of generalized rules of conduct, cognitive rationales of how the world is to be viewed, and socio-political norms and values, provides an orderly concept of what policing means for those engaged in the practical delivery of policing services (Chan, 1997; Van Maanen, 1978; Holdaway, 1983). It is then a mode of adaptation that enables officers to cope with the ironies and uncertainties of performing the police role. The occupational culture serves as a source of knowledge about 'doing' policing, establishing a set of background common-sense under-standings of what policing means and how in a practical sense it is accomplished.

Whilst there have not been any studies that have directly ad-dressed the issue of whether there is a distinctive detective culture, there is implicit evidence to suggest that the routines of detective work result in a radicalized and concentrated version of the police culture being found amongst detective officers (Hobbs, 1988; Sanders, 1977; Rachlin, 1995; Simon, 1991). This would be in line with the findings of other studies which have suggested that the culture varies according to rank (Reiner, 1991; Ianni and Ianni, 1983); the concerns of the particular police organization (Ericson and Haggarty, 1997; Wilson, 1968); and the particular role or specialism (Punch, 1985; Heidensohn, 1992).

Portrayals of police detectives have suggested that the CID is a bastion of 'macho values'. The detective is identified as the hard-working, hard-drinking, fornicating, and swearing crime-fighter. Hobbs (1988) locates the values of this version of detective culture as a reflection of, and stylistic appropriation of, devices used by those with whom detectives have contact. There is, though, some evidence to suggest that the trenchant machismo of detective culture is waning (Maguire and Norris, 1992), although my research suggests that this is not uniform and there are distinct variations as regards the pace at which change is occurring. Overall, the culture of CID is intensely pragmatic, concerned with getting the job done expediently, and underpinned by values which are conservative, machoistic, and action-orientated (Heidensohn, 1992; Young, 1991; Holdaway, 1983). These values are reinforced by a generalized suspicion of 'outsiders' and pessimism about human nature, together with a heightened awareness of potential dangers (Skolnick, 1994; Herbert, 1997) and a general sense of social isolation (Reiner, 1992; Van Maanen, 1978).

Organization and Environment

The values and norms of detective culture are inflected by the position of this aspect of police work within the structures of the organization and its attendant stratified status hierarchies. These cultural attributes that do much to order and structure investigative practices are shaped by the range of interspersed policy, procedural, product, and presentational discourses that effectively constitute the organization in a 'structural' sense (Innes, 2002). As such, the actions of police officers when responding to crimes and the products of such actions cannot be divorced from the context in which they are situated. Consequently, in order to understand how detectives 'do' investigative work, we need to understand the ways in which it is ordered by the organization of which it is a part and the environment that frames the organization. Policing 'on the ground' is contextually located, in that what is and is not deemed an appropriate course of action for an individual agent is conditioned by the social purposes and functions of the organization of which they are a member. Police work is a series of 'situationally justified actions' that are negotiated and ordered in accordance with the values, working rules, formal procedures, and interpretative practices established and reproduced through the structures of the police organization.

The way in which officers approach the problems encountered in police work, the accounts they produce in relation to such work, and their interactions with various other actors are 'framed' by the presence of the organization. This reflects a more general notion that forms of action and interaction are regulated by the structural contexts in which they take place (Goffman, 1974; Maines, 1977; Mead, 1934). Detective work is informed and shaped by a dialectical interplay between the ephemeral situational qualities of particular incidents and the more permanent structural qualities of the police organization. As such, the police organization provides a 'perspective' of how members are to view the world, render it meaningful and orderly, and make it suitable to act in (Weick, 1995). The presence of the organization mediates between the actions of the individual and the environment in which they are performed, encouraging those whose actions in effect 'perform' the organization to regularly act in ways and to assemble, use, and accept definitions of situations that are consistent with the organization's modes of working and its objectives. The hierarchical, administrative, and bureaucratic orders of the police organization provide a system of procedural, discursive, and cognitive relationships, regulations, and rules of various kinds, that shape the sorts of factors that have to be accounted for and negotiated at a practical level when doing policing.

For police officers, who are often called upon to make decisions and perform actions in complex and fraught circumstances, the organizational perspective encodes and interprets the environment, identifying its salient features. It provides shared understandings of the sorts of problems encountered, thereby establishing what are deemed appropriate actions and procedures, plausible interpretations, achievable ends, and expected outcomes. The organization does not of course exist outside of the actions performed by its individual members, rather it is both medium and outcome of these actions.

Becoming a Detective

The organizational perspective and the values of detective culture are acquired through experience and through the socialization processes associated with becoming a detective. Entry to the CID is, in a similar fashion to entry into the police, achieved through a combination of formal and informal socialization (Fielding, 1988; Sanders, 1977). The precise methods of selection have changed over time and tend to vary between forces, but a common factor of the selection procedures is that potential candidates should have served a form of 'apprenticeship' on crime-related work, where their suitability for entry into the CID is evaluated. This period of assessment may allow those already in the department not only to determine that this individual has the right basic skills, but also the right kind of personality to suit life as a plain-clothes officer, thus offering at least the potential for the cultural transmission of a particular set of values and attitudes between generations of CID officers. This apprenticeship period also serves to reinforce the sense that investigative work requires the possession of experientially acquired and refined 'craft skills'.

Although the formal element of instruction for new detectives has been modernized and new topics introduced[7] (Irving and Dunnighan, 1993), a significant proportion of the taught component of detective training retains an emphasis upon enhancing the trainee's knowledge of the criminal law. In contrast, most detectives encountered in this study continued to believe that the 'real' skills of crime investigation are learnt 'on the job', not in books.

When new detectives join the CID they will be 'mentored' by more experienced officers. It used to be that this mentoring was conducted purely on an informal basis, but it has now been established as a formal component of the instruction process, with continuous monitoring and assessment of the junior detective's progress. Despite this degree of formalization, it appears that there is a continuing belief that it is the informal elements of instruction that are most important in developing the skills of a junior detective. Hence, the mentoring relationship continues to be important in relaying and transferring the tacit and informal knowledges of detective work, of how to get the job done in 'the real world', and the recipe knowledge, working rules, and attitudes that will facilitate this (Ericson, 1993; Manning, 1997; Sanders, 1977).

Murder as a Public Problem

The police's approach to crime investigation and the response to homicides in particular are manifestly influenced by the factors and issues outlined above. In addition, however, the influence of a number of cultural discourses located in society more generally should not be discounted. A comprehensive understanding of police murder investigations cannot simply be content with an analysis of how detectives produce meaning, for murder investigations themselves are attributed particular meaning both by those who perform them and also a wider social audience. These cultural meanings impact upon detective culture and the practices detectives utilize in their work. In order to understand murder investigations then, we need to situate such work in its social, moral, political, cultural, economic, and legal contexts. Therefore, it is important to consider a number of more broadly based issues to do with the links between the police, state, law, and morality.

The academic literature on policing has repeatedly documented how the police's principal social function as an agency of the state is the emergency maintenance of social order (Bittner, 1970). They are part of the formal apparatus of social control, provided with a wide-ranging remit of intervention to regulate forms of both public and private conduct through the potential or actual use of coercive force (Banton, 1964; Reiner, 1992). As a consequence, the police are portrayed as part of the institutional order and are located as a particular site of symbolic power in society.[8]

In assuming responsibility for providing an immediate response to all potentially unlawful deaths, the police's intervention attests to the fact that the crime of murder is an issue about which there is considerable public and political interest and concern. This is confirmed by the degree of media attention in this aspect of their work, and by the fact that the police response is legitimated, aided, and structured through the principles and processes of the primary form of 'governmental social control', the law (Black, 1976). Indeed, the very way in which English law constructs the appropriate state-sanctioned response to murder as life imprisonment is further evidence of the degree of moral seriousness imputed to the commission of this act.

But if we are to understand the status and nature of police murder investigations, it is not enough to say that murder is a form of social problem for which the police provide a response. We must identify what sort of a problem it is. Who is it a problem for? And precisely why is it seen as problematic? The title of this book indicates that my interest lies primarily in the way in which murder forms a problem for the police and how they respond to it, although strictly speaking, it should be acknowledged that murder is not just a problem for the police, rather it is a problem for which the police have assumed responsibility on behalf of society, as part of the process of law.[9] However, as a public agency of the state, the involvement of the police effectively transforms the quality of the problem constituted by an act of murder. It moves, from being the sort of event that C. Wright Mills (1959) described as a 'private trouble', to become part of a 'public issue'.[10]

If one examines the actual act of murder, it is essentially a form of interaction between two people, the victim and their killer.[11] It is an incident that impacts profoundly upon those known to the victim and causes great distress for them (Rock, 1998a; May, 2000). It may also affect those known to the killer in a similar way. But unlike in small homogeneous societies, in a complex, heterogeneous, late-modern capitalist society, proportionately very few people will personally be affected in an instrumental sense by the untimely death of a small number of individuals.[12] We live, after all, in societies in which many of us are relative strangers. Nevertheless, certain of these essentially private acts impact profoundly upon the collective conscience and collective memory of society, and elicit moral outrage and demands for effective action. Mediated communication is central to such processes.

Murder in the Media

Narratives and representations of murder and its investigation are regular features of both fictional and factual mediated communications. And as Knox states, 'The act of narrating murder, for all its drive to make that act an aberration, and its actor pathological, makes murder culturally intelligible by reference to things known: that which is taken for granted, everyday, familiar and common to all' (Knox, 1998: 21–2).

In contemporary society much of our shared understanding of the world is obtained 'at a distance'. The reflected image of our culture that media organizations provide is thus crucial to how the symbolic and cultural formations, within which the work of the police is situated and understood, are produced and reproduced. Mediated representations of violent criminality and its control are a central way through which the established patterns of social order in society are legitimated and reproduced (Cohen, 1980; Hall *et al.*, 1978). In this sense, murders serve as vehicles for the articulation of otherwise diffuse and inchoate existentially based concerns about the state of social order, by journalists and other potential moral entrepreneurs. Effectively, there is an inversion of C. Wright Mills's (1959) model, in that the public problem of displaying the meanings of social order and deviance is accomplished via their personification and representation as dramatic private troubles.

Stories involving serious crime and its control feature regularly across different news media, because they tend to fulfil the institutionalized values of newsworthiness established and maintained by media operatives (Ericson *et al.*, 1987; Schlesinger and Tumber, 1994). At the same time though, these mediated narratives on deviance and the restitutive response to it provided by the police become crucial in the articulation of our cultural sensibilities, and help to define the normative boundaries of society.

In the majority of mediated narratives on homicide, the offence often tends to be fairly incidental to the overall narrative and message of the piece. Such communications are 'morality tales', whose implicit or explicit focus is principally upon the response to crime provided by the authorities and the capture of the dangerous offender (Sparks, 1992). In these tales, detectives tend to be portrayed as having knowledge and insight into the pragmatics of criminality and as being possessed of a particular ability to decode and understand criminal behaviour. As such, in many cultural representations, the detective is connotatively constructed as the embodiment of a deeply embedded rationality that can be traced throughout the 'episteme' of modernity. Through the application of a 'scientific' style of logic, method, and knowledge, the detective is able to suppress the chaos signified by the crime and the criminal, and thereby reassert order. Interestingly though, as society has shifted from modernity to late- or post-modernity, accompanied by a destabilization of notions of 'truth', the pervasiveness of the 'hegemonic' portrayal of the detective has declined. Increasingly, journalists have been willing to critique police practice and present negative accounts of the institution of policing. The reasons for this will be explored in the next section of this chapter. Overall though, there remains an established tendency for both fictional and factual mediated representations to emphasize the crime-fighting, action-oriented world of the detective (Sparks, 1992; Hobbs, 1988; Reiner, 1992, 1994).

In much coverage of policing then, mediated representations explicitly connect the police with the provision of an authoritative social response to heinous crimes and the capture of the dangerous offender. As such, as an aggregate measure it reproduces policing as a 'symbolization' of the provision of order and social control. Policing is portrayed as social authority in action and results in the reproduction of an ideological commitment to order amongst significant sections of the population—precisely those more powerful groups in society who have very little direct contact with the everyday realities of police work. It is in this sense that Peter Manning (1997) connects media portrayals to 'the police mythology'; a web of inter-linked iconographies and sensibilities, which in effect have functioned to maintain a degree of public reification of the police as a social institution.

As such, police work should not be understood simply as a series of actions and practices, it is at the same time a form of expressive symbolic communication. Social control strategies enacted through law signal cultural values, in addition to being mechanisms for achieving social compliance and regulation (Garland, 1990; Gusfield, 1981). Public acts of policing and law enforcement in relation to serious crimes are then carriers of meaning, saturated with a symbolic load, dramatically illustrating that there is a system of authority in society and mapping out moral boundaries.

Within the 'police mythology' there is, though, a distinct 'detective mythology', which portrays the detective role as the apotheosis of 'real' police work. It is based upon a 'ratiocinative iconography' centred upon a glamorous crime-fighter engaged in the identification and chase of dangerous and malevolent criminals. As is the case with the 'myth' of policing in general, the mediated representations of detectives and detective work have been central to the production and reproduction of this mythology.

Drawing upon these cultural narratives, we can identify how and why the investigation of serious crimes has been central in underpinning the ideological legitimation of policing and the reproduction of the 'police mythology'. More recently, however, popular support for the police has become ever more problematic and fragile, reflecting a new set of cultural sensibilities associated with what Garland (2001) terms the 'late-modern crime complex'. It is a development that has led the police role to be seen as increasingly contested for many people and communities. Against this backdrop, the symbolic significance of homicide investigations for the police institution has not declined. Indeed, if anything, such cases have increased in their symbolic importance. Where public confidence in the police's ability to control crime has been increasingly eroded, high-profile murder investigations provide a 'litmus test' where their investigative abilities can be publicly appraised.

A Contemporary Overview

Although the police response to murder has been central in manufacturing albeit increasingly temporary periods of public legitimacy, at the same time, it has also been an instrumental cause of why a sense of public legitimacy for policing has declined. There have been a succession of high-profile cases, many of which were murder investigations, where it has been shown that investigating officers were corrupt, unprofessional, or seemingly incompetent. The publicity provided by media organizations to these cases has done much to undermine general confidence in the police service.

Attempts to deal with the array of issues arising from what are generically labelled 'miscarriages of justice' are central to understanding many of the recent reforms that have been introduced in relation to the conduct of major crime investigations. As Ashworth (1998: 14) suggests, these cases demonstrated recurrent problems in terms of '. . . concoction or falsification of evidence by police officers, in non-disclosure by forensic scientists, and more generally in non-disclosure by the prosecution to the defence. In some cases there was oppressive conduct by the police during questioning with or without actual violence.' The reforms introduced in respect of such problems have been buttressed by other developments. I will now briefly review the various reforms that have impacted upon investigative practices over the last twenty years, and discuss some of the key factors that contributed to their introduction.

A number of legislative reforms were introduced during the 1980s and 1990s that have altered police investigative practice. Some of these developments, such as the Police and Criminal

Evidence Act (1984), have enhanced the degree of formal regulation of police actions. However, as Ashworth (1998) documents, in
the 1990s there have been several subsequent reforms, underpinned
by the politics of criminal justice policy and concerns about rising
crime, that have served to substantively enhance the investigative
powers of the police. Developments such as the curtailment of the
suspect's right to silence, and the introduction of changes in the
rules governing the disclosure of unused evidence, serve to remind
us of the complex nature of the politics that has arisen in relation to
investigative work.

The research findings that detectives often played little more than
a 'supporting role' in solving crimes, together with concerns about
corruption, led a number of senior police officers and policy makers
in the late 1980s and early 1990s to publicly question the efficacy of
the CID and its methods. The moral and political ambivalence they
felt about the role of detectives led them to argue that the majority
of crime investigations could be performed more efficiently and
equally effectively by uniform patrol officers. As a result, and as
part of a wider drive to 'rationalize' policing (Manning, 2001),
tenure arrangements were introduced limiting the amount of time
junior officers could spend in CID. It was hoped that such arrangements would also decrease the potential for corrupt practices to
become instantiated and accepted within police culture (Maguire
and Norris, 1992).

At around the same time, several of the most senior officers in
the police service pursued policies that effectively devalued the
investigation of low-volume serious crimes. They explicitly shifted
their focus and priorities to address the more immediate political
problem of effecting reductions in high-volume crimes, where
there had been massive rises and for which government performance indicators had been introduced. In doing so, they neglected
the symbolic dimensions of policing mentioned previously, and the
extent to which policing has always relied on a degree of 'front-
management'. More recently though, there has been something of a
reaction against the longer-term effects of these policies. Increasingly, there is concern that it has led to a crisis of confidence and
competence in respect of the abilities of senior detectives to investigate the small number of more complex and difficult, yet strategically important major crimes (Smith and Flanagan, 2000). So much
so, that one of the key agenda-setting bodies in British policing

recently urged that, '... because murder is the most serious of violent crimes, its thorough investigation is a fundamental police duty and should be recognised explicitly as a priority' (Her Majesty's Inspector of Constabulary, 2000: 116).

Some of the most important changes in the conduct of major crimes were introduced in the early 1980s, following the Byford Report into the failings of the police investigation into the Yorkshire Ripper murders (Doney, 1990). On the basis of the recommendations made, guidance was issued by the Home Office to all forces, concerning the management of large major crime investigations. As part of this, the Major Incident Room Standard Administration Procedures (MIRSAP) were introduced. MIRSAP revised the principles for the division of labour between investigators in a murder squad and the administrative procedures by which lines of enquiry and their resultant information were to be managed. Since its initial introduction, MIRSAP has been refined under the guidance of the Association of Chief Police Officers (ACPO) Homicide Working Group. These changes have been made, in the main, to take account of developments in the application of information and communication technologies in crime investigations. In particular, the introduction of the Home Office Large Major Enquiry System (HOLMES) has had an important impact upon how homicide investigations are conducted. HOLMES was the result of a Home Office programme first launched in the 1970s to evaluate the potential of microcomputers to enhance the capabilities of the police in major crime enquiries. Overall though, the development of MIRSAP and the introduction of HOLMES have contributed to a move away from the individualistic, autocratic orientation of the traditional approach to investigation, towards a more 'modern', rationalized, and bureaucratic system (see Chapter 4).

A further notable development in this area is that in 1998 the ACPO Homicide Working Group published the ACPO Murder Investigation Manual. The document deals with a number of issues pertaining to the development of common national standards in homicide investigations, including: benchmarking forces' performance; the exploitation of technology; the development of senior detectives' skills; the management of finite resources; the application of a modern systematic approach to murder investigations; and the introduction of increased professionalism. Any such changes at a national level have, however, been accompanied by a diverse and devolved set of local changes in policy and practice introduced by individual police forces. The current situation is, then, that whilst there are national guidelines that provide a degree of uniformity in a number of areas relating to how the police investigate homicides, there is also a considerable degree of local variation in terms of how investigations are conducted.

Important and rapid developments in the discriminatory potential of forensic science have further contributed to shifts in the conduct of major crime investigations. Many forensic technologies have become increasingly sensitive and thus useful, in terms of their application within major crime investigations. And although such developments may assist detectives when investigating otherwise intractable crimes, it is important not to treat such matters uncritically. When attending a crime scene, officers have to be increasingly mindful of the potential to disturb or contaminate potentially useful evidential physical material. As such, although the forensic science aspects of contemporary investigative processes are increasingly important, they are also increasingly complex, and subject to more management and scrutiny.

Overall then, the investigation of murder has been the subject of fairly intense scrutiny and reform. This has occurred because of the symbolic meanings that are attributed to it. For police and public alike, it remains as one of, if not the most, serious type of crime. Accordingly, this book seeks to enhance our understandings of how murders are investigated.

Conclusion

In summary, this study has two principal themes. The main focus is upon the investigative process, the interpretation and communication of information, and the social construction of meaning and understanding that is performed by the police when responding to murders. In examining this aspect of policing, I am particularly concerned to elucidate how investigative actions are ordered and structured by detectives and the various factors that impact upon the process as a whole.

There is, though, a secondary ancillary theme to the study, which contributes to broader debates concerning the links between policing and the moral, social, and political foundations of law enforcement. It is within the context of such debates that this study should be located and its significance lies as much in its exposition of these broader sociological concerns, as with its empirical explorations of the practices of police detectives.

The study is divided into four parts. This chapter, together with the three that follow, aims to set the scene for the substantive discussion, showing how patterns of homicide, the legal process, and division of labour within the murder squad shape investigative practices. Having set the scene, in the second part of the study I develop a theoretical framework to enhance our understandings of how detectives investigate homicides and why they employ particular methods, strategies, and techniques. Following on from this, in Part III, I turn to focus upon the process of investigation, mapping out the stages of the work conducted. The final part of the book draws the key themes together and relates them to a wider social and cultural context.

2

Murder

In both moral and legal discourses murder is constructed as a particularly heinous act that violates the fundamental principles of the sanctity of life. As such, it is identified as deserving a special status and punishment. Murder is a particular form of the category of offences defined in law as criminal homicide. For the purposes of this research, I am concerned principally with the two pre-eminent offences of criminal homicide, murder and manslaughter.[13]

As discussed in the opening chapter, criminal homicide in England and Wales, if considered in historical and cross-national perspective, and in terms of other types of crime, is a social problem of comparatively limited scope.[14] In contrast to its media profile, it remains a rare event. Reflecting such concerns, this chapter will seek to map out the broad national homicide trends and patterns, before providing a more detailed examination of the incidents studied during my research. Having done this, I will then move on to consider how police understand and make use of the patterns in the aetiology of criminal homicide.

Criminal Homicide in England and Wales

There are currently somewhere in the region of 700 criminal homicides recorded by the police in England and Wales each year, although as Figure 2.1 illustrates, the homicide rate has been rising slightly in recent years.[15]

In the postwar era, the homicide rate almost doubled from 347 recorded cases in 1948 to 650 in 1997. The average annual rise in homicide between 1977 and 1997 was 2.1%, which compares favourably with an average rise of 7.2% for all serious offences of violence against the person. Furthermore, any rise in the homicide

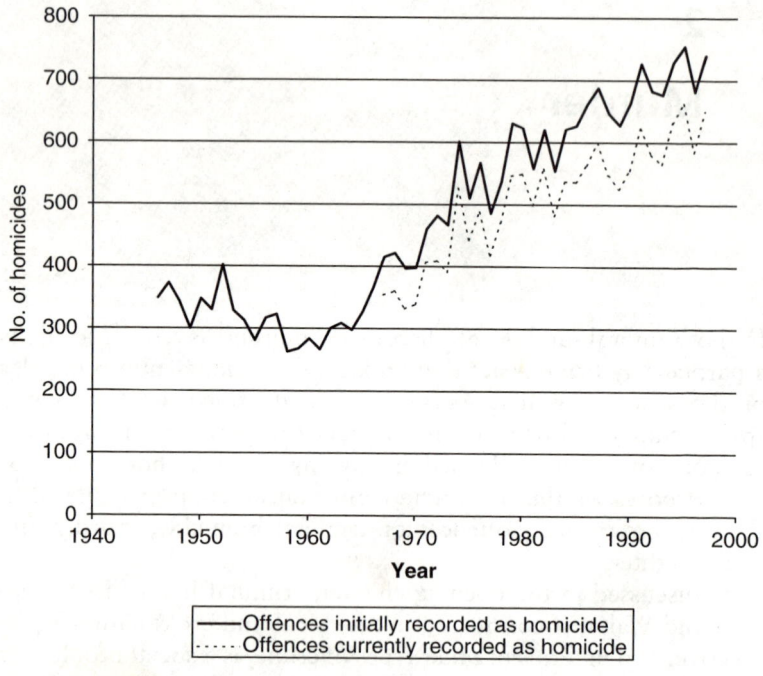

FIG. 2.1. Number of offences recorded as homicide by police in England and Wales, 1946–1997

rate has been far outstripped by the overall rises in property crimes over the same period.

Since 1967 the Home Office have collected statistics to account for the number of cases which are initially recorded as homicides but upon investigation are revealed to have been the result of some other cause. The broken line in the graph in Figure 2.1 reflects these data and demonstrates that about 14% of all cases initially recorded as homicide are reclassified after some investigation by police. This is an important point for the argument put forward in later chapters.

Despite any small rise in the homicide rate, it remains true to say that if we place these figures in an international context, what is evident is that the homicide rate for England and Wales remains comparatively low (Leyton, 1995; Lane, 1997; Levi, 1997). Whilst a comparative analysis of homicide rates between countries is fraught with problems, it is clear that countries with broadly similar economic, political, legal, and cultural institutions can experience widely differing rates of fatal violence.[16] Perhaps the most useful comparison that can be drawn in this respect is between England and Wales and the USA.

The homicide rate per capita in the USA has consistently been much higher than in England and Wales (Monkkonen, 2001), a factor that has served to boost its status as a public problem, and which in turn has led to a far greater amount of research on all aspects of homicide having been conducted in the USA than in Britain. However, the very fact that there is such a disparity in the homicide rates between the two countries means that caution is required in the importation and exportation of findings from one context to the other.

In England and Wales between 1988 and 1997, 61% of homicide victims were male and 39% female. On average there are about 12 offences per million population in England and Wales each year, but as Table 2.1 shows, the highest risk of victimization is to be found in children under 1 year old. The next most at risk group of the population is adult men aged between 16 and 30, where there is a homicide rate of 16.9 per million population.

Research on homicide has established as orthodoxy that most victims will know the person who kills them (Daly and Wilson, 1988; Polk, 1994). About 22% of all homicides in England and Wales involve current or former spouses, cohabitants, or partners,[17] whereas in the USA only about 8% of all murders occur in the context of long-term sexual relationships.[18] Indeed, during the 1980s, there is considerable evidence to suggest that the USA saw a decline in the traditional 'family and friends' contexts of homicide and a rise in the number of 'stranger' homicides (Lane, 1997; Jenkins, 1992), a trend that may be explainable, at least in part,

TABLE 2.1.   Variations in risk of homicide victimization by age

	Age						
	Under 1	1–4	5–15	16–29	30–49	50–69	70+
No. per million	40	9.4	4	16.9	14.5	8.8	7

Source: *Criminal Statistics England and Wales 1997*, Table 4.6.

by factors associated with developments in drugs markets (Bowling, 1999; Lane, 1997). These sorts of figures suggest that social and cultural factors do have an influence upon national and regional homicide rates and need to be accounted for.

The figures for England and Wales (1988–97) show that, on average, 79% of female and 56% of male victims had some form of prior relationship with their killer. For female victims, 44% were killed by a present or former spouse, cohabitant, or lover. Twelve per cent of female victims were killed by their children, whilst 5% were killed by a parent. A friend, acquaintance, or associate was responsible for the killing of a female victim in 16% of the cases where females were victims and only 12% were killed by someone whom they did not know. No suspect was identified in 9% of cases where females were victims.[19]

Where men are victims of homicide, the most common forms of relationship were that they were killed by: a friend, associate, or acquaintance (34%); a stranger (30%); a present or former spouse, cohabitant, or lover (8%); or another family member (12%).[20] In 13% of the cases no suspect had been identified by police.

The fact that most victims of homicide know the person who kills them is reflected in the causes of these kinds of assaults. The Home Office data show that in nearly 53% of all homicides between 1988 and 1997 the principal cause of the fatal assault was recorded as a quarrel, revenge, or loss of temper. These causes accounted for nearly two-thirds of homicides where a suspect was known to the victim(s).[21]

Despite the fact of sharing similar socio-economic systems, there is a very large gap between the US homicide rates and comparable figures for England and Wales.[22] At least part of the explanation for differences in countries' homicide rates seems to be linked to the availability of firearms within that jurisdiction. Levels of fatal violence in a society are, at least in part, a reflection of the lethal potential of the modes of attack used by offenders. Firearms are extremely effective (when compared with other methods) at causing fatal injuries, and 70%[23] of all US homicides are gun related. This differs somewhat from the profile of how death is caused in England and Wales, where firearms are involved in only about 10% of all incidents of fatal violence: 11% of all male victims and 6% of all female victims died as a result of being shot. Table 2.2 sets out

TABLE 2.2. Percentage of homicide offences by method of killing and gender of victim

Method	% Male victims	% Female victims	% Total victims
Knife or sharpened instrument	38	28	35
Blunt instrument	10	11	11
Hit or kicked	20	12	17
Strangulation/ asphyxiation	7	27	15
Firearm	11	6	9
Other[1]	14	16	13

Notes: [1]Includes explosion; burning; drowning; poison or drugs; motor vehicle; and not known. Based on Home Office data for the years 1988–97 inclusive.

Source: Criminal Statistics England and Wales 1997, Table 4.3.

the principal methods by which victims are killed in England and Wales.[24]

As can be seen, the majority of homicide victims in England and Wales are stabbed to death. One interesting gender disparity is that a far higher proportion of female victims are killed by 'manual means' (i.e. hit/kicked or strangled) than male victims. As will become evident, this difference is probably connected to issues of physical strength and the nature of the interactions in which fatal violence occurs.

It is important to reflect upon the fact that homicide is not uniformly distributed throughout England and Wales and that there are geographical clusters in certain urban areas (HMIC, 2000). This reinforces a phenomenon noted in some of the American literature on homicide, that they tend to occur more frequently in certain urban locations (Riley et al., 1997). For the purposes of this study, the distribution of homicides is significant in as much as it suggests that police forces may have different levels of experience in dealing with criminal homicide.

Homicide in the Criminal Justice System

Men are disproportionately over-represented as victims of homicide; they are, though, even more over-represented as suspects. Of those persons indicted for homicide, 89% were men.[25] Based upon an aggregation of the Home Office data for 1988–97 in relation to the criminal justice processing of cases of criminal homicide, it is possible to state that of all homicide suspects, 39% were men indicted for murder and convicted of that offence.[26]

The limited available data suggest that, in a significant number of cases, the police charge a suspect with murder, but the conviction obtained is for manslaughter, where wilful intent on the part of the offender does not have to be demonstrated by the prosecution. What is interesting about the figures comparing indictments with convictions is that they show that over the past ten years there has been a small but significant improvement in the proportion of cases where a conviction for murder is obtained. The figures in Table 2.3, based on a percentage calculated from the total number of murders and manslaughters, demonstrate this trend.

The data contained in this table reflect a longer-term trend in the postwar period that shows there has been a proportionate increase in the number of murder convictions when compared with convictions for manslaughter.[27] Figure 2.2 outlines these broader long-term trends, taking 1967 as a base year and showing the comparative percentage rise for convictions of murder and manslaughter.

This figure shows how there has been a rise in the percentage of convictions for murder, particularly at the expense of convictions for section 2 manslaughter. Another important development over

TABLE 2.3.   Percentage of suspects for criminal homicide offences indicted and convicted of murder

Year	Percentage of male suspects indicted for murder and convicted of murder	Percentage of female suspects indicted for murder and convicted of murder	Percentage of all suspects indicted for murder and convicted of murder
1988	37	13	34
1989	40	12	36
1990	36	13	34
1991	33	15	31
1992	35	24	34
1993	41	14	38
1994	41	34	40
1995	44	14	41
1996	45	21	42
1997	42	21	40

Source: *Criminal Statistics England and Wales 1997.*

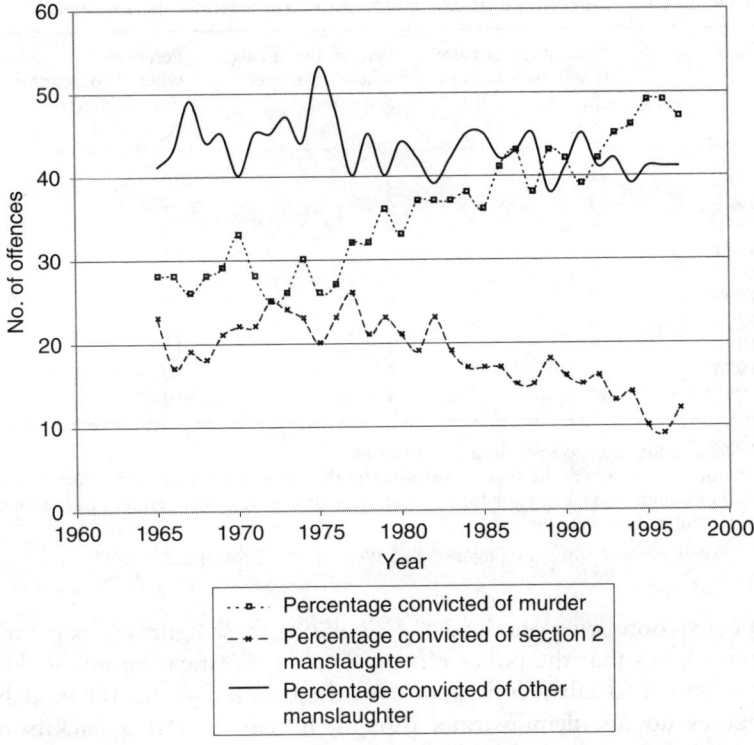

FIG. 2.2.   Percentage of total convictions by homicide type

this period is a decline in the number of convictions for infanticide. The Home Office data show that between 1965 and 1975 on average 17.4 women were convicted of infanticide. By the period 1985–95, this had fallen to an average of 4.7 convictions per annum.

A key concern in respect of this study concerns the effectiveness of the police in solving homicides. Table 2.4 summarizes the data for England and Wales where no conviction for murder, manslaughter, or infanticide was obtained.

The data in this table show that on average in 8.3% of offences recorded as homicide, the police were not able to charge a suspect and in an additional 4.2% of cases all suspects had been acquitted by the court. In 10% of all cases recorded as homicide, legal proceedings were either not initiated or were terminated without

TABLE 2.4.   Percentage of cases where no conviction was obtained

Year	Percentage of cases where no suspect charged	Percentage of cases where all suspects acquitted	Percentage of cases where prosecution not initiated or concluded[2]
1988	6	3	10
1989	9	4	9
1990	9	5	9
1991	6	6	11
1992	7	5	9
1993	7	4	8
1994	10	4	10
1995	9	5	11
1996	9	3	10
1997[1]	11	3	10

Notes: [1]Court decision pending in 190 cases.
[2]Includes cases where the suspect is found by the court to be insane; the suspect has died or committed suicide; or for other reasons proceedings were either not initiated or terminated.

Source: *Criminal Statistics England and Wales 1997*, Table 4.2.

a conviction being obtained.[28] Calculating these figures as percentages shows that the police effectiveness in investigating homicides has remained fairly consistent over the past ten years. What such figures do not demonstrate, though, is that against a backdrop where the number of homicides being committed is rising, more convictions for offences of homicide are being secured, whilst at the same time an increasing number of cases, in purely numerical terms, are going unsolved.

Murder: Study Data

The data for this study are based upon an analysis of all cases initially recorded as homicides in the police jurisdiction in which the study is located, between 3 November 1991 and 30 March 1997. This provides a data-set of 75 cases, involving 83 victims, of whom 61% (n = 51) were male and 39% (n = 32) were female.

The data in my study broadly reflect the national homicide trends. They are also in line with the findings of Mitchell (1990) whose quantitative analysis of convicted murderers in England was based on a larger sample of cases. Of the 75 cases, in ten there was currently no suspect identified, which included those cases still under investigation and three which were long-term unsolved. Three cases were recorded as 'no crimes' where the police investigation revealed that no criminal offence had been committed.[29] Five cases involved multiple victims: five men were killed in a single fire; in one case a mother drowned her two young sons; two young men were shot in a pub; a husband and wife were shot dead in their home; and an elderly couple were killed in their home. Excluding the offences that were not solved and the three 'no crimes', the police identified 83 suspects, consisting of 69 males and 14 females, who were either charged directly with an offence of homicide, or with assisting in some manner in the commission of the offence.

Victims

Figure 2.3 sets out the people who were the victims of homicide in my study, by age and sex. This graph illustrates several facets concerning the age of victims in the cases studied. Perhaps the most noticeable trends are the two dramatic peaks in the age distribution of male victims. Given the analysis of the national

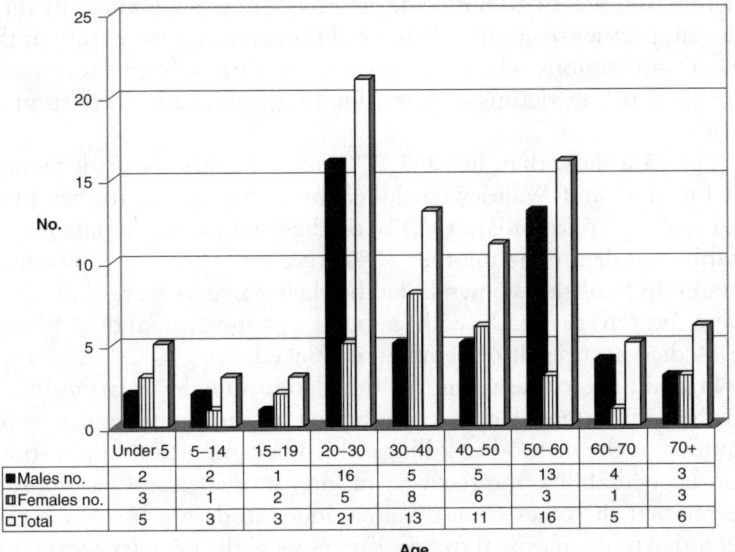

	Under 5	5–14	15–19	20–30	30–40	40–50	50–60	60–70	70+
■ Males no.	2	2	1	16	5	5	13	4	3
▣ Females no.	3	1	2	5	8	6	3	1	3
□ Total	5	3	3	21	13	11	16	5	6

Age

FIG. 2.3.   Victims by age and sex

data, the peak for young males could reasonably be expected. However, the second peak amongst adult males aged 50–60 is more surprising given the general explanations of the dynamics of the social interactions in which homicide arises (Daly and Wilson, 1988; Polk, 1994). One possible explanation is that the second peak is simply a recording effect, which reflects the small number of cases in the sample and the demography of the area studied.

In line with national data, the local data for my study suggest the victim is likely to know the identity of the person who assaults them. This also reflects the findings of other studies. 'Put simply, people don't kill each other because they are strangers. Homicide tends to involve exceptional tensions and emotional extremes' (Polk, 1994: 176). In 68% of the cases in my study, the police investigation showed that the victim knew their killer. Figure 2.4 sets out the nature of the relationships between victims and killers in more detail.

Of particular note in the cases studied is the fact that 33% of all male victims were killed by a friend or associate and a further 33% died as a result of an assault by someone unknown to them. The figures for female homicide victims show that 22% of the female victims and 9% of all homicide victims were women killed by their current partner or spouse. This would suggest that the nature of the social interactions when men are victims differs from those when females are the victims of homicide in a significant proportion of cases.

The data show that, in 1997, 47% of all female homicide victims in England and Wales were killed by a current or former male partner. In approximately 30% of these cases, the women were stabbed to death and another 30% were strangled or asphyxiated. About 15% of the women killed by their partners were shot, 10% were beaten to death with a blunt instrument, and a further 10% died as a result of being hit or kicked.

In addition to the nature of the victim/offender relationship, a further important factor contributing to how the police solve murders is the method of killing, which has important implications for the availability and recovery of forensic evidence. Once more it seems that the cases from the area under study are broadly representative of the national trends. Knives were the primary weapon in 35% of all the fatal assaults in the cases studied.

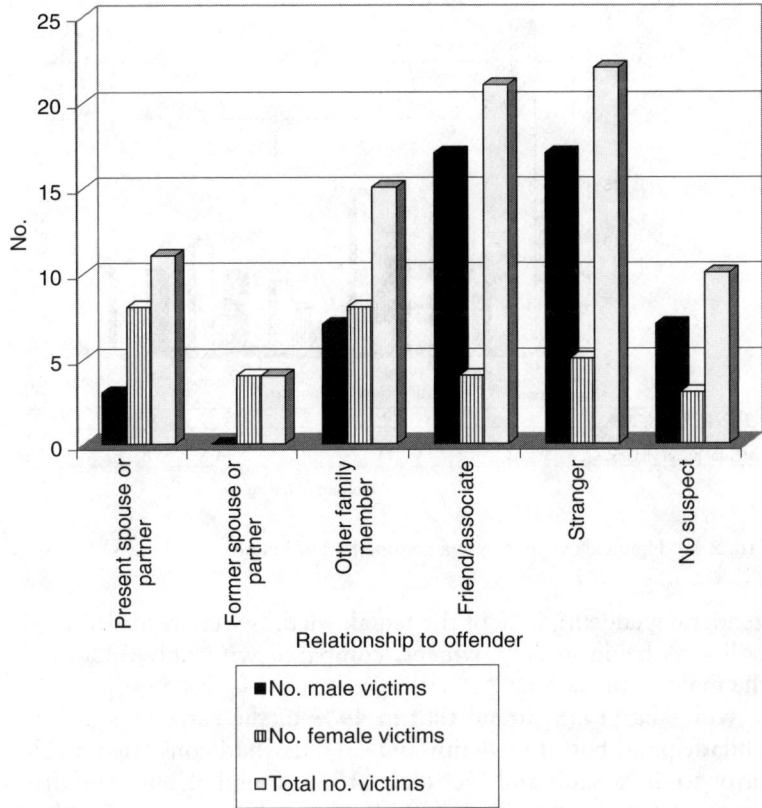

Fɪɢ. 2.4.   Victims killed by relationship to offender

Whilst the data recorded by the police do not directly address such issues as social class, they do provide a number of indicators as to the socio-economic status of homicide victims and their killers. Indeed, 45% of male victims were unemployed and a further 6% were in 'casual employment'. By way of comparison, only seven of the 42 female victims were defined as unemployed or in casual employment.

The data in Figure 2.5 show that the risk of victimization of homicide is disproportionately located amongst particular groups. By breaking down the figures along the lines of victim sex and employment, it can be seen that the distribution of such risks is

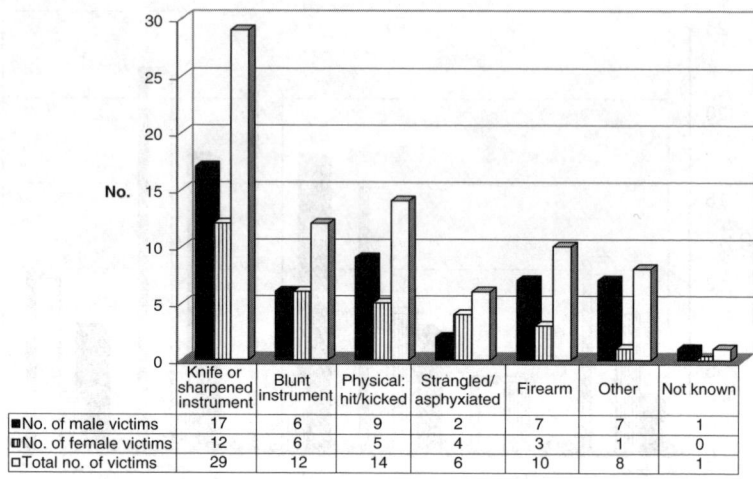

	Knife or sharpened instrument	Blunt instrument	Physical: hit/kicked	Strangled/ asphyxiated	Firearm	Other	Not known
■No. of male victims	17	6	9	2	7	7	1
▣No. of female victims	12	6	5	4	3	1	0
□Total no. of victims	29	12	14	6	10	8	1

Method of killing

FIG. 2.5.   Homicide victims by sex and method of killing

gender dependent: 53% of the female victims were recorded by the police as being in employment, compared with only 33% of all the male victims.

Wolfgang (1958) found that in 44% of the cases he studied in Philadelphia, both the victim and offender had consumed alcohol prior to the assault and Websdale (1999) found alcohol and drugs were related to a significant number of male-perpetrated multiple homicides. Alcohol also seemed to be an important contributing factor in a number of cases in my study. In 24% of all the cases, police enquiries revealed that both the offender and the victim had consumed a substantial amount of alcohol. The presence of alcohol may serve to act as a 'dis-inhibitor', which increases the propensity for the parties to try and resolve their dispute through violence.

Another correlation that was apparent in the data concerns the time of day when fatal assaults occur. Thirty-two per cent of all the incidents took place between 8 p.m. and midnight and an additional 25% occurred between midnight and 4 a.m.

In this discussion of the circumstances surrounding fatal violence, it is important to reflect upon the fact that there are a whole range of factors that are in a sense extraneous to the violence itself, but may influence whether the victim dies or not. What is evident from reading the case files is the extent to which death in homicide cases is sometimes less a matter of intention than the unfortunate confluence of a number of factors. In a number of cases encountered in the fieldwork, a victim received severe and potentially life-threatening injuries. However, due to a range of factors, not least amongst which was prompt and effective medical attention, the victim survived and the cases were dealt with as lesser offences. Indeed, many of these injuries were technically more severe than those in some cases where a fatality occurred. For example, in one case where a fight broke out in a pub, the victim was punched in the face and he collapsed and died. Similarly, in a second incident, this time outside a pub, the victim was punched once on the jaw, causing a massive sub-arachnoid haemorrhage which proved fatal.

Perpetrators

Of the 83 police suspects who were charged with an offence relating to the commission of homicide, 69 were males and 14 females. In 14 cases there was more than one person involved in some capacity in the assault. Where more than one party to the offence was identified, in seven cases both the primary assailants and their accomplices were male. In a further five cases, there was a female who acted as an accessory to the commission of the offence by male offenders and in two cases the primary assailant was female who was assisted in some manner by a male accomplice.

The issue of female perpetrators of homicide is worth reflecting upon briefly. In line with the broad patterns of offending, the data collected show that females commit far less homicide than males. It is also suggested that women often tend to have different motivations when they kill than men and that the crimes they commit frequently need to be understood against a backdrop of an increasingly abusive relationship (Websdale, 1999). However, the involvement of a woman as a suspect does tend to elicit particular media interest in a case, which in turn impacts upon the police investigation. The fact that homicide is itself not a common crime and female participation in it is even rarer serves to make such stories 'newsworthy' as there is '...an added factor of dissonance in placing women in the dock as publicly arraigned offenders' (Heidensohn, 1985: 88). This degree of interest results from the fact that the involvement of women in such acts of violence realizes a transgression not just of the moral contract of the sanctity of life, but also of the socialized sensibilities of the appropriate gender roles relating to the conduct of men and women. This transgression of moral/gender boundaries, as well as moral/legal boundaries by female offenders, has been labelled as the problem of 'double-deviancy' by Heidensohn (1985). Certainly in the cases in the sample, two separate incidents both involving a female offender resulted in a high level of sustained media interest in the case. A third case generated national media attention for a short time, although this was not maintained.

Morris and Blom-Cooper (1979) in their analysis of persons indicted for murder between 1957 and 1977 report that 40% of the individuals concerned were aged between 15 and 24. A more recent study found that over 60% of those convicted of murder were aged under 30 (Mitchell, 1990). Figure 2.6 provides a break-down by age and gender of those charged with offences related to homicide.

There is an obvious gender disparity present with regard to who commits acts of homicide, with men being very much over-represented (Jefferson, 1997; Polk, 1994). More detailed analysis of the data summarized in Figure 2.6 shows that 48% of the suspects charged were men aged between 20 and 34.

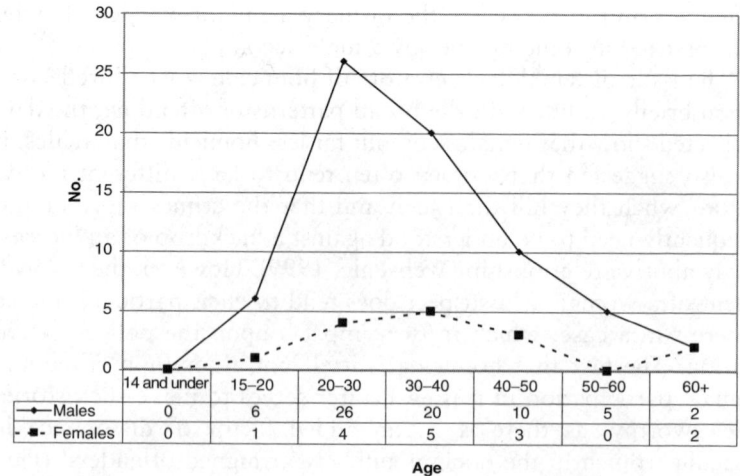

FIG. 2.6.   Offenders by age and sex

There has been very little work on the occupational status of murderers in this country. Mitchell (1990), in one of the few studies to examine this issue, found that 48% of the convicted murderers studied were previously engaged in non-professional employment and a further 46% were unemployed. In terms of the suspects identified by police in my study, 33% of males were unemployed and 41% were in casual employment. This is a higher proportion than were employed. Similarly, for female offenders, eight of the women were unemployed, five were in casual employment, and one was employed.

Further analysis of the data shows that in 12 cases (17% of all those incidents recorded as homicides) where a male killed a male, both the victim and suspect were of similar age and similar low socio-economic status, the predominant category being young males who were either unemployed or in a 'casual' work arrangement. There is, then, a degree of symmetry between the socio-demographic profiles of victims and offenders.

From the point of view of the police, at the start of an enquiry the location of where the offence has occurred is often taken to be an important factor. Amongst the cases studied, 18 of the incidents occurred in a property where both the victim and offender lived; 24 took place in the victim's dwelling; five were either in a public house or directly outside; six were in a public park or recreational area; in two cases the bodies were found in a remote rural area; a footpath or road was the setting for four cases. The remaining cases took place in a variety of other locations.

The Phenomenology of Homicide

The 'family and friends' context that is common to the majority of homicides suggests that in contrast to the typical mediated representations of such crimes, most criminal homicides are not committed 'in cold blood', but rather are 'hot-blooded' episodes occurring in 'emotionally charged' circumstances. And whilst an analysis of the socio-demographics and relationships of the parties involved in such incidents provides an indication of the broad patterns involved in this type of crime, perhaps the main limitation of such an approach is that it fails to capture the complex, chaotic, and confused nature that is typically part of the phenomenological reality of homicide.

If we want to understand the nature of the police response to homicide, a central focus must be upon how investigators, in making sense of an incident, reduce and resolve the confusion often typical of fatal interactions. It is vital, therefore, to attempt to understand the details and complexities of such events, and how they are 'experienced' and understood by their participants.

Monkkonen (2001) identifies that the philosophical essence of murder is that it is typically a perverse attempt to exert some sense of control over another person. This can involve trying to stop some behaviour, to change emotions, or to permanently assure compliance. Often, though, it is not a calculated form of social control, rather the acting out of an impulsive, emotionally driven, unreflective response to some perceived problem. In effect then, from the situated perspective of the instigator of the violence, it is enacted as a form of 'raw' solution to their problem.

Wolfgang's (1958) somewhat counter-intuitive concept of victim-precipitation, together with Luckenbill's (1977) discussion of 'righteous anger' in the 'situated homicidal transaction', have both pointed to some of the complexities involved in understanding how and why fatal violence occurs. But it is Jack Katz (1988) and David Matza (1969) who have perhaps been most instrumental in the development of an approach that is sensitive to the experiential subjectivities of 'doing' crime. Katz, in particular, draws attention to the emotional seductions and dynamics of crime that arise in the context of particular settings. His account is insightful in mapping out how emotion and passion often underpin fatal violence, and how there tends to be a tumult of existential confusion at work. As he puts it, 'When people kill in a moralistic rage, their perspective often seems foolish or incomprehensible to us, and indeed, it often seems that way to them soon after the killing' (Katz, 1988: 12).

In many instances the instigation of the use of violence is impulsive. Indeed, the death of the other may not be the objective of the attacker; it may be to hurt the victim or rather, '... it attempts to achieve the existentially impossible goal of obliteration, of annihilating or wiping out the victim' (ibid.: 33). This approach helps us to understand why in a number of cases in the current study there is evidence of what might be termed 'overkill', that is, violence far in excess of what was actually required to cause the death of the victim. For example, in a fight that took place between two young men in a pub, the pathologist's report recorded that the assailant had beaten the victim with his fists and once the victim was on the floor, he was kicked in the head, before the assailant concluded the assault by stamping repeatedly until the victim's skull collapsed. When he was interviewed by detectives, the suspect gave this account of his actions:

I hit him twice with my left fist to the right-hand side of the jaw, then I pushed him twice with my left fist to his left side of the rib-cage, he fell to the ground and I kicked him and then stamped on the left-side of his face with the full sole of my foot . . . at this stage I didn't realise that the guy was seriously injured . . . I was just really angry, very angry . . . I wouldn't use the word clinical it was just, um, an act of sheer anger.

In this example, the killer, a former boxer, can only really explain the extreme violence he used as an expression of the anger that he was feeling towards the victim.

In the moment of performing violent acts, many perpetrators say that they are seemingly overwhelmed by emotional sensations typical of what Matza (1969) termed 'dizziness', feeling both in and out of control of their self. They feel as if they are somewhere between directing and being directed by the dynamics of the situation. As such, their posthumous accounting for their actions is often typified by an attempt to explain and rationalize their behaviour, through the use of a number of 'techniques of neutralization' (Sykes and Matza, 1957). The following example, taken from a case involving a female assailant, illustrates how emotion is implicated in the instigation of violence. The extract is from an interview between police and a friend of the assailant, who went to the police because the suspect had told her important information about the crime.

She turned up and said 'Something awful has happened . . . She's pushed me over the top. I've hit [victim's name] . . . I've hit her with a hammer. I think I've killed her'. . . . I said 'Did you hit her more than once?' She said 'I think so. I don't think she can survive what I did. If only she'd leave me alone. There was a row in the kitchen . . .' I said 'Did you hit her on the head?' She said 'Yes.'

This account also provides a sense of how the offender was trying at least partially to neutralize her sense of guilt by blaming the victim for provoking her.

Of course, not all homicides can be explained as an outcome of emotional circumstances. In many cases, the role of the perpetrator is more calculating and rational, factors often made evident by their actions prior to and in the aftermath of the crime. However, this attention to the role of emotion in homicide and the complexities that tend to be involved in situations of unlawful death provide some indication as to why in a number of cases what started as a seemingly trivial altercation rapidly escalated to fatal violence. It is important also for understanding some of the investigative problematics that regularly confront police. In choosing to provide an account of their actions to detectives, especially when those actions have been motivated by anger, it may be that the suspect is engaged in producing a reflexively oriented construction of the meaning of what they have done, as much for themselves, as for the police. Consequently, the problem for investigators is not just that of ascertaining whether a suspect's or witness's account is 'true' or 'untrue', although this is often a core concern. Detectives also need to be aware of the subtle shadings present in what they are told by both suspects and witnesses.

Police Talk

One way in which police cope with the ambiguities and complexities that frequently inhere to the job of trying to ascertain how and why a homicide occurred is through their formal and informal communications. During the fieldwork, it was noted that detectives routinely talked in terms of a number of different 'types' of murder. Such forms of organizationally situated police talk, based upon systems of interpretation, categorization, classification, metaphor, and trope, encapsulate a set of shared 'common-sense' understandings that assist officers, both collectively and individually, in attributing meaning to their work and the wider social world (Garfinkel, 1967; Goffman, 1981; Cicourel, 1968). Labelling incidents as belonging to a particular type is, in Weick's terms (1995), a form of 'sense-making'. It connotatively evokes (albeit in a simplified form) the key issues and core problems that investigators are likely to encounter, and figuratively constructs them in an appropriate form for the organization. In turn, this informs the selection of investigative strategies. As David Sudnow (1965) describes, such classifications assist officers in making sense of an incident by identifying what are the 'normal' qualities of and issues for cases 'of this kind'.

Drawing upon the data collected, it is possible to identify seven types of murder that police officers referred to in their conversations with each other. Within a number of these categories there were also several identifiable subclassifications which were regularly used by them.

- Domestic homicides: are those incidents where the cause of the fatal act is held to stem from an argument or a general deterioration of the relationship between a husband and wife, common-law partners, or between people in a long-term relationship.
- Argument-motivated (or confrontational) homicides: are those incidents where the death of the victim was the outcome of an argument between two people which rapidly escalated to violence. From the police point of view, this label was frequently used to cover the scenario where young men in public settings use violence as a form of social control.
- Child murders: involve the death of an infant or child. Officers frequently identified these as the most difficult cases emotionally.
- Criminal cause murders: can be defined as those cases where the death arises as a result of either the victim or offender (and in some cases both) engaging in some form of unlawful activity. Frequently, the death of the victim stems from an 'instrumental' application of violence as opposed to the more 'expressive' forms of violence that are to be found in domestic and argument murders (Block and Block, 1992). There were several subclassifications used by police to cover different sets of circumstances, including 'burglary gone wrong', 'drugs murders', 'revenge murders', and 'robbery murders'.
- Sexual murders: take place in the context of a violent, sexually motivated assault. An important distinction worth noting is that police referred to 'homosexual murders' as a specific subset of all sexually motivated homicides. In part, this seems to reflect the particular problems that were experienced by police in responding to such crimes.[30]
- Stranger murders: were used as something of a general category by police to refer to those cases where the victim did not know their attacker. As such, it was frequently used in tandem with some of the other classifications.
- Serial murders: are the rare cases where there are several victims of the same offender.

It can be seen that the classifications that the police used were closely allied with issues of motivation for the offence. Motivation was a significant factor in terms of how officers developed a sense of what happened in the assault and consequently how they selected lines of enquiry to pursue within an investigative strategy. Understanding why the offender might have performed the act in a particular way is central to assembling a plausible understanding of the incident as a whole. Once an investigator is able to infer the reasons why the particular victim should have been the target for a fatal assault, they will have at least some sense of who might want to kill the victim. This in turn can be used to direct the search for the offender.

The discursive system of classifications used by officers assists them in rendering the complex and often ambiguous reality of the circumstances in which murders occur both relevant and appropriate to investigation. This reflects a wider sense in which, 'In their street talk police officers use stories to represent to each other the way things are, not as statements of fact but as cognitive devices used to gain practical insight into how to do the job of policing' (Shearing and Ericson, 1991: 491). In talking about murders and differentiating between the different types of murder, detectives were implicitly selecting and emphasizing the matters likely to be of particular concern and that have to be accounted for in responding to different incidents. This classificatory system is grounded in real experiences, but is an aggregated interpretation and synthesis of these collective experiences which effectively serves to establish the significant characteristics of different types of homicide.

Such figuratively enacted representations provide a sense of order to the work conducted. They are sense-making devices that provide officers with a commonly held stock of background expectancies about homicide and its participants. The labels that are applied by police effectively function as a form of coding, which allows them to construct at least a partial sense of what has taken place within a fatal interaction and thus a possible investigative response. However, these ideal types also communicate moral concerns and values which indicate how police should think and feel about such issues. For whilst all murders tend to be viewed as 'bad' by police officers, certain types of homicide elicit particular reprobation. Child murders, sexual murders, and 'out of the blue' stranger murders generate particular feelings of concern; they also tend to receive a large amount of attention from the media and would seem to be viewed as particularly reprehensible.[31] Broadly speaking, police sentiments seem to reflect those of the public at large in this area and the different classifications that they employ would appear to recognize that some homicides have a particular symbolic status.

Classifying homicides in this way thus operates in a similar way to how folk tales function in broader cultural contexts (Douglas, 1966; Needham, 1979; Geertz, 1973). It communicates tacitly held police knowledge and has both instrumental and expressive functions. The classifications relay knowledge which assists police officers in terms of how they conduct their investigations, but they also communicate the moral values and schematics which underpin the instrumental factors.

Academic and Practitioner Criminologies

The classifications used by the police effectively mirror and in a sense figuratively encapsulate many of the findings of academic criminological research on homicide. Indeed, there is a manifest degree of overlap between the practically oriented classifications detailed above, and those resulting from the work of criminologists such as Polk (1994), Mitchell (1990), and Daly and Wilson (1988) amongst others.

For example, the identification of domestic homicides by the police as a separate category reflects the fact that the cause of the murder is likely to be located in the 'private' relationship between the victim and perpetrator and the enactment of a futile gesture of control. This dominant narrative also features in Websdale's (1999: 79) summary: 'In many ways men's lethal violence is the final assertion of their power and control over women and, paradoxically, an acknowledgement of their loss of control'.

The 'state of morbid possessiveness' that Websdale (1999) describes is echoed in Jack Katz's (1988) discussion of cases where the partners had previously separated. Here the male offender's actions were typically marked by a final attempt at reconciliation and, when this failed, a fatalistic nihilism—'if I can't have you then no one can'—appeared to consume them. This use of fatal violence as a nihilistic form of social control is well illustrated in one of the cases in my sample, where a 55-year-old husband visited his estranged wife at her new home and pleaded with her to return to him. When she refused, he went outside to his car, removed a shotgun from the boot, returned inside, and shot his wife twice. He then turned the gun on himself. In a further two cases, the male partner committed suicide after killing their female partner.

In all the incidents involving former partners and in three where males killed their present partner, it was recorded by police that the primary motivation for the fatal assault was that the woman had either left, was in the process of leaving, or had threatened to leave her male partner. Overall, of the 14 incidents in my sample which involved spouses or common-law partners, seven were men killing their current female partner, three were women killing their male partner, and four cases were men killing a former spouse or partner from whom they had previously separated.

A notable characteristic of domestic homicide cases was that they often involved high levels of violence. One such case was where a 57-year-old husband came to believe that his 40-year-old wife was a prostitute and having an affair. One evening he came home from work and confronted her about his suspicions. In the course of the ensuing argument, he picked up a 3-inch kitchen knife and stabbed her 15 times.

In the majority of domestic homicide cases, the violent act seemed to arise quite spontaneously and quickly, against a background of progressively mounting tension within the relationship. When interviewed by officers, many of those who killed their partners said that the relationship had been worsening for some time and that in this context their partner said the wrong thing to them at the wrong time and they 'snapped', responding with extreme violence. The following brief extract from a police interview with a husband who killed his wife is typical:

Things had been going from bad to worse, not just at home but I was having trouble at work you know... and then that day she just kept pushing me, just saying things to wind me up and then I couldn't stand it and she said something and I lost it... I completely lost it and I hit her and she fell to the floor and I kicked her. Then I think I picked up a knife and stabbed her...

Such losses of temper are important factors in explaining how and why murders occur. 'Whether the victim be male or female, it seems that the most common motive for unlawful homicide is some sort of personal emotional reason: that is the offence is committed in the course of a quarrel or in a fit of temper' (Mitchell, 1990: 58).

Violence as a manifestation of an emotional outpouring has also been identified by criminologists as an important characteristic of confrontational homicides, which accounted for 27% of the cases in my sample. This police classification is to all intents and purposes the same as Polk's (1994) concept of the 'status confrontation', where a male kills another male in a public setting. In his 'anomic' explanation of the emotional and physical dynamics of such incidents, Polk (ibid.) argues that many such incidents are 'caused' by a perceived slight to the masculine status of one or other of the parties. An extract from a police interview with a man involved in an incident that was classified by police as a confrontational homicide illustrates some of the relevant issues:

I was sitting drinking my pint and I went to the toilet. A man came in directly behind me . . . He came and stood at the next urinal to me and kept looking at my penis while I was urinating. I turned sideways a bit to stop him and um I was wearing a pair of jeans with button up flies and um as I was doing them up he was staring at my crotch . . . um . . . I punched him twice in the face . . . um . . . 2 or 3 times to the body . . . um . . . he fell to the floor and I . . . um stamped on his face, I'm not sure how many times, more than once anyway.

Although not relevant to the above incident, the presence of a social audience is frequently significant because the opportunities for withdrawal from physical confrontation without a loss of 'masculine honour' by one or other party are thereby restricted. This is reinforced by a belief that attainment of peer status through any other means than 'masculine violence' is constrained through a lowly socio-economic position. 'Through it all resound the joint themes of masculinity and lower social class position. Extreme violence in defence of honour is definitively masculine and lower or under class in its makeup' (Polk, 1994: 92). Similar understandings inflect the police use of the term confrontational homicide. But for them, the presence of an audience to the confrontation is important in terms of identifying potential witnesses.

Equally significant, though, is the fact that often in these incidents the eventual victim is not a passive subject to the encounter, but an active agent in the escalation of violence (Katz, 1988; Luckenbill, 1977; Wolfgang, 1958). For detectives, a key investigative and legal problem in this type of case is identifying who initiated the confrontation and who instigated the violence. There is frequently a degree of 'role ambiguity' in terms of who emerges as victim and who as offender from such encounters.

Females were primary offenders in two similar cases. In one incident, the 17-year-old offender had heard rumours to the effect that her boyfriend had been seeing another girl, serving to illustrate that such motivations are not exclusively a masculine affair. In a rage, she visited the girl's house and finding that she was not present, threatened the girl's father with words to the effect, 'tell your daughter to stay away from my boyfriend or else'. When the other girl returned home, upon receiving the news she telephoned the protagonist and arranged to meet her later at the boyfriend's house in order that this 'misunderstanding' could be settled. When the two girls met, the offender produced a knife and stabbed her rival. There was a similar case to this involving two males, where in a dispute over a mutual paramour, the 67-year-old man stabbed and killed his 80-year-old rival.

The fact that homicide can result either directly or indirectly from participation in other forms of criminal activity has been discussed by both Katz (1988) and Polk (1994). From an investigator's point of view, establishing such a link was an important way of identifying potential suspects for the death, that is, they could look for suspects amongst people known to participate in certain forms of criminal behaviour. In addition, though, separating these offences captured the sense in which they sometimes posed unique problems for investigators. For instance, 'drugs murders' frequently presented particular problems for investigators because of the fact that many, if not all, of those persons who would be of interest to the police enquiries would be heavily involved in the drugs scene. As a consequence of this, the information that these people can provide is held by police to be problematic and unreliable. The following quote from a detective superintendent gives an indication as to what the police perceive as the central investigative problems in drugs murders: 'It was your typical drugs murder. When we got in there it was bloody obvious that the victim was high, everyone there was high ... we even had to peel the fucking dog off the ceiling.'

Reflecting wider public sentiments, sexually motivated murders and stranger murders were often seen as being amongst the most serious by police officers. The label stranger murder tended to be applied by police in a somewhat generic fashion, to cover those cases where the victim and offender did not appear to have any prior association, and the motives for the assault were not easily identifiable or conventionally rationalizable.

Within the sample, there are three incidents where the offenders' primary motive for the offence was connected to sexual intercourse with the victim. One of the victims was a work colleague of her eventual assailant. The second victim had met a man in a pub and they had then driven to a remote beauty spot. When she refused to have sex with the man, he assaulted her extremely violently, kicking and stamping on her head and then fled. The third female victim was a prostitute who was beaten with a blunt instrument and strangled by a 'client'. The three sexual murders in the sample were characterized by an extremely high level of violence in the assault. As a result of this they were investigated very thoroughly and a large amount of resources were directed to the enquiry in view of the 'public danger' that these offenders were felt to constitute.

One case from the sample exemplifies the principal issues involved in stranger murders. The victim was a prostitute who was murdered by a male. There was an extreme degree of violence within the assault, where the offender tried to cut the victim's head off with a 6-inch steak knife. The motivation of the assault was deemed to be pathological and to have stemmed from the offender's disturbed sense of reality rather than any especial sexual motivation. Many of the homicides that were labelled as stranger murders by police featured an extremely high level of violence within the attack.

Whilst I have not discussed all of the police classifications in detail, what is emerging from this discussion is a sense that there is considerable overlap between the academic criminology of homicide, and the largely experientially grounded understandings used by detectives to inform their investigative response to such crimes. In a sense then, the discursive classificatory system used by detectives encapsulates similar forms of knowledge, and provides police with a pragmatically oriented way of understanding the causes of homicide, the motivations for fatal violence, and the problems involved in its investigation.

Conclusion

In this chapter, I have examined the key patterns of homicide and how police officers understand this type of crime. The cases in the sample are broadly representative of the national trends and reflect the fact that the majority of murders involve people who are known to each other, a factor that has significant implications in terms of how the police investigate and solve such crimes. In approximately 40% of the cases in this study, the crime was essentially solved for the police, either through the offender making an admission at the scene, or due to the fact that the crime took place in a public setting where there were witnesses who could identify the offender to the police. Overall, in about 30% of the cases in the sample, the identification of a suspect was directly attributable to the investigative work performed by police.

An important element in relation to the analysis of the data were the obvious links between notions of masculinity and violence. Males are far more likely than females to kill; they also constitute the majority of victims of fatal violence. Permeating the commission of homicide is a theme of 'macho display'. The acting out of masculine status repeatedly emerges as a central cause of fatal interactions, where one or other of the parties involved needs to demonstrably express a particular version of their masculine status and power.

The most obvious instance of this are sexual murders. However, as was discussed, issues of male sexuality and status are also important in relation to domestic murders and confrontational-argument murders. In the former category, it appears often to be the case in the background to the attack that the male's 'sexual possession' of the female is perceived to be threatened. In the latter group of offences, the most common scenario is a fight between young men in front of a public audience, often motivated by a situation where their masculinity, and by implication reproductive capacity and status, has been challenged by another.[32] To withdraw from such a challenge would be perceived as resulting in a further loss of status.

Further to this, though, there is an important division in the symbolic status implicitly maintained between the two categories of domestic murder and sexual murder. The incidents that tend to be labelled as sexual murders are those where the attack is committed by a stranger to the victim and they are often high-profile, strategically important cases for the police. Such incidents are often the cause of great public concern, generating lots of media attention and significant levels of police resources are made available for their investigation. Contrast this with the label of 'domestic', which carries with it connotations of an almost private matter. It seems plausible to propose that such divisions may at least partially reflect deeply embedded moral sensibilities regarding the morality of sexual relationships. Sexually motivated jealousy and insecurity, and the *crime passionnel* by a male partner that are typical of domestic homicides can almost be empathized with, in a culture in which the normative moral standards of sexual conduct aspire to lifelong fidelity. The 'sexual' murder committed by a stranger who does not in any sense have a claim to legitimate proprietary 'sexual rights' over the victim is treated more seriously and as being possessed of more symbolic significance for society as a whole.

The discursive system of classification that the police use to distinguish between types of homicide can be seen to serve two related functions for police investigators. First, it provides a retrospective summary catalogue of police experience in dealing with these kinds of matters. All of us develop cognitive maps of the world which influence how we act and interact with people, places, events, and things in our everyday lives. The police typologies operate in a similar fashion, in that they do not reflect the minutiae and details of each individual case, but rather they are a mechanism for the communication of aggregated police experience and how cases involving similar issues have been investigated previously. Secondly, given the chaos, complexity, and confusion that regularly attends the phenomenological reality of homicidal incidents, the typologies the police make use of serve to simplify the seeming complexity of a particular incident, thus enabling officers to develop a sense of understanding about what are likely to be the key facets of the crime and consequently what actions they should take. The fact that police routinely talk in terms of different types of murder is indicative of the fact that different circumstances frequently involve different investigative problematics that have to be resolved. Classifications provide a sense of what are likely to be the significant issues and problems in terms of producing an authoritative account that makes sense of the incident, so as to establish what has occurred and who was involved.

3

Law

Detective work is informed and structured by the legal context in which it is undertaken. The law and legal system are a direct influence upon how detectives conduct their enquiries. Law defines what acts are defined as crimes and establishes the criteria for differentiating between offences. It also allows police a range of powers to assist them in carrying out their enquiries. However, as it structures investigative work, the law and legal system are reciprocally structured by the work police perform. The police enact law, and the products of their enquiries constitute the basis upon which the subsequent legal work of the criminal justice process is based. Thus the relationship between investigative work and the legal context which inflects and permeates it can be conceptualized as one of structuration (Giddens, 1984, 1993). The first part of this chapter examines how law and the legal system regulate investigative work. In the second half, the focus shifts to consider the ways detectives are able to actively negotiate such constraints, so as to shape and inform the wider legal process of which the investigation is a constituent part.

The Legal Frame

The influence of the law and legal system upon investigative practice can usefully be conceived of as what Goffman (1974) terms a 'frame'; that is, a mechanism that orders past, present, and future thoughts, experiences, and actions. The legal frame is enacted by detectives and other socio-legal actors as a 'mode of rationality' that conditions and shapes how they think about, act towards, and understand offences, and also their affective responses to such matters. It provides a bounded set of principles and procedures through which the attribution of responsibility for a range of proscribed actions can be divined. This concept of law as a mode of rationality recognizes that the legal frame is not simply conditioning of police practice, but that there is a degree of reciprocity present in the relationship. Investigative actions are regulated by the legal frame, but at the same time the police perform both 'gatekeeping' and interpretative functions, in terms of when, where, how, and why the law is invoked in particular settings.

Socio-legal perspectives on law enforcement have drawn attention to the process of negotiation and interpretative interaction that results when the classificatory system of law as it exists 'in books' is used by field-level officials 'in action' (Hutter, 1988, 1997; Hawkins, 1984). Rock (1973) thus suggests two basic analytic elements of law, the creation of authoritative rules and their enforcement. Developing this position, police homicide investigations can be understood as being situated in a legal context that is shaped by the extant framework of legal rules and definitions, and the social processes of their enforcement. Law establishes the principles, functions, and structures within which and through which the police operate as crime investigators. In this role they are key actors in the operation of an adversarially based system of enforcing the law, where their actions are concomitantly regulated by the system of which they are a part.

Law frames the fundamental principles and objectives of the criminal justice process, which the police investigation seeks to uphold, operationalize, and fulfil. It defines what activities constitute criminal behaviours and puts in place a range of reflexively organized institutions, which act to provide authoritative responses to such prohibited activities. However, the investigative activity of collecting and constructing information, so that it is relevant to the concerns of other participants in the legal process, is a key factor in determining the ways in which the institutions of law are enacted.

When constructing an account of his investigations, the detective is involved in a process of transforming an individual event into categories which have a character of permanence and exactness. These categories are drawn from the available stock of categories stored within the police and wider legal organisations. Use of these categories allows the detective, his super-ordinates, the prosecutor, and the other court officials, to accept his account as 'the facts', and therefore to act as if they were in a state of perfect knowledge, and as if this perfect knowledge has fairly stable constitutive elements. (Ericson, 1993: 18)

The function of the police investigation, the production of 'valid' knowledge for the legal process, is established by the details and specifications of law. Law determines the structural relationships between the participating institutions and actors, and how they should properly be constrained in performing their respective roles in terms of what are considered to be legal and appropriate actions. However, in terms of the way in which the police-led interactions produce the valid knowledge for the legal process, that is, the lines of enquiry they do or do not make, the questions they do or do not ask, the information they do or do not provide, and the interpretations they select, the police are structuring of the criminal justice process. It is this process of structuration that gives rise to the sense of law as a 'negotiated order' that will be addressed later in this chapter.

Legal Reality

The law as an instrument of social control represents the primary way in which the democratic state justifies and legitimates its interventions into the lives of its citizens. For police officers, law establishes what is a crime and who is a criminal, how decisions should be made in respect of the application of such labels, and the formal consequences that should flow from such an application. Law is not the sole source of power by which deviancy is attributed to a person or act. Indeed, crime is a sub-class of a wider range of deviant behaviours (Becker, 1963). What it does do is to provide an authoritative definition of 'criminal' to particular acts and set in place mechanisms through which the presence of criminality can be determined.

In attempting to perform this role of classifying social behaviours, the central problem encountered is that social life consists of complex events and encounters, for which there are a myriad of ambiguities, perspectives, and interpretations. The law, though, lays claim to being a body of knowledge and a set of rationalizing principles, which can be used to establish the 'truth' of events. Its main ritual, the criminal trial, is held to be the embodiment of the method by which responsibility, guilt, and innocence can be established and validated. Therefore, how 'legal truth' is divined from 'social reality' is extremely consequential for the legal process.

The Anglo-American model of criminal justice is based upon a system of adversarial advocacy, which is characterized by a search for 'proof' rather than 'truth' (Sanders, 1997; Rock, 1993), although in the ideological rhetoric of law the two are maintained to be more or less commensurate. This prioritization represents a pragmatic solution to the difficulty of replicating 'reality' and establishing 'truth' in the artificial environment of the courtroom. Rather than seeking an 'absolute truth', in establishing 'what happened' and 'who (if anyone) was legally culpable', the adversarial system recognizes the potential for competing versions of reality between participants, and tasks defence and prosecuting counsel to construct their cases accordingly. As such, law can be seen to operate with a parochial conception of 'reality'. It places 'epistemological' and 'ontological' boundaries around the events with which it is concerned in accordance with its principles and interests. In so doing, it 'lifts' particular conflicts out of their social and historical contexts, and focuses them around a limited number of key issues and allegations. This process presents events as far less ambiguous and less complex than the phenomenological reality of the incident might otherwise suggest (Rock, 1993; McConville et al., 1991). The legal conception of reality holds that 'truth' in everyday life can be subjective and relative, and as such, the legal case which abstracts from an infinitely complex realm of phenomenological and existential experience needs to be viewed as a particular form of social construct. The legal process objectifies the quality of deviance by establishing its core facets and reifies the diagnostic categories used to divine its nature. The delineations it makes are clear and concise when compared with the phenomena of 'social reality'.

'The case' is a central concept in the adversarial system. It represents the bounding of reality and the ordering of understanding and events that occurs through interactions with legal discourse:

A case was a deliberate simplification that obscured some issues, giving luminosity only to what were called the 'facts at issue', the facts that were deemed to be causally related to the commission of the offence. It was so constructed that it tended to strip away volumes of context and history ... It was designed to ignore many of the tangled social relations, hurts, incidents, motives and emotions that could be woven into personal disputes, concentrating on but a few matters. It was intended to shed greyness and ambiguity... (Rock, 1993: 31)

The problem of how to bound 'reality' is thus structured by a number of legal notions such as material relevance, reasonable doubt, and admissibility (McConville *et al.*, 1991; McBarnet, 1981).

Constructing a case involves defining the nature of the issue to be considered and then ordering and linking together individual pieces of evidence in such a way as to provide a coherent and logical narrative account of the incident. As such, the individual facts that evidence suggests and the conclusions that are drawn upon the basis of the available evidence have to be arranged with reference to one another and with reference to the facts and principles upon which they depend for their probative rationality.[33] Thus, when performing 'case work', the law provides police with a set of scripts and vocabularies of motive to follow, in order to translate the incident concerned into a form that is meaningful when viewed in relation to the legal frame.

As Tamanaha (1997) identifies, essentially law establishes 'what are to be counted as the facts'. Legal 'facts' are based upon evidence, a form of knowledge that is produced and organized according to certain 'epistemological' rules in an attempt to ensure its validity and reliability. The role played by evidence reflects the sense in which certain established 'common-sense' facts (or truths)[34] can be taken to suggest the presence of other facts (or truths), with the former acting as the warrant for the latter.[35] Producing and presenting evidence in support of an account of a crime is governed by a number of central principles that underpin the whole legal process. For example, there is the principle that sufficient evidence must be provided to prove 'beyond reasonable doubt' that a suspect is guilty. Furthermore, there are regulations governing how evidence is to be identified and collected, contained in the rules of evidence which are based upon judicial discretion and other allied regulatory constraints within the Police and Criminal Evidence Act (1984). These various principles maintained in law influence the work of police investigators in more subtle ways than is often credited. For example, in establishing what types of evidence and how much of it has probative value in respect of a certain offence, the law encourages detectives to pursue certain lines of enquiry at the expense of others, in order that particular kinds of evidence should be established. Together these epistemological and procedural principles establish law as a mode of rationality that permeates how the investigative role is enacted.

Definitional Power

An important aspect of how law is enacted as a mode of rationality is the way in which it establishes a series of definitions that can be applied to a situation, thereby identifying it as a crime (or not). This definitional power of law and its relevance to understanding police crime investigations generally is well illustrated by the case of homicide and murder.

Murder is a subset of the legal category of criminal homicide. The term homicide refers to the killing of one human being by another and there are several sub-categories of homicide. Murder is a common-law offence and is established through the presence of the *actus reus* and *mens rea* on the part of the accused. Manslaughter can be adjudged to be either voluntary or involuntary. Voluntary manslaughter includes both the *actus reus* and *mens rea* as for murder, but it is allowed under certain circumstances that the mind of the person committing the fatal act may be affected to such a state that they cannot be held legally liable for their actions. These circumstances are provocation, diminished responsibility, and acts of suicide. Involuntary manslaughter covers those cases where the accused killed another lacking the quality of malice aforethought, but none the less demonstrating a lesser degree of *mens rea*. There are three types of involuntary manslaughter: killing by gross negligence; killing with subjective recklessness as to death or bodily harm; and killing by an unlawful and dangerous act. Infanticide is the offence committed when by any wilful act or omission the death of a new-born child is caused.

A killing will be considered unlawful unless it occurs: in self-defence or in order to prevent serious harm; where an officer of the law employs reasonable force in the execution of their duty; where it happened by accident or misadventure; or where a criminal is executed in accordance with his/her sentence (Ashworth, 1993).

Broadly speaking, although as indicated above not exclusively so, the extent of moral culpability for a homicidal act, and consequently the degree of punishment in law, is related to how deliberate the act is adjudged to be. 'Hot-blooded' killings that arise out of highly charged emotional confrontations are held to be 'less bad' than 'cold-blooded' killings, although importantly, as Heidensohn (1992) has suggested, legal definitions associated with notions such as 'reasonable provocation' have a gendered aspect, favouring masculine patterns of violence and discriminating against the legitimacy of the violence of 'women who fight back' against abusive partners.

As should be apparent from the discussion of the phenomenology of homicide, the work of the police in terms of deciding upon which is the correct definition to apply to an incident is often not clear-cut. Overall, the qualitative distinctions between different crimes, and between crimes and non-crimes, are often more subtle than is generally understood. If we consider for a moment the relationship between an act of murder and a killing that results from justifiable self-defence, the result of the two acts is the same—an individual is dead. But there is a legal distinction drawn between the two acts, according to the circumstances in which they took place. The legal classifications that are selected and applied to incidents are very often not self-evident and uncontentious. Indeed, if they were, such matters would not require a complex legal process in order to define them. It is the law, buttressed by some sense of popular morality, that specifies the differentiation between the sets of circumstances which set the classification of the act, for example, murder, manslaughter, accidental death, suicide, and so on. But it is the actors of the legal process who establish the facts of the case and work to attribute an appropriate classification to it. It is a basic point, but one that is worth making, that the crime of murder necessarily involves the killing of a human being, but not all such killings are murders.

In order to 'fit' different legal definitions to situations, detectives engage in a double movement of interpretation. The circumstances of the incident have to be interpreted so that a decision can be made in terms of whether the particular legal specifications fit those of the incident. At the same time, the legal definition has to be interpreted so as to test whether it usefully encapsulates the qualities of the potential crime. Such interpretative work is very significant in the earliest stages of the police's response to a suspicious death, for if an investigation is to be launched by police, the circumstances of the incident must be interpreted in such a way as at least potentially to fulfil the criteria of a crime.

The majority of murder investigations start with the discovery of a body, although there are a small number of cases where an investigation has been launched prior to the discovery of a complete corpse. Even where there is a body available to investigators, the circumstances in which death occurs can often appear ambiguous. Therefore a decision has to be reached whether a crime may have occurred or not.[36] As Jack Douglas's (1967) work demonstrates, in such circumstances establishing the cause of death is often based on patterns of inference and interpretation applied in conjunction with a set of common-sense understandings about how and why deaths occur.

A number of officers interviewed could recount past instances where common-sense reasoning had contributed to the classification of an incident. The following field note provides one such example:

Over lunch and the officers at the table were telling 'war stories', discussing past cases they have been involved in. Many of the stories were suffused with humour, one of them recalled how at 'the double shooting at [place name] when [officer name] was the duty inspector called to the scene. He was all ready to call it a double suicide until someone pointed out to him that the fact that the shotgun wasn't still there possibly suggested otherwise.' This generated a few chuckles.

Similar stories were told on other occasions that demonstrated how a similar logic could be used to avoid setting up a costly murder investigation into incidents where the cause of death was suicide. During an interview one officer described how:

We got a call to turn out to this house where the body of a man had been found and the uniform chief inspector was jumping up and down saying it was a murder and we should do this and that. But the thing is once you've been to a few autopsies and what have you, you get to learn that death is a process and the body can do some unusual things. So I was saying 'no slow down, hold on', and it turned out that all the blood that was there, which convinced [chief inspector's name] that this bloke had been murdered, was the result of his internal organs haemorrhaging.

In the early stages of an investigation distinguishing between murder and suicide may be particularly difficult. An example of the sorts of issues raised in respect of producing an authoritative classification was provided during the fieldwork period, and although not witnessed directly, was the subject of much discussion amongst officers. An extract from my field notes documents some of the issues:

In the HOLMES office at headquarters ... two detectives came in who have been involved in a couple of 'jobs' that have been running. They talked to the other people in the office. The discussion revolved around a case where the body of a male and female were found in a burnt out car at [a semi-rural location], well known to be popular locally with courting couples. A homicide investigation was established and from the conversation it appears that three potential scenarios were developed by the investigators and used to inform the early lines of enquiry. The first was that the couple were having an affair and had been found out by a jealous partner. The second scenario was that the man had committed suicide after killing the woman. The third that they had entered into a suicide pact. The officers who were on the enquiry said that the enquiries into the backgrounds of the victims suggested that the latter option was most likely. Although as one said 'we didn't find a note, which is a bit strange and what you might have expected'.

More importantly though, they went on to recount how, the following day after this first enquiry was commenced, a third dead body was found nearby. The early enquiries indicated that it was unconnected with the other two and they recounted that the circumstances here were far less ambiguous and it was obviously a murder. Evidently, as a result, the majority of the detectives who had been despatched to investigate the double death, now thought to probably be a suicide, were transferred to the second incident, which was unequivocally a murder.

This extract indicates some of the difficulties that may inhere in defining an act as a particular form of homicide. In particular, establishing the motivation underpinning the death can be a complex piece of interpretative work.

Objective Actions and Subjective Intentions

One way in which the legal frame structures the investigation of murder is by establishing that in order for a prosecution for this type of homicide to be successful, it must be demonstrated that the suspect was possessed of criminal intent. As a subjective state of mind, criminal intent is more difficult to prove than that of criminal action, due to the fact that actions are external and observable and hence imbued with a greater degree of 'reality value'. This disjuncture between the objectivity imputed to physical actions and the subjectivity of intention and its impact upon the process of law has been discussed by Jack Douglas (1971: 111) where he identifies how 'The basic goal is to make the internal, subjective experience externally observable—to make the external an "index" or sign of the internal'. This need to establish or 'objectify' the quality of intention resonates throughout the investigative actions of the police. There is a general tendency within the investigative method-ology employed by the police, given the aforementioned problems with providing objective proof of subjective intention on the part of the offender, to try and seek proof of intent in all cases.

Detectives claimed to approach serious crimes as 'worst case scenarios'. Particularly in the early stages where the facts of the case were being established, the official policy was to investigate all suspicious deaths as potential murders. They would actively search *for*, and make interpretations, that suggested that the case is one of murder rather than one of manslaughter.[37] One detective explained that there is a rational basis for treating crimes in this way.

You have to think that each case is a murder, until proven otherwise you have to treat each case as a 'worst case scenario', because if you don't and later on something comes up which suggests that your interpretation was wrong and this person was probably murdered, you're gonna have a real problem, because the evidence is likely to have gone and you're left holding 'a crock of shit'. On the other hand, if you start off collecting all the evidence on the basis that it could be a murder, you may waste a couple of days finding out you were wrong, but at least you are sure.

If investigators do not know who the offender is, then determining their state of mind and degree of intent is rendered intrinsically problematic. On many occasions, experienced detectives were able to 'read the scene' and the pattern of injuries to construct an inference about the extent of the offender's premeditation, although these inferences would often have to be revised as the investigation progressed.

If, as a result of their enquiries, the investigators satisfied them-selves that proof of intent was not available, then they would settle for a charge of manslaughter. However, it was fairly obvious that on a number of occasions detectives felt that defendants were charged with a lesser offence simply because the police could not obtain sufficient evidence to substantiate a 'factually correct' charge of murder. These issues were illustrated in one case where there were three individuals suspected of involvement in the murders of two victims. The police were extremely unhappy with the Crown Prosecution Service's decision to charge only two of the suspects with murder and the third with 'attempting to pervert the course of justice, namely by destroying or concealing potential evidence', in connection with the murders. This is documented in a field note.

Outside and the three police officers were pretty angry. During the course of the exchanges the officer in charge of the investigation said to me 'The three of them went there with the intention of killing the two victims, they all knew it was going to happen and the bloody problem we've got is that we can make it stick against two of them, but there's nothing concrete that we can use against [suspect 3's name] to prove that he was in on it.'

A pragmatic solution to resolve such difficulties is routinely adopted by investigators, where certain actions on the part of the killer are used as 'signifiers of intent' and are held to provide an indication of their internal, subjective motivations.[38] The killer is constructed as 'the author' of the criminal act, in which either their past behaviours, or their actions preceding the event, can be interpreted as 'signifiers'. As such, the actions of the individual are held to be a part of, or reflection of, 'the author', which if interpreted correctly can be taken as an objectifiable signal of the subjective causes of the act.

An example of the use of signifiers of intent in this way was observed on one case where considerable attention was paid by investigators to trying to establish whether the knife used as the murder weapon was brought to the scene by the assailant, or whether it was already present at the scene of the crime.

A significant line of enquiry continues to be trying to establish whether [suspect 2] brought the knife with him, or whether he picked it up off the side once they were in the property. Several officers are revisiting a number of witnesses who know him in an effort to establish if anything else could be generated that can put him in possession of a suitable weapon and possibly whether he was carrying it that night. Meanwhile, a couple of others are looking at what knives were out on the side.

The investigators maintained that if it could be demonstrated that the suspect had brought the knife with him, this could be used to suggest that he had come to the scene with the intention of causing harm to the victim. Similarly, in a different case, when lines of enquiry established that their suspect had made threats to harm the victim some three months prior to the victim being found dead, this was interpreted by detectives as constituting a signifier of intent and was used to support a charge of murder against the suspect. A more general example of this kind of inferential work is the way in which at the crime scene detectives will, with the assistance of the pathologist, examine the patterns of wounds and level of violence used in the assault as an inferred indicator of the intentions of the attacker.

The search for signifiers of intent, from which logical inferences can be drawn about the *mens rea*, is then a central undertaking of the process of investigation. The custodial interview is one setting in which this search becomes particularly important.[39] A brief extract from an interview with a suspect serves to illustrate how the police deal with the problems of ascertaining the level of intent. The male suspect had been involved in a fight in a pub where another man had died.[40]

P   Would it be fair to say that you wanted to hurt him?
S   Quite obviously I did want to hurt him.
P   Mmm.
S   It wasn't my intention to do him any serious harm.
[...]
P   When you hit him what was going through your mind?
S   Um.
P   What were you trying to prove?
S   [Pause] Er, I wasn't really trying to prove anything I was just um, just really angry and just lashed out in anger.
[...]
P   Would you say that you were controlled in what you did, or would you say that you lost your temper?
S   No, that I lost my temper, lost my temper.
P   Why did you kick him in the head?
S   I don't... I was just really angry, very angry.
P   Do you not think that doing something like that would cause serious injury?
S   Um, oh yeah. I know I suppose it's a possibility yeah, of course it's a possibility yeah.

In the exchanges above, the interviewers were trying to determine the level of premeditation to the offence. The questions show how in discussing the suspect's actions the police were trying to negotiate an account of the event with the suspect that exploits, to some degree, the suspect's ignorance of the law and fulfils certain legal requirements in building the case. If it could be shown that the suspect knew that he was likely to cause severe injuries to the other man, then this could be used to attempt to justify a charge of murder rather than manslaughter.

One of the primary objectives of investigative work is to effect a translation of the incident into a form appropriate to legal discourse and its associated definitions. At the same time, and as a constitutive part of this translation, the legal definitions are interpreted in such a way that they are relevant to the particular circumstances and qualities of the incident subject to investigation. The range of subjective and objective elements that are constitutive of the often opaque phenomenological social reality of an incident involving sudden, and potentially unlawful death do not necessarily fit neatly with the classificatory distinctions and definitions maintained in legal discourse. The law enacted as a mode of rationality allows that only certain things must be proven and certain issues are of consequence for the purposes of the decisions it is called upon to make. Therefore, translating social reality into 'legal reality', and conversely interpreting legal definitions in relation to the complexities of real-life incidents, is an important component of crime investigation work.

Police Investigative Powers

The ability to engage in this interpretative work is shaped by the range of investigatory powers that the law provides police in order to expedite the investigative function. Importantly though, at the same time as promoting and facilitating certain investigative strategies through the provision of these powers, the law also seeks to regulate how they are applied. Law is, then, in terms of the powers that it makes formally available to detectives, both a regulatory mechanism and a productive, facilitative resource. In this sense, the regulation can be understood as a two-way process: at the same time as it constrains, it also opens up a field of action. 'The provision of powers may also be positive in defining what police may and may not do: "law has the great virtue of limiting what it grants." The combination of empowering and restricting is a characteristic ambivalence of liberal governance' (Dixon, 1997: 295). This sense of the law as simultaneously constraining and enabling serves to counteract the mediated image of the detective as operating in an environment in which they are seemingly immune to any form of sanction or control. The use of these powers will be discussed in more detail in due course.

The Legal Process

The final principal way in which the legal context can be seen to influence the work of police investigators is through the structure of the adversarial legal process itself. Previous accounts of crime investigation work have already noted the significance of case constructionism in understanding police work (McConville *et al.*, 1991). But even prior to the final presentation of evidence at the trial stage, there are a number of legal proceedings which serve to structure not only the content and form of the trial, but also the investigative work that precedes them. This is most evident in the 'prosecutorial review' function, performed by the Crown Prosecution Service (CPS) (Ashworth, 1998).

In effect, the CPS mediate between the police's investigative function and the wider legal frame. They advise police on matters of evidential sufficiency, compliance with formal requirements in case-building, in addition to providing scrutiny and advice over decisions to charge and prosecute suspects. On major crime enquiries, the CPS are involved at a comparatively early stage and may provide ongoing advice to the police in respect of decisions to charge. The Head of CID summarized the working relationship between the police and CPS on major crimes thus:

Generally speaking you don't involve them until you get to the suspect stage and then very often only when the suspect's in custody. In murder enquiries, there won't be many enquiries now where you don't have a conference with CPS before you charge someone... You don't need their sanction to charge, but on murder enquiries you're a bit unwise if you don't get them on your side, because if they don't think you've got enough evidence, then at the pre-committal stage they'll pull the case.

This senior detective did recognize, though, that there was potential for disagreement between police and CPS:

If we're satisfied that there's enough to charge, then we'll try to convince them of this. Normally they are more critical than we will be, that in itself is not a bad thing. They'll be more... the standard of evidence they are looking for is going to be higher than mine. I want to get this person charged and from experience I know that if I'm happy that the person's done it and there's some evidence to support this, things can only get better...you could go ahead and charge without CPS, but they'll 'pull the job' if it doesn't meet the criteria that they apply. I wouldn't want to run a job without their support.

The data from this study suggest that the CPS do have an important impact upon police decision-making in major crime investigations. Representatives of CPS were not only in a position to evaluate police evidence, but they also made interpretations of legal stand-ards for the police. They set out which facts of the prosecution's case must be proven and to what degree this must be done, before charges can be laid.

There are several pre-trial stages, such as the committal proceed-ings and pre-trial review, which further serve to influence the work of the police, in particular around matters relating to the disclosure of evidence. The extent to which these pre-trial proceedings can structure the 'reality' that is contested at trial is demonstrated by a double murder in the study. The suspects were arrested quickly and a substantive case against them was rapidly established. However, the police were struggling to establish a motivation for the offence. Eventually, several lines of enquiry produced some evidence to suggest that the shootings were connected to serious, international criminal activities. These criminal connections in effect explained several anomalies that had, until this point, been troubling the police in terms of understanding why the crime had occurred. At the pre-trial review, though, it was decided that to introduce such matters would overly complicate the facts at issue and no reference was made to this aspect of the police enquiry throughout the trial. Both defence and prosecution presented their cases in such a way that such issues were of little relevance to the version of 'reality' that they sought to promote.

The police enquiry is central to the construction of a case, but the police are not the sole agency with constructive powers in the process. The adversarial legal system has evolved a number of structural mechanisms that complement and supplement the con-structive agency exercised by the police. Obviously, prosecution and defence counsels have an ability to delimit and arrange the issues of the case in court. Indeed, the presentation of the case in court provides further editing and framing of the material of the case, in order that the issues appear clear-cut and unambiguous. Investigators are aware of the scrutiny that their work will be subject to at trial and therefore the good investigator tries to anticipate any potential weaknesses and act accordingly. As such, the proceedings of the trial stage can be seen to have an anticipatory structuring effect upon the work of investigators.

Negotiating Law

Having examined some of the ways in which the legal frame structures the investigative work performed by detectives, I will now turn to focus upon some of the ways in which detectives negotiate these potential constraints upon their actions. Socio-logical studies of the work of law enforcement officials have rou-tinely drawn attention to the role of discretion in terms of how they make decisions about how, when, and why to enforce laws (Hawkins, 1992; Wilson, 1968; Hutter, 1988). Discretion is part of the process by which police officers and other enforcement agents negotiate the legal frame that surrounds and permeates their working practices. For the purposes of this study we do not require a detailed discussion of discretion, only a map of its main aspects.

Discretion arises from the need to interpret and apply often fairly general legal formulations and prohibitions to the specific nuanced qualities of a situated incident. It is then part of the process of translation whereby officials decide how a law should be applied (if at all) to the incident in question and vice versa (Hutter, 1988). Thus discretion is the legitimate authority to construct an interpret-ation of what has occurred and to determine how the law and what it allows might be implemented.

This interpretation of the literature on discretion provides a starting-point in terms of thinking about how police investigative actions are neither wholly constrained nor unconstrained by law. In order to enforce the law, the potential enforcer is engaged in an interpretation of the incident in question and also an interpret-ation of the law. They have to decide what the law means, judge whether the case before them is covered by it or not, then decide what action is applicable and how this should be justified and accounted for.

Administrative Controls

Central to understanding how, when, and why officers use discretion and interpret rules in particular ways is the role of the police organization. As discussed previously in Chapter 1, the police organization establishes routines, conventions, and standard procedures that mediate between individual members' activities and the external environment in an effort to ensure that the actions of officers and the products of these actions are legally valid. Thus the organization establishes forms of administrative regulation and control over the conduct of individual officers.

In their discussion of the nature and logic of rules in police work, Smith and Gray (1983) demonstrate that rules as they pertain to the social processes of policing and law enforcement are not static or absolute, neither are they irrelevant. Rules bring clarity about an area, but they also open up areas of negotiation in the process of enforcement, being both constraining and enabling. Due to the ways in which they are formulated, they also allow for a degree of discretion in terms of how they are used to inform decisions. Therefore, in thinking about the legal dimensions of detective work, we need to retain an awareness that rule compliance and deviation are situated in a broader context.

Particularly when thinking about rule-breaking, a matter which has been of some concern in both academic and policy-based discussions of detective work, an important consideration should be who deviates from legal principles, and when, how, and why do they do it. Just because people do not always obey the law, it does not mean that they never do. Historically, the fact that the more dubious instances of police 'discretion' seem to have taken place in 'low-visibility' conditions, providing an opportunity for the construction of uncontested post-hoc accounts with a 'legalistic gloss', is in itself indicative of the fact that contravention of legal and bureaucratic rules is recognized as potentially consequential by the actors doing it (Reiner, 1992). The very fact that it is felt that a 'gloss' should be applied to dubious activities suggests that, to some degree, formal rules have to be taken into account.

Smith and Gray's (1983) analysis makes clear that the bureaucratic, hierarchical structures of the police organization establish a set of procedural rules, guidelines, and norms that function to condition the activities of officers, supplementing and augmenting the formal prescriptions established in law. These internally based procedural rules provide for a degree of organizational self-governance by the police, as senior officers seek to monitor and effect a degree of discipline over the activities of their subordinates. As Maguire and Norris (1992) identify, such forms of administrative control are more pronounced on major crime enquiries than for other investigations, a theme reiterated by a detective interviewed in this research.

You should be under closer supervision in this sort of enquiry than on normal day to day crime work. You're having a daily briefing in the morning when you're expected to update the whole team about particular lines of enquiry that you've been involved with, so you get a degree of scrutiny there. The paperwork that you are doing is seen by far more people and in a far more inquisitorial way than any paperwork that you are doing on division.

In directing the work of those under their command, senior officers on a murder enquiry are concerned to try and ensure that the lines of enquiry being performed are conducted in accordance with organizational policy. These organizational policies are, at least in part, intended to ensure that the investigative actions performed comply with legal rules and requirements. This returns us to the anticipatory structuring effect that the adversarial system has upon investigators. Experienced detectives are aware of many of the mistakes that can be made when conducting complex investigations and the 'lines of attack' that defence counsels will try to exploit at trial. As such, they try to utilize their experience and that of their colleagues to ensure that, as far as possible, mistakes are not made and possible attacks can be countered or defended. One experienced senior detective said:

Allegations over blatant misconduct go back a long time and a lot of lessons have been learnt. Things have been done wrong...but in terms of actual individual officers transgressing...I would have thought that incidents of that are far higher in normal CID work than in major crime investigations...I've sat through a lot of those trials and I tend to find that the level of cross-examination on murder trials certainly more recent ones...is generally more civilized because I think papers have been scrutinized that closely that generally speaking all the obvious things should have been done. You do occasionally get 'cock ups' but you don't usually see some of the horrible 'cock ups' you see in other cases because a lot more scrutiny has been given to it...the officers go through a ritual in that the defence more or less know what the answers are going to be.

As this officer makes clear, there are a range of administrative controls present within the investigative system, including policies, procedural guidelines, regulations, and bureaucratic structures.

These administrative controls are numerous and cover a whole gamut of diverse activities from first actions at the scene to statement taking. In addition, they are supplemented by more informally based systems of internal disciplinary surveillance. A number of SIOs stressed that when an enquiry was in progress it was important that either they, or their deputy, should be aware of all information coming into the enquiry and the progress of ongoing lines of enquiry. One way in which this was achieved was to read all statements, messages, and reports. To quote one senior investigating officer SIO, 'When it comes back "not seen"..."not done"..."alibi not checked out", then I'm picking up the fact that someone out there isn't doing what they should be and they'll be in for a bloody roasting'. This supervision by senior detectives was typically supplemented by placing officers with particular experience in strategic roles within the murder squad. If implemented properly, the social organization of the murder squad should provide a range of integrated administrative controls through which the ongoing work of the detectives can be regulated, to ensure that it is compliant with the law.

Law as an Investigative Resource

Detectives are subject to a combination of legal control and administrative control, but beyond this, the law and the way it is structured create an 'enabling environment' for detectives (Ericson, 1993). Detectives are able to use their formally endowed investigative powers in a negotiated fashion to assist them in achieving their objectives. The law is thereby available as a resource that detectives both use directly and draw upon in more oblique ways, whilst conducting their enquiries. I will now examine some of the various ways in which detectives use the law.

Amongst the most important sources of information for police in homicide investigations are suspects and witnesses. Owing to the circumstances in which such offences tend to occur and the seriousness of the crime, many people often volunteer information to the police in order to assist them with their enquiries. As the next extract illustrates, this can include people and groups from whom in ordinary circumstances the police would not expect to receive co-operation.

Outside and the detectives spotted two men, they went over to them telling me to 'stay back and out of the way'. I have heard the names of these men talked about several times previously and it is obvious they have been involved in 'stirring up trouble' in the area. They have a reputation as 'local hard men' and have several convictions each. The detectives and the men were in a corner discussing something for about 10 minutes. The detectives then wandered back to me, the other two men walk off. The two officers then recounted how the men have told them some interesting 'intelligence' about some rumours that have been going round the village as to the motives for the attack.

However, such co-operation is not always available. For various reasons, people may be resistant to providing information to the police. In the cases studied, for example, some suspects refused to answer questions put to them by police with the intention of trying to avoid incriminating themselves. For similar motivations, the friends and family of suspects often withheld information when questioned. Perhaps more unexpectedly, people who knew the victim sometimes did not provide a full account of their knowledge about the victim, in an attempt to protect the deceased's memory. This latter issue was illustrated in one case observed:

The investigation has stalled somewhat and so several detectives have been tasked to re-visit the friends of [victim name]. They have established some details about the victim's past now, which they believe may have some bearing on why he was killed, but which they are sure at least two of his friends must have had at least an idea, but when last interviewed they did not mention it...Two officers reported in, saying that one friend has confirmed the police's suspicions. They said that they didn't tell the police originally because they didn't think it was important and given this, they thought it would be better for the surviving relatives if they did not know about it.

Witnesses may not volunteer information because they are frightened of the potential repercussions of becoming involved, or they are hostile to the police. This is particularly problematic for police when a killing happens in a community that is broadly opposed to the police. A sense of this is provided in the following extract from my field notes.

This afternoon out with the SIO and his deputy on [housing estate] which has quite a bad reputation. You could practically feel the hostility in the air—everyone was in plain clothes, but it was fairly obvious from the stares that the officers got that everyone knew who they are. Conversations with residents were few and far between, and fairly curt. Typically, the answers were 'I don't know nothing' and 'No I haven't heard anything'. The SIO seemed to take it more or less in his stride and afterwards in the office there was some joking about it.

People edit and construct the information they are prepared to relay to the police with a whole host of purposes and intentions. At the core of the detective role is the paradox that those people who have most information about criminal activities are the criminals themselves, but they also have the least incentive to provide any such information to the police. In an effort to deal with some of these problems, the police may try and use their powers to persuade the person to relay the information to them. On occasions, this use of legal power(s) represents a particularly creative attempt to develop leads and clues.

The Use of Investigative Powers

The most obvious way in which the law is enacted as a resource in detective work is in the application of substantive and procedural law. The police often complain that the law is overly restrictive of their activities and serves as an impediment to effective and efficient investigations. However, the range of coercive powers that the law makes available to the police establishes it as a significant investigative resource (Dixon, 1997; Ericson, 1993). The ability to place suspects under arrest, to question them in custody, and to search and seize their property, amongst other powers, are obvious ways in which the law acts as a resource for detectives.

However, as Hobbs (1988) argues, detective work is entrepreneurial in nature, and detectives frequently use their legal powers in the manner of a 'commodity' that can be traded in exchange for information from witnesses and potential suspects. Detectives will often use the 'low visibility' of their working environment, in conjunction with their discretion, to try and make a 'deal' for an entrepreneurial 'trade'. Hobbs (ibid.) details how detectives would pester particular targeted individuals so that the subject would seek to initiate a deal with the intention that the detective will then 'go away'. Several versions of this sort of negotiation were observed in my study. When dealing with an individual whom officers believed to be in possession of useful information, the officers would sometimes deliberately overstate the charges against an individual and threaten them with arrest and/or prosecution, using the subject of the encounter's ignorance of the law to convince them to tell the police what they wanted to know. On other occasions, detectives promised to 'turn a blind eye' or reduce charges for crimes where they might usually intervene, in order to persuade a person to tell police what they know. The working environment of detectives often places them in a position whereby substantive and procedural laws can be employed in a strategic fashion to generate information.

'Unorthodox' methods that seek to use the law can be found in almost all areas of investigative work and have been variously described as 'jerkology' (Rachlin, 1995), 'offering the out' (Simon, 1991), and 'bargain and bluff' (Hawkins, 1983). These studies have shown that the efficacy of such strategies is at least partially dependent upon the subject of the encounter. Detectives 'tailor' the selection of a particular strategy according to their perception of the 'type' of person they are dealing with. The degree of manoeuvre available to detectives is generally greater for low status, poorly educated persons with little experience of police procedures, than for middle- or upper-class persons who can be expected to have a more developed sense of their rights.

Using Law to Circumvent Legal Rules

The rules of evidence and the procedural legal powers provide a range of prohibitions in terms of how the police should generate, gather, and construct evidence. But there is in between those methods that the law encourages and those it prohibits a 'grey area' which the police liked to term as 'being within the spirit of the law'. It is here that the law may be manipulated and used in such a way as to circumvent certain legal restrictions.

As has been discussed, the law as it exists 'in books' is encapsulated in somewhat broad and ambiguous terms, in order that it should be applicable to a range of real-life circumstances. For detectives, the meaning of standards such as 'beyond reasonable doubt', 'reasonable grounds', and 'oppressiveness' is open to interpretation. They are malleable and plastic, and can be 'worked' according to the situation or problem, allowing for a degree of manoeuvre in terms of how investigative tasks are undertaken. As one senior detective described it, '...that's what good investigation is all about. It's not about breaking the rules, it's about finding legal ways round restrictions.' This ability to use and manipulate the law in a creative fashion so as to find legal solutions to legal problems was held to be a core skill of a good investigator. Particularly in respect of more difficult cases, such methods were seen to be both legitimate and to play an important part in constructing the police case.

In negotiating potential legal constraints upon their actions, there was frequent recourse to entrepreneurial tactics by detectives involving the use of persuasion, deception, and innovation.[41] The due process controls in law explicitly control 'how much' of each of these tactics may be used. For example, too much persuasion becomes entrapment, but even in a circumscribed form, detectives are able to employ such tactics to enhance their structural power advantage in dealing with witnesses and suspects.

One tactic that detectives use to legally circumvent resistance or impediments to their actions are 'misdirections', where they essentially 'trick' people into providing them with information. The term 'misdirection' is conventionally used to refer to how conjurors and con-men during their 'act' perform a specific action to distract the audience's attention, which allows them to effect the procedure of the trick itself. In a similar fashion, detectives often used techniques of misdirection to disguise or mask their real motives for interacting with a subject in order to extract information from them. Where people were reluctant to co-operate with them, detectives would often try initially to persuade people to assist them, because the law requires a lesser degree of regulation over police conduct where a person voluntarily co-operates. However, where co-operation was not forthcoming, they might decide to try and trick the person concerned into providing assistance.

An example of how detectives use 'misdirections' to test their suspicions and to collect evidence is provided by a case in which a prostitute had been violently murdered. The enquiry had been running for two days and house-to-house enquiries were under way in the local area. A man of a distinctive physical appearance approached officers and handed them a camera film saying he felt it might be of some relevance to their enquiries as it contained photographs of the building where the victim lived and was killed. The officers noticed that on his left cheek were several recent looking, longitudinal, parallel scratch marks. As is standard practice on major enquiries for all persons with whom the police have contact, the man was asked to fill out a personal description form and a house-to-house enquiry form. Significantly, to one of the questions on the latter form 'Have you ever been inside the scene?', he answered 'no'. The officers were suspicious of this man and as one of the detectives who served on this investigation recalled, 'Basically, we decided to "play a hunch" and take a closer look at him. There were several things going on, the fact that he lived near the scene, he had pictures of it and he was to put it bluntly a bit odd, which just made you think "hello" something's not quite right here.' It is a well-established psychological paradox, of which detectives are aware, that particularly in more pathological killings, the murderer often feels 'a need' to involve him or herself in the police investigation in some way.

The police enquiries launched into researching this man's potential involvement revealed that a man of similar physical appearance was known to be a regular client of the deceased prostitute. As a result, a decision was taken to visit the man under the auspices of making further enquiries about the camera film's contents. As two officers were walking up the stairs to visit the man in his bed-sit flat, they noticed a dark brown stain on the carpet, which looked like blood. They entered into a brief conversation with the suspect and asked him, 'Would you mind coming down to the station to answer a couple of questions so that we can get a statement about the pictures you've taken?' This is the misdirection, using the pretence of the pictures, when they have already identified him as a potential suspect. The man agreed to attend the station and he was interviewed for just over one hour, with an officer taking notes 'for the purposes of preparing your statement'. It was then suggested that his fingerprints be taken 'just for elimination purposes'. A further interview was conducted for one and a half hours, during the course of which the suspect was asked 'Have you ever been inside [the scene]?', to which he replied 'no'.

What the police had not revealed to the suspect was that the forensic search of the scene had identified a fingerprint on a door-frame in the victim's blood. During the second interview the suspect's prints were compared with the mark found at the scene and they were found to match. As a result of this he was arrested. The following day his bed-sit flat was searched and substantial amounts of forensic evidence recovered.

Using Law to Construct Innovative Solutions

A further way in which law can be used by detectives is in the creation of innovative solutions to problems in obtaining evidence. The police view of the law is that it tends to state what cannot be done, rather than what can. Therefore, novel ways of collecting evidence may well be employed by detectives if they feel that such techniques do not contravene the law.

A particularly good example of how such 'legal entrepreneurship' (Maguire and Norris, 1992) may be employed by police officers was provided in a story told to the researcher during the fieldwork.

A while back we were investigating a sexual murder and we had good forensics linking the suspect with the crime, my general feeling was that if we were going to 'run' the case we needed to strengthen the link. Now what I thought of was that because during the assault the assailant had bitten the victim's breast, we could use this as conclusive proof that this was our man... And we had managed to recover an impression of a quite, quite a distinctive bite-mark. The law at this time said that suspects could not be forced to provide a dental impression for comparison and he was, understandably, refusing to do so. In order to by-pass this, I got, when his meal was delivered to his cell, I got one of the officers to put an apple on the tray. As soon as he bit into the apple they re-entered his cell and whisked the apple away. We then got the bite on the apple compared with that from the victim and lo and behold they matched.

This innovative approach was disclosed to the defence at trial and the judge allowed it.

Developing solutions to investigative problems and lawfully circumventing legal restrictions was seen as a key ability for detectives. As one put it,

If you're not allowed to take their fingerprints, but they're sitting there and you give them a cup of tea or take from their home numerous bits of writing paper and test them to see if there's prints on them, that's perfectly legitimate, perfectly within the rules. That's what good investigation is all about. It's not about breaking the rules, it's about finding legal ways round restrictions, nobody would argue with that.

Another technique was described thus:

You lock the suspects at either end of the cell block, then you walk down the corridor and shut the cell block door and then wait inside the cell block, with note book in hand to record their conversation. Works like a charm. Of course the defence might try to make it an issue, but there's nothing to say you can't do it and if you've got the necessary authority then put a tape recorder in there... again you'd have to argue it and it would be open to scrutiny afterwards, but anything you do is open to scrutiny.

Many people might choose to question the ethical basis of such techniques. The police, though, were of the opinion that provided such innovative methods were disclosed and available to be scrutinized by the judge and defence counsel, then they were worth trying.

The law as it is employed by officials 'on the ground' may be characterized as a resource that is available to assist in the achievement of specific objectives. Detectives are skilled and adept at using the law as a resource when investigating crimes. They are able strategically to deploy procedural law and substantive laws in their attempts to accomplish their objectives.

Law as Negotiated Order

The first task for investigators on a major crime enquiry is to assess whether or not a crime as defined in law has potentially occurred. Once it has been established that a crime has been committed and a suspect identified, the main function of the investigation (and detectives would argue often the most difficult), the incrimination of the suspect, can be pursued. Incrimination involves both the collection of information and its interpretation by investigators, in order to establish and corroborate evidence that provides 'reasonable grounds' to arrest and detain the suspect.

Once a suspect has been identified, then considerable investigative effort is directed towards constructing the available information into evidence. Collected together, the various pieces of evidence should provide a detailed narrative account, setting out what happened, who was involved, and how. This whole process of case construction is shaped and influenced by the 'bounded reality' of the law. Each piece of evidence is an artefact of the legal process as a whole and of the case to which it refers.

The standard police textbooks define the police investigation as a logical search for the truth, which should be undertaken to establish possible suspects, eliminate those not responsible, and support charges against those who are (Maguire and Norris, 1992). However, as we have seen, the nature of legal truths and logic is more problematic than such normative accounts suggest. Law is enacted as a mode of rationality in investigative work, where facts and truths are constructed, inferred, and assembled, rather than merely described: '... the police participate in the construction of evidence. Evidence is not something "discovered" or "unearthed", but is produced by all the parties (victims, witnesses, suspects, lawyers and police) involved in the investigation of the case and in this process the police are the main actors' (McConville *et al.*, 1991: 36).

Law works with a particular notion of what constitutes reality and how it can be 'known'. As such, the police investigation is a key element in the legal process, as it is where the information that will be used by the subsequent elements of the system is collected and constructed into a case (Ericson, 1993).

Police perform a key role within the legal process. They not only exercise power over the collection of information, but they are also involved in defining and ordering the relevant information.

The most pervasive and persuasive form of power is the power to define and produce reality. This power is in turn dependent upon other power resources, including access to relevant knowledge, knowledge about how that power is socially distributed, the differential availability of legitimate accounts for actors, and the visibility of the process by which accounts are generated ... This power is exercised over what might be accepted as a legitimate account of reality, and through the particular account of reality that is given as it influences a particular course of action. (*ibid.* 17)

This definition of a reality that is manufactured through the police's investigative activities is structured by particular legal standards and concerns, which seek to ensure the reliability and validity of the account.

I have described how the law and legal process frame the investigative actions and interpretations of detectives and are recursively organized by this work that they condition. As such, we can conceptualize the law as a form of negotiated order in crime investigations. It is a form of governance over the activities of investigators, allowing forms of creative and adaptive application which enable officers on the ground to deal with situational contingencies. Conceptualizing law as a negotiated order in police work brings to the fore the fact that its enforcement involves a complex, dynamic, and multi-faceted relationship between the police, laws, and the legal system. As a consequence, rather than seeing the law as a fixed quantity, it is probably more valid to view it as being possessed of a 'plastic' or malleable quality.

... law should be seen, not as having some fixed essence, but as an adaptable set of practices, discourses, techniques and modes of regulation. It can provide both broad discretionary, pragmatic adaptability and a clear rule-based regime. Its great strength as an ideology and as a mode of domination and accomplishment is that it can do both and switch between them. (Dixon, 1997: 318)

Neither the structures of law that contribute to the situational context of police investigations nor the agency of the investigators in producing a particular legally valid 'reality' can be fully understood independently of the other. There is a continual mutual influence between legal discourse and the activities to which it refers. This mutuality is most usefully understood in terms of the reflexivity that is present between the law as 'authoritative rules' and as a social process of enforcement. Each aspect is both shaping and being shaped by the other in a number of ways.

Conclusion

The generic term of 'murder investigation', regularly used to describe police homicide investigations, in fact refers to two aspects of their work. First, they have to investigate whether 'a murder' as defined in law has actually taken place and secondly, if it has, the circumstances of the killing and the identities of those involved. Strictly speaking, therefore, the police work can only be definitively labelled as a murder investigation retrospectively, once the trial stage of the legal process is concluded.

This chapter has been concerned to demonstrate how the legal frame impacts upon and shapes the investigative actions of police detectives. The law and legal process can be thought of as a mode of rationality, in that it provides particular techniques, strategies, and ways of thinking in respect of the problem of how to produce a justified and validated account of a past incident, where it might be expected that there are multiple explanations of its causation and how it unfolded. As a mode of rationality oriented towards the proof of guilt beyond 'reasonable doubt', as opposed to the divination of 'absolute truth', the legal process can be seen to recognize William James's (1975: 97) dictum that 'Truth happens to an idea. It becomes true, is made true by events.' The process of law is then an apparatus for producing an 'objectified' account of what happened in an incident and on the basis of this deciding who, if anyone, is legally culpable.

Understanding law as a negotiated order provides us with some sense of why, although police do on occasion contravene the law and other formal rules, on major investigations they are, for the most part, content and able to try and operate through and within the law. The law not only regulates police actions, it also provides a panoply of powers that enable the police to investigate crime. This does not mean that the police do not operate in 'grey areas' around the boundaries of legality. Indeed, this ability to creatively use and adeptly negotiate legal constraints is a core skill for a detective and is used to overcome resistance from witnesses, informants, and suspects. A comprehensive theory of police major crime investigations must account for the reciprocity that is manifested between the structural qualities of the legal frame and the agency of law enforcement officials. Murder investigations are structured by, and structuring of, the legal frame. In short, they are structurated by law.

4

The Social Organization of Murder Squads

In this chapter I consider the social organization of murder squads, focusing in particular upon the functional division of labour which is established amongst the members of the enquiry team. The roles of the key players and the division of labour that is established between them are organized in such a way as to form an infrastructure that supports the investigative process. This organizational system acts to co-ordinate and control the actions of the individual investigators, in an effort to ensure that the whole enquiry is conducted in an efficient and effective manner. In a murder investigation where there might be anything up to 30 investigating officers, a lot of the lines of enquiry are synchronous and as such, the design and operation of the organizational system is an important issue in terms of understanding homicide investigation work.

The Transition from Autocratic to Bureaucratic Structure

As discussed in the opening chapter, perhaps the most fundamental change that has occurred in recent year with regard to how the police investigate murders has been the increasing distinction and separation of the roles in the enquiry team. Prior to these changes, the investigation of serious crimes was very much autocratically centred on the figure of the senior investigating officer (SIO). Since the early 1980s there has, however, been a shift in emphasis away from this traditional ethos, with its connotations of the detective as a 'super-sleuth' expert on criminality, towards a more rationalized and bureaucratic organizational system, regarded by some police officers as constituting a more 'modern' approach.

For over a century after the murder committed by Daniel Good in 1842, the police processes and procedures for the investigation of murders remained more or less unchanged. There were, of course, various developments in the realm of forensic science which served to improve aspects of the police response (Cole, 2001). But overall, the established investigative systems for the most serious crimes, based around the figure of 'the man from the Yard', appeared to be sufficiently effective and robust that no fundamental revision of the basic tenets seemed to be required. It was an approach that did much to enhance the image and status of detective work both within and outside of the police. Although reformed somewhat in the 1960s, by the late 1970s and early 1980s this system was increasingly under pressure. The reasons for this are worth documenting briefly.

The man from the Yard mode of investigation had done much to embed a degree of standardization in the police response to serious crimes. However, as a system of investigation, it was reliant upon the personal skills and abilities of the senior detective concerned. A senior detective described some of the problems:

The senior investigator was located very much in a 'hands on role', they would be involving themselves in all the major aspects of a case and would tend to 'carry the job in their head'. This was fine if you had someone who could work like this, but potentially disastrous if he couldn't cope or if he got it wrong. There was no sense of objectivity or accountability in the system. Very often the senior investigator would be the only person who knew all the details of an investigation and anyone else on the job was involved only in as much as you followed instructions.

Whilst this system seems to have been effective in a large number of cases, there were of course obvious limitations. Several of the more experienced officers interviewed were able to recall examples where the officer leading an investigation had developed a theory or 'hunch' on a case and became fixated on this, ignoring contradictory evidence or possibilities. The organizational structure was such that if the SIO concerned made a mistake in directing the investigation, there were only very limited checks and balances to identify or counter it. It was too easy for the officer in charge to develop what was referred to on several occasions as 'tunnel vision'. The less senior officers in an enquiry often had only a partial understanding of what they were investigating and, sometimes as a result of their limited knowledge, significant items of evidence were missed. The almost total concentration of power and the knowledge of the investigation in the figure of the SIO meant that it was often hard for anyone else to evaluate the progress of the investigation and equally difficult to rectify mistakes when they were made.

The move away from this autocratic model of investigation to a more systematic and bureaucratic approach did not happen instantly. There was a deeply entrenched belief within certain sections of the police culture in 'the old way of doing things', and the fairly radical set of organizational reforms introduced in the 1980s took some time to gain acceptance. Subsequently, though, the basic organizational system that underpins murder enquiries has evolved and developed, albeit incrementally. The system that was developed in response to the perceived need for modernization is based around a certain degree of standardization nationally as regards the structure for police major crime investigations, an objective that, with the recent publication of the ACPO Murder Manual, has become more explicit. Within this structure, there is, though, a degree of flexibility to allow for the different range of circumstances in cases and for local conditions.

Within the current investigative system for major crimes there are four principal roles:

The Senior Investigating Officer   The SIO is in charge of the overall investigation and assumes a 'command and control' role. They are involved in strategic decision-making rather than 'hands on' involvement in all the details of a case.

The Major Incident Room   The major incident room (MIR) is the administrative centre of the investigation. It is responsible for breaking down the SIO's directives and strategies into specific tasks, that in police parlance are termed 'actions', which can be undertaken by individual officers. The MIR is responsible for the co-ordination of the investigative effort and it also acts as a store for all the information collected. Members of the MIR also undertake to provide an analysis of the information collected by the investigation, to research how it links together, and as such maintain a record of the enquiry's knowledge about the offence.

The Outside Enquiry Team   The members of the OET are the detectives who under direction from the SIO and MIR actually perform the physical research and investigation of those people, places, events, and objects that are thought to be of relevance to the enquiry.

Forensic Support   The forensic support functions are comprised of a number of specific roles which collectively assist with the highly technical and specialized work involved in identifying, collecting, processing, and interpreting physical materials related to the crime. This work frequently plays a vital part in assisting investigators in terms of developing their understanding of how the incident happened and who was involved in it.

The social organization of the murder squad in this way enacts it as a form of bureaucracy. There are clearly established responsibilities between team members who undertake work associated with their specified roles. Overall, the rationalized division of labour is intended to reduce the seeming complexity of the environment and to allow for information to be identified, processed, and managed in a fairly standardized way.

The overall effectiveness of this modern system relies upon actively involving all of the constituent roles to a far greater extent than was previously the case under the traditional autocratic system. Ensuring effective and timely communication between the respective roles is therefore a central concern of this mode of organization. Its functioning requires a greater degree of knowledge dissemination amongst all members of the team. If investigators are to be able to spot potential leads when they are conducting investigative activities, then they have to retain up-to-date knowledge of the current direction of the other lines of enquiry. In order to facilitate this degree of awareness amongst the team members, daily briefings are held where officers report on their latest findings and an exchange of ideas and hypotheses is encouraged.

In practice, this form of bureaucracy has much in common with a model of 'cybernetic hierarchy', in that the SIO and MIR are the 'high' information units which direct the 'high' energy units of the OET and the forensics teams. But in turn the activities of these latter units condition the work of the former ones. However, before I discuss the nature of the organization any further, I will first describe how an investigation is established.

The Logistics of Setting Up an Investigation

The present discussion of the procedures and sequences of actions that are involved in responding to a sudden death will not consider the investigative content of actions taken in the initial response phase—that will be dealt with in later chapters. Rather the focus here is upon the more mundane aspects of what happens, in terms of selecting officers, accommodation, and acquiring equipment.

Early Stages

Dead bodies are found in many ways, although in common with most types of crime, the police's knowledge of the occurrence of a suspicious death depends principally upon them reacting to reports from members of the public. There are three main response scenarios that can be identified, and again as with other aspects of this type of work they have a situated rationality according to the circumstances of the incident. In the *emergency response*, a victim, witness, or assailant will phone the police requesting assistance and provide them with details of the assault. Particularly in the case of domestic murders, it is very often the offender who calls the police. Similarly, in argument-confrontational homicides, there are frequently witnesses to the fatal interaction who call the police. The second scenario of reporting is that which arises when a neighbour, friend, or family member becomes concerned about the whereabouts of *the missing victim* and reports this to the police, as a result of which the victim is discovered. Another common form of reporting is where a member of the public *finds the body* and then relays this information to the police, usually via the telephone.[42]

The initial response to these scenarios will usually be provided by uniform officers despatched to the scene. The first officers arriving at the scene of a sudden death are tasked with a range of activities. They have to locate the victim and check that they really are dead. If not, then their primary function is to administer first aid (Geberth, 1995). In a significant number of cases when the police respond to incidents of fatal violence, the suspected offender is still present at the scene. In this situation, the attending officer will arrest the suspect. More generally, the officers providing the initial attendance are required to collect information from any witnesses, to note carefully the condition of the scene upon arrival, and to take such steps as may be necessary to protect any evidence that may be present at the crime scene (ibid.).

Once it has been confirmed that there is a death in suspicious circumstances, the initial response officers will notify the police control room. When such a report is made, a filter mechanism comes into effect within the police organization. This notifies a range of appropriate personnel, including the divisional commander, that a major investigation may be launched. In addition, a doctor will attend the scene to certify death. Members of the CID will be notified and will progress to the scene and they will assume responsibility for the investigation, with the chain of command shifting as more senior officers are brought into the enquiry. The report will also be quickly passed to the Head of CID who will appoint a senior investigating officer from a pool of officers who have received specific training for this function.[43] Once the divisional commander and the SIO have attended the scene and assessed the situation, the investigation proper will commence. The main activities in the first few hours involve pursuing any urgent lines of enquiry, commencing the work involved in processing the scene, and gathering together the members of the investigating team and establishing the major incident room.

Initial Assessments of the Scene

In the earliest stages, the SIO has to make a decision as to whether the incident is potentially a crime. If it is, then they must make a provisional assessment, if possible, as to what type of homicide it is likely to be. Although this provisional assessment can be refined, it is nevertheless consequential in terms of securing resources for an investigation in the earliest stages. Such decisions are made under a considerable amount of pressure and in the face of limited information. Therefore, the SIO has to be particularly concerned, whilst waiting for the pathologist's expert interpretation and the initial interpretations of the distribution of material at the scene, to try and make sure that a murder is not mistaken for a suicide or natural death and vice versa.

The SIOs studied were particularly concerned that if they misinterpreted the scene and set up a murder investigation, and it was later shown to be a death from natural causes, then they could be subject to criticism for wasting substantial resources from the force's budget. On the other hand, if they attributed death to natural causes and a post-mortem revealed the presence of 'foul play', then they will have impeded the likely effectiveness of the investigation. One of the fundamental tenets of investigating murders held by the police is the fact that the first 24 hours after the crime has occurred are the most important for an investigation. The following comment was typical in this respect, 'Everyone will tell you that it's the first 24–48 hours that are most important. If you haven't picked up a decent lead by then, you can be fairly sure you're in for the long-haul.'

The ability to make an accurate decision based upon limited information was held to be one of the key skills of an experienced detective. Death, even when it is from natural causes, can be 'messy' and lots of blood can serve to confuse the interpretations of those who are not experienced in the processes of dying. Many of the more experienced detectives, who had attended a lot of deaths and post-mortem examinations, had developed a formidable knowledge of the biological processes of dying. The way in which they talked about death, dying, and how to differentiate between natural causes and homicides cast them very often in the role of 'bar-room pathologists'. Experience of the range of circumstances in which people die and are killed, and what happens to their bodies, was held by these officers to be a crucial factor in enabling them to avoid making wrong assessments. As one detective said,

Sometimes you just walk into a room and something tells you it's not right... you can't always put your finger on what it is, but you get this feeling that it's wrong... you think I've seen something like this before and when others might 'dive in' you can take a step back and view it more critically... and usually you're proved right.

Their knowledge of such matters could be used to prevent setting up an expensive investigation where what on the surface appeared to be suspicious circumstances were in fact a result of some natural process. Conversely, in those cases that appeared to involve death from natural causes, their 'gut feelings' could be used to go against first impressions and to investigate the incident as suspicious. The general rule to investigate all suspicious deaths as per a murder until such time as this possibility is disproved was, though, subject to a range of structural pressures that seemingly influenced the decisions taken.

Examining the Body

In addition to the notification of the police investigative personnel, arrangements will be made for a number of other specialists such as scenes of crime officers (SOCOs), specialist forensic scientists, and police photographers to visit the scene. Their roles are to identify and collect any 'contact trace materials' potentially available and to record the distribution of evidence at the scene. As will be discussed in more detail presently, a key concern is to try and minimize the potential for the contamination of the scene and consequently access to it should be tightly controlled. One person who is routinely provided access is the Home Office pathologist, who provides expert advice to police in all suspicious deaths. It is now common practice for the pathologist to conduct an initial examination of the body *in situ*, in order to assist them in their subsequent autopsy.

The autopsy is a detailed medico-legal examination conducted by a pathologist and usually attended by one or two more senior members of the murder squad. The stated intention of the pathologist's role is that they should identify the cause of death for the police investigators. Such analysis is obviously of importance in terms of establishing whether the death was caused by human agency and thus warranting further police investigation. In addition, though, the pathologist is regularly able to provide the police with a significant amount of detail concerning the circumstances surrounding the death. On one of the cases studied, this aspect of the pathologist's work was exemplified.

In the briefing the SIO reported some of the details from the autopsy. In conducting the examination of the body the pathologist suggested that it looks as if the victim had been hit and punched several times in the head. During this assault he fell on the ground where it appears that he was kicked in the head and chest. At some point during the attack the assailant(s) then jumped on the victim's head and chest at least several times, causing serious damage to the victim's face and rib-cage.

Pathologists can draw upon a documented body of research which suggests that wound patterns are not random, together with their own experience, to show how the type and site of particular wounds and injuries on a victim can be interpreted to reconstruct the interactional dynamics of the assault.

Offence Grading

Resources were, in principle at least, made available for murder enquiries according to a formula based upon a threefold classification of murders employed by police.

Grade A: A grade A murder was formally defined as 'a major crime of grave public concern, e.g. where the victim is a child, multiple murder or the murder of a police officer'. The Head of

CID when interviewed understood them thus: 'Category A murders are whodunit murders where there is not an obvious offender. They're normally of national or certainly regional importance in terms of the publicity they generate, the amount of concern they create in the public's mind... they're the biggest.'

Grade B: According to one SIO, grade B murders were

Not the cleared murders, the more 'run of the mill' murders, either where you know who the offender was but you hadn't got your hands on him, or where the offender was in custody but you were having difficulty proving it. Or where it didn't generate a large degree of public feeling but it was one that still had to be cleared.

Grade C: Were officially defined as a major crime where the identity of the offender is apparent upon investigation. But as the following comment from the Head of CID makes clear, this system of classification is fairly flexible, 'Category C are more domestic murders where people are "nicked" immediately or it is pretty obvious whodunit such as child deaths, although child deaths could very often be an A, but if it was the parent type they'd be category C'.

The grading of an incident was attached to a formula intended to establish the correct level of resources for different types of enquiry. The exact number of officers employed in the enquiry team was a matter of professional judgement for the SIO, but as a guide the following numbers were recommended in the force studied:

Grade A: an initial maximum of 38 officers, consisting of:

two detective inspectors;
six detective sergeants;
30 detective constables/constables.

Grade B: an initial maximum of 16 investigating officers:

one detective inspector who may also be the deputy SIO;
three detective sergeants;
12 detective constables/constables.

Grade C: an initial maximum of 11 officers:

one detective inspector, who may be the SIO;
two detective sergeants;
six detective constables/constables.

In practice though, the availability of personnel and resources for major investigations was shaped by the overall level of work being conducted by the organization. This was particularly so when several major investigations were being run at the same time.

The distinctions in the grading system are not intended to portray any conceptions of the relative moral values of victims, but rather are designed to reflect instrumental concerns about targeting appropriate levels of resources to particular cases, to ensure overall levels of investigative efficiency and effectiveness. The grades are justified on the basis that they reflect organizational experience of the fact that certain types of homicide are likely to require more resources if they are to be solved. Having said this though, even if it is not their formal function to do so, the boundaries that are established between the categories do appear to reflect broader public opinion about murder. Thus, it can be argued that the police response to homicide is, to a certain degree, structured according to the particular symbolic status that is attributed to the different types of murder. Certain murders are recognized by the police as generating 'grave public concern', and as a reflection of this, additional resources are made available in order to try and ensure that these strategically important crimes are investigated successfully.

The police organization's evaluation of seriousness is then constructed, with several factors being taken into account. The grade attributed to a particular incident is determined in accordance with the status of the case (e.g. solved/unsolved); its apparent solvability; the status of the victim (e.g. child, police officer, etc.); the nature of the assault; and the degree of publicity generated by the crime. The distinctions that are made are not purely qualitative, they are also quantitative. Most murders involve people with prior acquaintance and are therefore comparatively easy to solve. The rarer types of murder are also more likely to be harder to solve. Furthermore, it should be noted that if required, the initial grading can be revised to take account of new developments once the investigation commences.

Getting and Maintaining Resources

In the force studied, the more senior SIOs, the staff for the major incident room, and SOCOs were specialists based at force headquarters. All the other staff on murder investigations were officers based on divisions who, when a major crime occurred, were transferred across to the investigation. Consequently, in terms of staffing major incidents there was frequently ongoing negotiation between the SIO, the divisional commander from the area where the body had been found, and sometimes commanders from surrounding areas, for adequate staff to run the enquiry. Generally speaking, it seemed that in the early stages of an investigation officers were readily made available to the SIO for their investigation. However, if the enquiry 'dragged on', then there was increasing pressure for officers to be returned to 'normal duties' as the levels of staff extraction required to service a major enquiry could impact upon the provision of more routine policing services.

There were potential problems with this system as one of the SIOs interviewed identified, 'There are formulas laid down . . . but it is the retaining of resources after say the first couple of weeks when the heat has died down, or even when people have been charged and you have all the work to do to get it to court, that you sometimes hit problems'. There were then evident difficulties with the approach utilized. However, for the force concerned, maintaining a permanent murder squad would not have been cost-effective. Furthermore, the presence of divisional officers on a murder enquiry allowed them to use their 'local knowledge', built up through their experience of policing the area, to assist the investigation.

Senior Investigating Officer

The senior investigating officer (SIO) is the detective with overall command of the investigation and responsibility for all aspects of the enquiry. They will implement the investigative methodology, setting the particular lines of enquiry that are to be pursued and the order in which they are to be undertaken. It is a demanding role. As one experienced SIO described it, 'Murders will stretch any experienced detective and particularly difficult murders will stretch him to the umpteenth and anybody who tries to tell you that it doesn't, doesn't know what they are talking about'.

The SIO is supported by a management team whose role is to assist in directing the investigative effort.

One of the key changes as regards the shift from an autocratic to bureaucratic system has been the developments that have been made to the role and responsibilities of the SIO. In the modern system, they are very much cast in a policy and strategy role, and are no longer involved in carrying out actual lines of enquiry. Nevertheless, solving 'big cases' was still perceived as being important to the career of individual officers. Conversely, under-performing or making mistakes on a high-profile case was seen as likely to impede an officer's career chances. As one SIO commented,

There are certain cases which turn into real high-pressure situations. Where there's pressure at an organizational level, because the media are creating problems and the Divisional Commanders want their people back on 'normal' duties. There's also pressure from upstairs [ACPO ranks] because it's costing a fortune everyday to keep the thing running. When this happens, as an individual you personally can come under pressure and you need a fair degree of experience to be able to cope with the strain and have the confidence to follow your best judgement without getting overly worried about what happens if you're wrong. Although it's not meant to, you'd be silly to think that making a 'right royal cock-up' on a high profile case isn't going to affect your standing. But in these situations you have to be careful, because it has happened on a number of occasions to me when 'sticking to my guns' and not listening to what others think and say, has eventually produced a result on a case that looked 'dead and buried'. You need a degree of 'bloody mindedness' in this job, a degree of tenacity and now and again an ability to take a calculated risk. Those people who toe the line all the time tend not to make the best investigators.

Within this quotation there are a number of points made which reaffirm my earlier comments regarding the fact that certain investigations, for a variety of reasons, are attributed a particular degree of symbolic importance within the police organization. In addition, the passing reference to 'normal duties' would implicitly seem to support the more general idea that homicide investigation work is ascribed a particular degree of status amongst some police officers.

The rank of the SIO appointed to a particular incident by the Head of CID was nominally determined in accordance with the grade attributed to the crime. As with all bureaucratic organizations though, the formal policy cannot be assumed to be commensurate with practice. There were several informal factors that were observed to contribute to the assigning of an individual SIO to a particular case.

The force's formal policy recommended that an SIO in charge of an active major crime investigation should have no other command responsibilities for the duration of an investigation. However, due to the general pressures on police resources discussed previously, in the force studied this was no longer viewed as being a practical option. The Head of CID was aware of the problem and described it in the following terms:

[SIO name] has got stuck with two or three jobs because quite simply because we haven't got anybody else. So we're stuck with the circumstances of not having anybody else to put on a job ... very often and most of the time you don't have the luxury of using particular people's skills for a particular murder.

During the period of research, the most experienced and senior SIO in the force was always involved in at least three cases. On the cases to which he was assigned, he would be closely involved in the early stages of each new investigation and when any significant developments occurred or when critical decisions were required. For the most part though, the day-to-day running of these enquiries was performed by the deputy SIOs, who were usually experienced detective inspectors. For the more 'common' types of homicide, there was also a move towards using less senior officers as SIOs.

The influence of these informal factors seems to reflect trends and concerns about the role of the SIO that are being expressed at a national level. In a recent study, Smith and Flanagan (2000) identified that there are concerns nationally as to whether current arrangements allow SIOs to build up the requisite 'investigative management experience'. This is particularly pertinent in relation to unusual or rare forms of murder, where the opportunities for individual officers to gain experience are limited.

In effect, the use of SIOs and deputy SIOs in the fashion described earlier was seen as one way of addressing this issue by the Head of CID. He envisaged it as constituting a kind of 'mentoring scheme', which could at least partially resolve 'the experience gap' and 'bring on' new officers by providing a degree of supervision as they gained experience. However, the potential effectiveness of any such strategy was offset by the primary concern to ensure that the crime was solved in an effective and efficient manner.

Another important consideration in respect of assigning SIOs to particular cases was location. Each of the detective superintendents, depending upon where they lived, assumed a professional advisory role for a particular area within the county. They did not have a direct line responsibility, but informally each had their own 'patch' which they kept an eye on, and they would, where possible, take responsibility for any major crimes that occurred in their ritory. In practical terms, this was also felt to have its advantages, in that SIOs were expected to work very long days during the investigation and it avoided them travelling excessive distances between their home and where the investigation was based.

There were also informal networks operating within the pool of SIOs, in that the more experienced officers would often provide less experienced colleagues with advice about how they might best proceed with their case. There were then four principal factors which nominally underpinned the assigning of an SIO to a case: rank; availability; location; and experience. However, as should be evident from the above discussion, frequently the practical realities meant that it was simply whoever was available when the incident occurred.

In terms of the conduct of the investigation, the SIO is responsible for strategic decision-making, identifying and setting the lines of enquiry, and providing an overall direction to the work being conducted. A record of all such decisions is kept in the policy file. This document records details of the investigative strategy that the SIO has used and why, as well as various policy statements which are used to regulate the activities of the team. It is intended to help the SIO to retain a coherent focus upon the facts of the case and an analytic approach to the investigation. It also allows for a degree of accountability to be brought to bear upon the strategic direction of the enquiry. The document is disclosable material at trial and may also be used in any internal police reviews of the investigation.

The Major Incident Room

The major incident room (MIR) is the administrative centre of the investigation. It is located between the roles of the SIO and those of the investigating officers. The officers who formed the staff of the MIR in the force studied were specialists based at police headquarters and they would run all the incident rooms that were set up in that jurisdiction. In policy documents the purpose of the MIR is described as being, 'To eliminate the duplication of effort and to aid the SIO to establish priorities and ensure the best possible use is made of manpower and equipment' (ACPO Working Group on Major Crime Investigation Reports 1 and 2). Maguire and Norris (1992) identify five formal aims of the MIR system:

- to provide the officer in charge with an accurate record of the state of the enquiry;
- to show the state of the enquiry and outstanding work;
- to provide the enquiry with an accurate record of all people and vehicles connected with the enquiry;
- to record information in a manner that allows suspects to be located;
- to provide a record to aid legal decision-making.

More analytically we can identify that the MIR is concerned with *investigation management* and *information management*.

Investigation Management

The investigation management function is concerned with the co-ordination and direction of the investigative activities performed by the murder squad. Officers in the MIR were responsible for translating the SIO's policy and lines of enquiry into specific 'actions', which members of the outside enquiry team could undertake. Actions are the basic unit of activity within a major crime investigation and are directions to perform a specific task. An action was usually assigned to a pair of investigating officers, although it could be a larger team and it was their responsibility to research this as directed. The following are selected actions from a case file and provide a sense of how such instructions are formulated. The code T/I is an instruction to 'trace and interview' and is differentiated from T/I/E which is 'trace, interview, and eliminate', which was generally only used when a person has been identified as a suspect. Each action has a reference number (e.g. A4) followed by the time it was raised and the day, then the task to be performed is set out.

A4 [time] [date] T/I [name] re knowledge of victim and 3 other old ladies...

A7 [time] [date] Information received from [Town name] police that they have been investigating [victim name] on allegations of fraud. Contact to get further details...

A11 [time] [date] Enquiries with local taxi firms to see whether any fares to deceased's address...

Once an action had been completed, it was returned to the MIR and the resultant information/evidence was entered into the system. The detectives are then assigned a new action to complete. Overall, the investigation management function allows the SIO and other officers in the squad to maintain an up-to-date sense of the state of the investigation, the number of lines of enquiry outstanding, and so forth.

The investigation management work performed by the MIR is crucial to the overall performance of the murder squad. Officers within the MIR have to try and make accurate and reliable assessments of the information that results from the various actions that they set. This is because the information is used to generate subsequent actions and thus unproductive actions will generate irrelevant information. This can lead to the team following a large number of 'false trails' and the enquiry as a whole entering a 'low productivity spiral' where large numbers of irrelevant actions are set. The bureaucratic structure of the system does not avoid the investigation following false trails, but should allow for such problems to be addressed and rectified when they arise.

As such, an important dimension of the investigation management function was the implementation of the administrative controls discussed previously. As one detective working in the MIR described,

If the system is being used properly I will know and so will the members of the team how long you've had this enquiry, what you've done on it and I can go in and see what you're doing because I can see the statements you take, officers' reports you put in . . . there's an awful lot of potential scrutiny there but it is still not going to stop someone from going out and doing and saying things that they shouldn't, but that's life. But the checks and balances that are in there if you're running the system properly should actually be quite tight.

As this officer intimated, although there is potential for oversight in the investigative system, this was not always realized as a result of the system not being run correctly. Similarly, an SIO commented how 'I read all the statements, officer's reports and messages . . . even if it is only skim reading. If I don't know the answer to a question that I'm getting, then I put a note in the margin or send back a list of questions [to the MIR] saying "What do we know about this?".'

Information Management

As the previous example makes clear, the investigation management provided by the MIR is intimately connected with information management. The information resulting from actions is assessed and analysed by the MIR staff and used to generate any follow-up enquiries. It is then indexed and stored for future use. Thus, we can see how the MIR is enacted as something akin to Couch's (1996) notion of a 'knowledge centre' within the investigative system. It interprets and stores the information in an appropriate form for the investigation.

Information management as enacted by the MIR is concerned both with the storage of the information and being able to research these data. It thereby allows officers to maintain a sense of the state of the enquiry's knowledge about the incident and thus also highlights areas requiring further development. In the force studied, incoming information was assessed by the MIR staff in order to evaluate its relevance to the ongoing investigation, the idea being that highly relevant material should be 'fast-tracked' through the system, so that it could be acted upon immediately. This method was used to overcome a problem with the alternative approach, which was based upon incoming information being processed on a 'first-come first-served basis'. This created problems for investigations in that where there was a lot of information to be processed by the MIR, highly relevant information could take some time to be processed, thereby stalling the progress of the investigation. However, the fast-track system also created problems, in that there was a possibility for it to become overly focused upon a particular theory about the crime, precluding consideration of alternative hypotheses.

HOLMES

The MIR can perform the investigation and information management functions in one of two forms. For small enquiries, the MIR can, in accordance with the Major Incident Room Standard Administration Procedures (MIRSAP), be 'paper based', where the work is done with original documents. Increasingly though, the majority of investigations use the Home Office Large Major Enquiry System (HOLMES), a computerized information storage and retrieval system.

HOLMES was introduced as part of a series of reforms in response to the criticisms made by Lord Byford in his report on the Yorkshire Ripper enquiry. As with other information and communication technology systems, HOLMES allows the police to routinely store, index, and cross-reference large amounts of complex data far more easily than in its 'raw form'. Maguire and Norris (1992: 69) summarize what are seen to be some of the main advantages of HOLMES: 'The HOLMES based inquiry system encourages a much more thorough, professional and rational approach to major investigations, with in built checks and balances'.

Although overall it has had a positive impact upon investigative practice, HOLMES does have a number of problems. Particularly in the years following its introduction, the potential benefits of the system were misunderstood by investigators. One long-serving senior officer interviewed recalled how

Many SIOs didn't really understand how the system worked, there's been a belief post Byford that you put the HOLMES system in and you'll clear the murder and that is very flawed. Investigating major crime is much more sophisticated than that. There is too much reliance on HOLMES as the panacea of all ills. The content put into HOLMES is done by humans, without that the system doesn't work. It can only ever be assistance to the mind in analysing large amounts of data.

Similar problems can still be identified in terms of how HOLMES is used by some SIOs. Because it allows for the management of large amounts of information, some SIOs appeared to assume that HOLMES had to be given large amounts of information. On occasions, it was observed that with more planning and thought the SIO could have focused the investigation, without having to rely upon the operations of HOLMES being worked through to filter out the irrelevant material. Furthermore, compared to contemporary information and communication systems, HOLMES is dated, complex, and difficult to use.[44]

MIR Staff

Having discussed the main functions of the MIR, I will now briefly examine the respective roles of the staff who contribute to the performance of these functions. An extract from my field notes will provide a sense of how the work is typically divided and shared by the members of staff in the room.

In the major incident room D.I. [name] the Enquiry Manager is at a desk fairly near the door into the room. On his desk he has two trays, an 'in-tray' and 'out-tray', he also has a pad where occasionally he jots a few notes down. The system is that any information coming into the room in document form should go through him. It seems that he spends a fair proportion of his time reading incoming documentation checking its correctness and trying to spot any potentially relevant material contained therein. When officers from the Outside Enquiry Team come into the room either to pick work up or drop it off he often chats with them, seemingly it is a way of picking up extra details and adding a bit of 'rich' texture and detail, to what is contained in the documents. Overall, his role is though to formulate a judgement about the validity and reliability of the information and to indicate the speed with which it needs to be acted upon or entered into the system.[45]

Sitting behind the Enquiry Manager is [name] the Action Allocator. His job is to log the documents onto the system giving them a unique reference number and 'raise' actions and assign them to members of the enquiry team as they come in looking for work. He has several in-trays on his desk. Material classified as Grade A by the Enquiry Manager is believed to be directly relevant to the progress of the enquiry and consequently is acted upon almost instantaneously. The other trays cover Grades B to D, where information is viewed as being less relevant. The Grade B tray has only a few documents in it whilst the Grade D tray (irrelevant material) has a pile about 6 inches deep. Also on his desk is a HOLMES terminal.

Once the Action Allocator has done his thing, the document is passed to the two typists sitting at the back of the room. They type the information onto the system. The original is then filed.

Sitting next to the Action Allocator at a desk is the Analyst, who is responsible for the research and analysis of all the information pertaining to the enquiry.[46] The Analyst researches the information on the HOLMES database and also has access to other databases which he uses to try and identify links with 'nominals' in the enquiry or discrepancies in the information, to highlight new lines of enquiry and suggest possible suspects. Thus he looks at people, places and things mentioned in the incoming documentation to see if they can be connected with any previous information held by the police. He also does intelligence searches to try and 'dig up the dirt' as it was described upon one occasion about potential suspects. Linked to this he spent some time creating ANACAPA charts setting out the established relationships between some of the victims' friends and other people who are featuring in the case.

One of the responsibilities of the Analyst is to produce up-to-date 'sequence of events charts', which graphically display how all the information collected by the team links together. The current chart was stuck up along two of the walls of the room in which the MIR was situated. This not only assists in keeping all officers informed of the current status of the investigation, but it also allows for any particular 'gaps' in the current state of the investigation's knowledge to be identified.

Particularly in relation to the Analyst's role it was noticeable that there was throughout the day ongoing discussion about the various people being researched and discussion of various scenarios and explanations. In effect this sharing of information seemed to operate as a way for the Analyst to check whether the stories and explanations he was developing were plausible and in accord with the facts of the case as the other people in the room were aware.

To briefly summarize, the major incident room is the administrative and knowledge centre of the investigation. Through its work it creates what is effectively an audit trail of the investigation, providing a record of the investigative actions performed by detectives and the information that results from them.

The Outside Enquiry Team

The officers of the outside enquiry team (OET) are the detectives who actually perform the investigative function for the enquiry. They were usually drawn from the divisional CID in the area in which the crime had occurred, although, as a means of alleviating the staffing pressure on the divisional CID system, detectives sometimes worked with uniform constables in plain clothes. In practice, this system supplemented the general investigative knowledge and skills of the SIO, with more detailed local police knowledge 'on the ground'. OET officers were assigned actions by the MIR and tasked to research persons, places, events, and objects of potential relevance to the lines of enquiry specified by the SIO. They usually worked in pairs and were responsible for ensuring that the information they obtained in respect of their tasks was as detailed and as accurate as possible. On more complicated enquiries, the OET was often headed by an experienced Detective Inspector; for less complex cases, the role would be performed by a Detective Sergeant.

   Pairs of investigating officers were also sometimes grouped together, in order to pursue particular themes within the lines of enquiry and develop the knowledge in this area for the entire team. In one of the investigations observed, a 'thematic' strategy was introduced by the SIO:

In the morning briefing the SIO appeared to be trying to focus the lines of enquiry a bit. He named six officers and said 'I want you lot to take the lead in looking into [victim name's] bank account and financial dealings. It looks like her cheque book and credit cards have been taken by the offender and we need to be checking her finances in more detail. Get onto the bank and liaise with them see if there's been any action there over the last 48 hours, also be prepared to move if there is any "action" on her accounts.'

In this case, grouping officers was used as a way of getting some required work done in an intense and concentrated fashion. On a different enquiry, a similar strategy of developing seven work groups to focus upon particular issues was developed. The SIO specified that:

Seven teams are to be set up each supervised by a detective sergeant.
1. Victim enquiries.
2. Relative enquiries.
3. Business customers.
4. Services to premises.
5. Other matters subject to investigation.
6. Intelligence unit: M.O. suspects and similar offences etc.
7. House to house teams.

The use of work groups in this fashion was an attempt to develop particular in-depth knowledge amongst officers of an aspect of the enquiry, in order that they should be particularly effective in identifying new leads and clues. Such an approach also has the benefit of minimizing the potential for cross-contamination of evidence.

On large investigations, the outside enquiry team sometimes also included specialist search teams and house-to-house enquiry teams. Search teams are specially trained in techniques of searching for physical evidence. House-to-house teams are used to question all residents within a specified area surrounding the scene in an attempt to trace potential witnesses and/or suspects.

At least one officer was often appointed as a family liaison officer (FLO) and whilst they play an important 'caring' role for the surviving family, they may also have an instrumental function for the police investigation. The police often needed to establish details about the victim's life as a means of trying to identify potential suspects and in these matters they were very much reliant upon the family's co-operation. The FLO was often important in facilitating a degree of co-operation.

Forensic Support

Forensic support services are available to murder investigations via a combination of police and non-police personnel. In the majority of cases, the search, identification, seizure, and analysis of physical evidence from relevant locations and people was performed by specialist police SOCOs. On occasions where particular specialist skills, knowledge, or equipment were required for a particular type of analysis, outside expertise was brought in. The analysis of most types of physical evidence was done by the Forensic Science Service at various laboratories around the country.

In addition to these key roles, there were a number of additional posts which might be included within the team. These included an administration officer who was responsible for the management of the budget for the investigation. If it was a large enquiry, then a specific officer would be appointed as exhibits officer to manage the physical evidence. It was also established practice to appoint a media liaison officer from the public relations office, to take responsibility for and co-ordinate the media interest that the cases generated.

The Organizational Structure

Having detailed the role of each of the principal functions in the organizational system in isolation, it is now appropriate to link them together to provide a sense of how they collaboratively support the investigative process. It is a structure which effectively serves to regulate the activities of police officers, but it also imbues their individual actions with a degree of coherence and rationality. In particular, the separation of the SIO's command function from the processing and analysis work conducted by the staff in the MIR, and the investigative work of the OET, at least in principle, provides an opportunity for mistakes, omissions, and wrongdoing to be identified and corrected. Figure 4.1 provides a schematic of how the various parts are connected in practice.

Figure 4.1 shows how and why the different aspects of investigative work performed by the different functions in the organizational system mutually condition the work and are conditioned by the work of the other components. The links between the elements

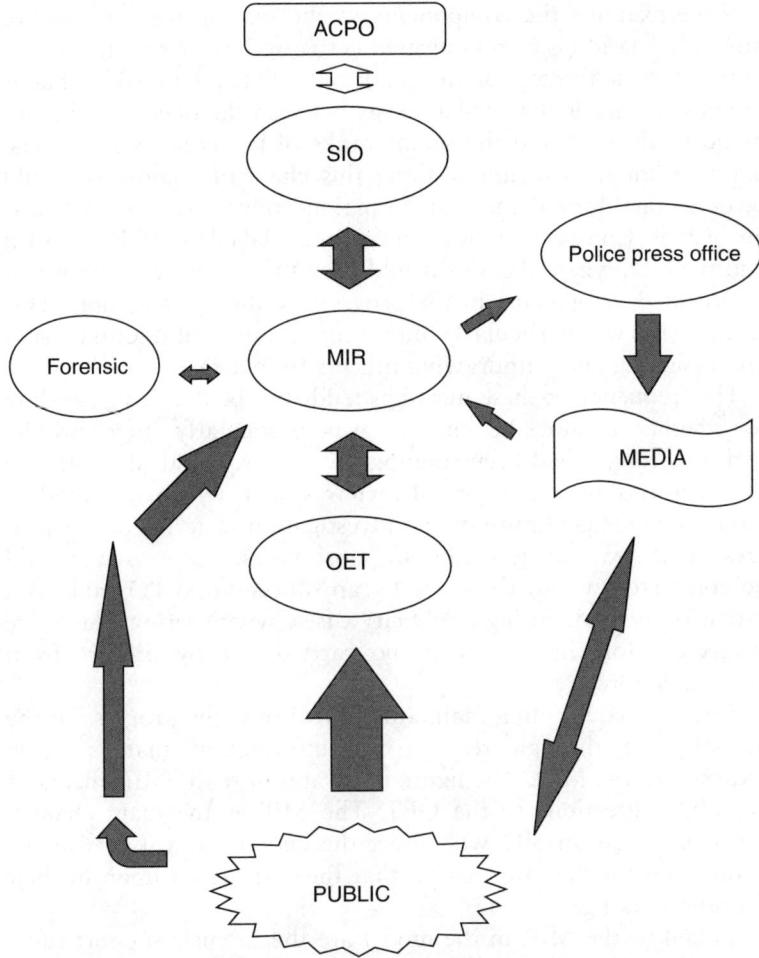

FIG. 4.1. Formal communication flows in the police investigative system

are communication channels whereby directions are given and the results fed back. The model also introduces the sources of information that are external to the police organization (i.e. the public and media), and shows how the information that they provide flows into the system and is dealt with.

If we examine the components of the system, we can observe how information is communicated between the different functions. If we start at the top of the model, the first relationship that is of consequence is that which exists between the operational command of the SIO and the senior ranks of the police service. The main forum for exchanges along this chain of command would be occasional formal and semi-formal meetings between the Assistant Chief Constable Crime/Operations (labelled ACPO ranks) and the SIO, where the SIO would keep the senior ranks informed of recent developments in the progress of the investigation. This relationship was particularly important in respect of resource issues and assigning and withdrawing officers from a case.

The frequency of these meetings tended to be decided according to whether or not the enquiry was particularly 'high profile' and how long it had been running. In the force studied, built into this relationship was a formal review system which was used to monitor the expenditure of the investigation in terms of the progress that was being made. In most cases, the review would be conducted within the force by an officer of ACPO rank. But provision is made in high-publicity cases, where serious flaws are suspected, for the review to be carried out by officers from an outside force.

The SIO would often maintain control over the progress of the investigation through reading the information that is being returned to the MIR. The figure illustrates how the MIR mediates the SIO's directions to the OET. The MIR is the main channel through which an SIO will direct the enquiry and it is also the main store for the information that they will draw upon in their decision-making.

Linked to the MIR in the model are the forensic support functions and the police intelligence sources. What Figure 4.1 does help to show is how the information from members of the public as witnesses and information providers flows into the system via the enquiries made by members of the OET. Publicly provided information can also become available to the investigation if members of the public phone in directly to the MIR. In addition, new information may become available to the police as a result of enquiries carried out by journalists interested in the case. In certain investigations, the media provide an important interface between the police and the public.

Informal Communication

The above model of the organizational structure of the murder squad is based upon formal communication and bureaucratic procedure. However, the fieldwork data strongly suggest that in addition to this formal codified transfer and exchange of information, there is a considerable amount of informal organizational communication which is an important aspect of how the work is ordered and conducted in practice. This finding is in accord with other studies of organizational life where it has been shown that organizations are not structured solely by formal communication channels, and that important information is not relayed just at an official level (Weick, 1995). The interactions that take place between the individuals who are located within and are constitutive of an organization's structure are of some significance in shaping the work that is undertaken: 'Social relations, coding procedures, interpretative practices and working rules, derived in part from the occupational culture, shape, constrain and pattern messages regardless of their informational content and form' (Manning, 1988: 34). Ethnographic observations made it evident that the formal communicational structures were routinely bypassed and circumvented by officers. The reasons for this are profoundly social and are connected to getting the work done effectively and efficiently. In Figure 4.2 I have tried to map the more significant of the informal channels of communication that were observed.

Bureaucratically oriented information processing systems, such as the murder squad, are notoriously cumbersome compared with the adaptive and flexible capacities of informal networks of social actors. Informal communications were used by murder squad detectives in a variety of ways, but especially when they wanted to bypass the system in order to get something done quickly, or where they did not want problematic actions or contentious information entered on the system which would thus register as part of the formal account of the investigation.

Informal communications were often the first stage in testing a new theory as to what happened. This was illustrated during the following scene:

The SIO sauntered into the MIR with his hands in his pockets. He asked the people in there how it's going and so forth. He then said particularly to the analyst but the others as well, 'what about if we put [name of a relative

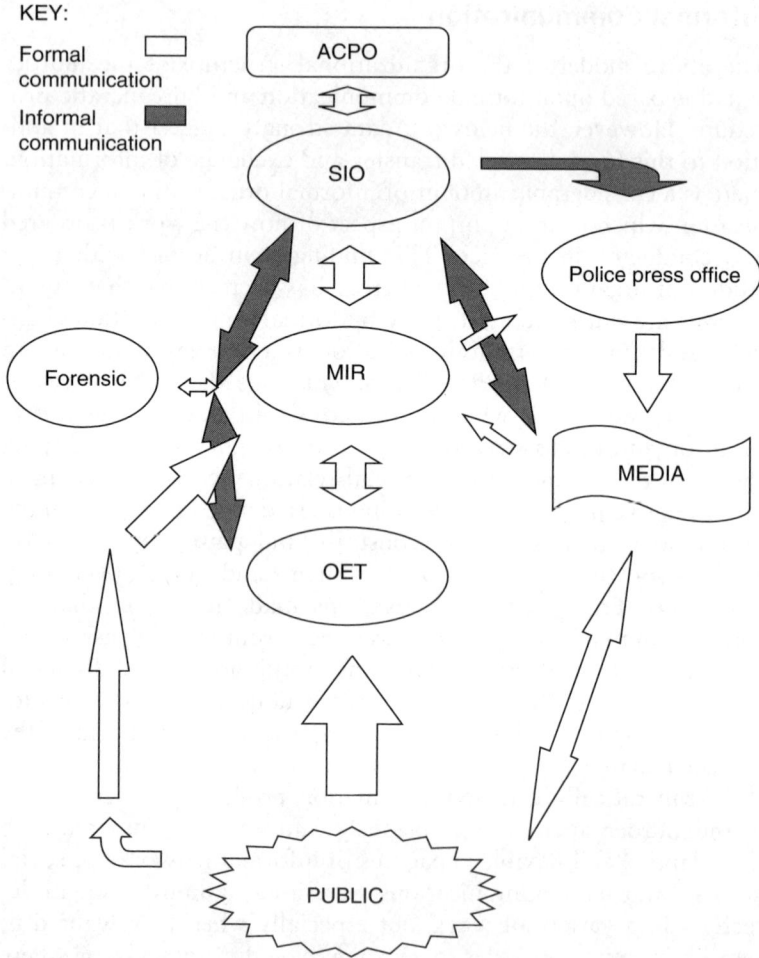

KEY:

Formal communication ▢

Informal communication ▮

FIG. 4.2.   Formal and informal communications in the police investigative system

of the victim] up for it, he's certainly capable of doing it. Is there anything that says we can rule him out?' There then followed a discussion of the merits of this theory. It started off quite enthusiastically, but as they discussed more details the enthusiasm waned somewhat. After five minutes or so, there seemed to be broad agreement that this was an unlikely scenario.

These informal patterns of communication were an important aspect of the work of detectives, as it was at an informal level that possible new interpretations of the evidence and general theories to explain aspects of the crime were often considered and debated. The information processed and stored in the MIR is used at the trial stage to provide a definitive account and record of the results of the police investigation and how it was conducted. However, there may be occasions when, for some reason or other, it is not advantageous or it is not possible to have a particular activity or reason recorded on the system. For example, there was often a fairly free flowing exchange of ideas and hypotheses between team members, as they speculated about possible motives for the attack and so forth. But the SIOs did not want all of these unsubstantiated interpretations to be recorded in the system, as this might have offered potential 'avenues of attack' for defence counsel at the trial stage. Therefore, as one might expect, the products of the police investigations that result from the investigative systems that have been described bore all the hallmarks of being formally constructed accounts. They made no reference to the many informal communications between officers that went on 'behind the scenes', and which were important to the ways in which the formal account was constructed.

Conclusion

The social organization of the murder squad is established around a division of labour and the identification of particular task environments within investigative work. In effect, we can conceptualize the murder squad as an information processing system which is designed to support the process of investigation. It is a system that is based around both formal and informal patterns of communication. HOLMES is increasingly important to the investigative information processing system as it allows for the handling of large amounts of complex data to be routinized. Major investigations often have several significant lines of enquiry being enacted concurrently. HOLMES is important in this respect because, in performing information and investigation management functions, it enables quick changes in the direction of the enquiry and rapid re-framing of the information held, should the need arise.

SIOs are often under a great deal of pressure from both within and outside of the police to 'get a result' when investigating a murder. The organizational structure that is deployed in respect of major investigations is intended to assist the SIO in ensuring that the investigation is successful and that its objectives are achieved in an efficient manner. Of course, the system does not foreclose the possibility of making mistakes and following false leads. Indeed, aspects of the design of the investigative system can contribute to the likelihood that the investigation will stall because needed information is waiting to be processed. Or alternatively, the design of the system can increase the risks of an investigation becoming overly focused upon an established line of action.

PART II

Toward a Theory of Crime Investigation

5

Information Work

The investigation of crime is fundamentally a form of information work. It is concerned with the identification, interpretation, and ordering of information with the objective of ascertaining whether a crime has occurred, and if so, who was involved and how. In the previous chapter I was concerned with examining the social organization of the murder squad and how this establishes a framework for the performance of investigative activity. In this chapter, the principal focus is upon the substantive nature of the information work that is performed. This provides a starting-point for this section, where I am concerned with developing a conceptual toolkit and theoretical framework through which we can better understand the practices involved in homicide investigation work.

Information, Intelligence, Knowledge, Evidence

Information can be defined as data that has been ordered and communicated. It is organizationally encoded data about some aspect of the world (Manning, 1988). As Mackay (1969) suggests, information reduces uncertainty, and we have received information when the sense of what we know about some aspect of the world can be reviewed and possibly altered. In the context of a crime investigation, information is meaningful data of potential relevance to the investigative activities of the police, either related to a specific crime being investigated, or some other matter in which the police may have an interest. In order for it to acquire these meaningful qualities, the information must be selected and interpreted, so that it can be understood and made sense of within the setting of the police organization.

In this sense, information can be distinguished from 'noise', which is non-relevant or meaningless data from the perspective of the actors within the police organization. As such, what is understood as information and what as noise is socially produced according to the interests of particular officers and the organization in which they are situated. Information can also be distinguished from the higher-order qualities of 'knowledge', which is information that has been interpreted and classified in such a way that it makes a positive contribution to the investigator's understanding of the crime. Whereas information is still possessed of a potential degree of ambiguity in that it can be subject to multiple interpretations, knowledge is constructed in such a way that social actors act towards it and use it in the belief that it has a 'factual' status (Mead, 1932). Moreover, there is a sense of an established inter-subjective agreement attached to the meanings that knowledge is ascribed. Information becomes knowledge when it is situated in a context established by other information available to investigators so as to facilitate understanding. An important distinction between information and knowledge in relation to crime investigation is that the latter is established as being reliable, 'objective', and valid, and can be used to constitute the basis for future police actions. As such, it can be seen that all information is not knowledge, but knowledge is a particular mode of information. The social production of information, its interpretation, communication, and use so as to form knowledge, constitutes the basis of how contextually situated social actors make sense of their actions, interactions, and environment.

In addition to the translation of information into knowledge, police also use information as 'intelligence'. Intelligence is information that has been analysed with the purpose of creating a future field of action for the police, in order to generate further knowledge. It tends to be derived from covert methods of collection (Marx, 1988), although this is not always the case. The final mode of information in crime investigation is evidence. Evidence is knowledge and the warrants for this knowledge that have been formatted according to legal discourse. It is information that has been selected and can be understood and represented in accordance with the rationale of the legal frame.

Evidence can take different forms: it can be 'personal evidence' that is provided by an individual based upon their perceptions and memory; or 'physical evidence' which is based upon an analysis of the 'physical residue' of an event (Kind, 1987). It can also be: *direct* or *circumstantial*; *corroborative* where it tends to support a view already formed; or *indicative* where it points strongly towards a particular individual (ibid.). In sum then, in responding to an incident of criminal homicide, the police activity is directed towards the collection of information, in order to manufacture knowledge and evidence that enables them to identify and prosecute a suspect. It should be stressed, though, that all the knowledge that is manufactured by police in relation to a case may not be converted into evidence due to strategic decisions to exclude it, reflecting the politics of adversarial justice.

The 'value' of the information that results from the police's investigative activities can be either 'immediate' or 'deferred'. The former refers to a situation where the relevance of new information to the investigators is obvious, either because it establishes a new 'fact', or because it reinforces already established knowledge. Frequently though, information has 'deferred value' where its importance and relevance is confirmed only due to new information becoming available at a later stage of the investigation. The links between information with 'immediate' and 'deferred' values are illustrated in the following case.

The murder related to a man who had been shot dead on his front-door step. The police investigation had been in progress for about three weeks, during the course of which it had been established through interviews with the victim's neighbours that a few weeks prior to the killing, a man had been in the street concerned, conducting a wildlife survey. At this point in the investigation, this was not deemed to be a high priority line of enquiry. A few days later a woman phoned in naming her husband as the killer, information with immediate value to the police. Through researching this lead, the deferred value of the information about the wildlife survey was revealed, in that the description of the wildlife researcher matched that of the man named. The police had several witnesses who could place their suspect in the location of the crime, prior to the shooting. They used the information to suggest that at the time of the survey the suspect was 'casing the job'.

The distinctions drawn between the different modes of information are indicative of how over the course of an investigation the qualitative content of the original information is altered as it is selected, interpreted, encoded, and decoded by police. The same unit of information can be subject to a range of interpretations and thus have several different meanings, according to the perspective of the person performing the interpretation and the context in which the information is viewed. This is important inasmuch as the meaning of a piece of information may not be the same to a witness as it is to a detective, or a suspect. The police's interpretation may prove to be especially significant though, inasmuch as they are structurated in a position of power, wherein they act to define the public account.

Information Sources

The information that detectives use to construct their account of the crime is collected through a range of investigative techniques and strategies, from a number of different sources. As will be discussed presently, an important characteristic of the process as a whole is that a lot of irrelevant information is frequently collected. Therefore, central to the progression of the investigative process is the management of information flows and the processes by which relevant material is separated from the irrelevant.

Police searches for information are broadly speaking either 'focused' or 'unfocused' in nature. The former refers to lines of enquiry directly targeted towards the establishment of specific details from specific people and/or locations. An example of this would be the routinely implemented line of enquiry to collect information about the victim from their family and friends. In contrast, unfocused search strategies such as media appeals and house-to-house enquiries are examples of what the police termed 'trawling for information'. They are performed in the hope that through making contact with the public, new information will be forthcoming from as yet unidentified individuals. An extract from the SIO's policy file on one case in the sample shows how a combination of these 'trawling' and more focused strategies are introduced at an early stage of an enquiry to try and generate some more substantive investigative leads:

The main lines of enquiry are to be:
1. Identify the deceased.
2. Forensic examination of the scene and exhibits.
3. House to house enquiries.
4. Check for further sightings of estate car mentioned by witness.
5. Missing Persons Bureau to be checked.

As can be seen, points 1, 2, and 4 are focused lines of enquiry in that they are quite well defined in terms of their objectives, whereas points 3 and 5 are examples of unfocused 'trawling' enquiries. The principal sources of information for a homicide enquiry can be divided up into five main kinds: physical trace materials; co-present eyewitnesses; non-co-present witnesses; self-incrimination; and police intelligence.[47]

Physical trace materials: The importance of forensic analysis to modern crime investigation cannot be understated. Technologies for the analysis of physical trace materials connected to a crime scene have advanced incredibly rapidly over the past 20 years, but the fundamental principles of forensic analysis remain valid. Essentially, forensic evidence consists of the physical residue associated with the offence, which can, through scientific analysis, be used to create a bi-directional link between some aspect of the victim, the offender, and the crime scene. The principles of forensic evidence are based upon Locard's famous maxim that 'every contact leaves a trace', which proposes that where any two pieces of matter come into contact, each will in some way affect the other. Thus in the performance of a criminal act, the perpetrator will leave traces of their identity on the objects with which they have contact. The presence of these 'contact traces' is held to work in conjunction with the principle of individuality, which proposes that two objects may be indistinguishable, but no two objects are identical. The combination of these two principles constitutes the fundamental premise of forensic science—that given the appropriate scientific techniques and given sufficient data at the crime scene, the imprints or traces left by the offender at the scene of a crime can be detected and interpreted in such a way as to establish a substantive link between the offender and their crime (Robertson and Vigneaux, 1995).

Physical trace evidence within the context of police investigations can be employed in three main ways. It can be *corpus delicti* evidence where it substantiates a legal element of the offence. It can also be used by police officers as *associative evidence* to connect one element of the crime (e.g. victim, offender, or scene) to one or other of the other elements. *Tracing evidence* is physical material, which is used by investigators to identify and locate the offender (Swanson *et al.*, 1996). The police use contact trace material as

forensic evidence to either: identify some particular characteristic of the offender; directly identify the offender; associate the
perpetrator with the scene; prove an element of the crime;
identify victims; eliminate potential suspects; or associate one
offence with another; and provide the investigators with lines of
enquiry.

Over the course of the twentieth century as science has advanced,
the discriminatory power of forensic science has greatly improved
and hence its usefulness to the police has also increased (Cole,
2001). Techniques of DNA recovery and analysis epitomize the
nature of such developments, in terms of how they have very
rapidly become established as standard investigative techniques.
It is important to be aware, though, that accompanying this exten-
sion of discriminatory potential and thus usefulness in assisting the
police to solve otherwise intractable crimes, the increased sensitiv-
ity of forensic analysis technologies has meant that the materials
themselves have to be treated increasingly carefully, if they are not
to be damaged or contaminated in some manner. The types of
materials that can be subjected to forensic analysis are very diverse.
However, in general, the analysis will distinguish either 'class' or
'individual' characteristics (Swanson *et al.*, 1996). It is also important to remember that, depending on its discriminatory value, particular items of physical evidence can form the basis upon which a
suspect is either incriminated or eliminated.

There are then limits to the value of and uses to which forensic
evidence can be put by investigators.[48] Nevertheless, forensic evidence continues to be seen as a vital part of the modern major crime
investigation by police officers. In particular, it tends to be used by
police to substantiate and prove their case against the suspect. The
following quotation was typical:

It's not impossible, but these days you'd be hard pressed to get a case past
CPS without some forensics there to support it. That doesn't mean you can
look to the results of scenes of crime tests or forensic tests to solve the case
on their own, because that won't do either. Ideally, if you're going to stand
a good chance of winning the case, as an investigator, you're looking for
good forensics as well as other types of evidence, such as an eyewitness.
You want a combination of factors lined up.

Detectives also used the symbolic capital of forensic evidence when
interviewing suspects to try and persuade the individual to confess

to a crime. By making the suspect aware that they have materials implicating them in the crime, but often withholding the precise nature of the evidence, detectives would try and encourage suspects to implicate themselves.

Individual pieces of forensic evidence can then, depending on the quality and quantity of physical material available, either assume a principal or minor role in the case that is constructed by the police enquiry. As a result they will either support, or be supported by, other pieces of evidence, in order to substantiate the police account. However, although frequently vital to a police investigation, the full results of forensic tests were often not available for up to three months. It was a common situation in the early stages of an investigation that the police were working with forensic evidence whose findings were preliminary and provisional. This had a manifest influence in terms of the way in which forensic evidence was incorporated into the investigative strategies.

Co-present eyewitness evidence: Co-present eyewitness evidence involves direct observation by someone of an activity that is in some way directly connected to the crime. In Goffman's (1981) terms, it is evidence from someone who was in 'perceptual range of the event'. In two of the 20 cases studied in detail, the presence of an eyewitness who actually witnessed the fatal assault was an extremely important aspect of the police case. In a number of the other cases, important information was provided to the police by witnesses who did not actually see the fatal blow being struck, but who were nevertheless able to enhance the investigator's understanding of the crime in some fashion.[49]

Non-co-present witnesses: Non-co-present witnesses provide information to the police that does not pertain to them having directly observed the criminal incident. They are often consulted by the police in order to collect contextual information which may assist them in understanding why the crime happened. Frequently, this will involve people such as the family and friends of the victim and any suspects. As part of this approach, where there are no established co-present eyewitnesses to identify a suspect, enquiries with non-co-present witnesses are one of the ways that potential suspects may come to light, due to members of the public forwarding their suspicions about particular individuals to the police.

Self-incrimination: Although in some cases suspects do not co-operate with the police, due to the circumstances in which fatal interactions take place, in a significant number of cases suspects are an important source of information for the police. Through custodial interviews the investigators will try and encourage the suspect (or suspects) to implicate themselves in some way in the crime. Although the absolute reliance upon confession evidence as proof of guilt is supposedly no longer maintained in contemporary investigations, the custodial interview remains a key stage in the investigative process (Ainsworth, 1995). It is used to encourage the suspect to incriminate themselves in the crime, to produce new information about the crime, and to establish the details of any potential alibi that a suspect may have, which can then be checked out. Particularly in relation to self-solving murders, the suspect may be co-operative with detectives. However, encouraging self-incrimination by the suspect is an important objective in all suspect interviews (Ericson, 1993). It seems that a significant proportion of suspects make some form of incriminating statement during interviews (Gudjonsson, 1992).[50]

Alternatively, even if a suspect does not choose to co-operate with the police, skilled detectives can turn this to their advantage. If they can demonstrate that any account being provided by the suspect is false or even partially false, from the police point of view, this effectively undermines the suspect in the eyes of the jury.

Intelligence: Increasingly, the police are making use of intelligence sources on murder enquiries. Police intelligence sources can be divided into two main types: informants and databases. The use of informants, or in the current argot Covert Human Intelligence Sources (CHIs), in police work and their effectiveness is difficult to quantify. The fact that the informant's co-operation is motivated through some form of exchange means that there are often particular ethical and practical problems involved for the police. However, when a murder happens in an area with poor police–community relations, informants provide a way of potentially circumventing a significant information blockage.

The use of informants undoubtedly raises particular problems for the police in terms of managing people who are likely to have some involvement in criminality. Nevertheless, the 'insider knowledge of the criminal milieux' that they provide means that informants are regularly consulted on murder enquiries. A case in the sample provides an example of how an informant's evidence bolstered the police case. The informant was a prisoner who shared a cell with the suspect whilst the suspect was being held on remand. The prisoner testified to the court that whilst the two of them were sharing the cell, the suspect had revealed to him details about the crime that only the police and the killer could have known about. This evidence supplemented the details that had been collected by other lines of investigative enquiry.

The second source of intelligence that the police draw upon are a set of national and local computer databases of information about individuals who are suspected of, known to be, or have been involved in criminal behaviour. As Matza (1969) amongst others makes clear, stored information has always been used by police to assist them in identifying potential suspects. The point to be made, though, is that increasingly sophisticated information management and communication systems allow for more data to be stored and to be available more quickly, to more officers. In effect, they expand the organizational memory (Marx, 1988).

Particularly on hard-to-solve cases, the use of intelligence sources was a regularly employed strategy. Various police intelligence databases, both at a national and local level, were consulted to generate possible suspects, often on the basis of the *modus operandi* (MO) used in the assault. The MO could be used to identify offenders who have committed crimes in a similar fashion in the past, or alternatively, to identify other past crimes (either solved or unsolved) that share similar features. Another routinely employed search strategy was to look at the patterns of crime around the time and location of the homicide, in an effort to identify 'known offenders' who might have been 'active' around the relevant time. The use of 'methodical suspicion' (Matza, 1969) in this way is illustrated in a case where the offender had obtained entry to the house via a downstairs window, whereupon he had sexually assaulted an elderly woman, before killing both her and her husband. Focusing upon the sexual deviancy and the way in which access to the property had been gained, the SIO stated that suspects should be identified from the intelligence files according to the following criteria:

Parameters as follows—1st priority: person's [sic] who've come to notice for indecency and burglary. 2nd priority: persons come to notice for indecency. 3rd priority: persons who come to notice for burglary. 4th priority: persons come to notice for other offences.

The results of this research were recorded the next day:

Results of research into M.O. suspects—indecency/burglary 10 persons; indecency 11 persons; burglary 67 persons; other 143 persons.

Overall, from this discussion we can see how police routinely seek to access a range of potential information sources. This is reflected in the ways in which lines of enquiry are directed towards different subjects and areas. The following extract from an SIO's policy file on a double murder investigation provides a sense of how a range of investigative actions are set concurrently in order to target a range of different information sources:

House to house enquiries in vicinity of [road name] and [scene].
Forensic examinations including forensic scientists from Huntingdon Laboratory at the [scene], on the bodies outside the public house, at the post-mortem and [suspects' addresses].
After positive identification of victims, families to be informed.
Full background enquiries and profiles of victims.
Full background enquiries re. suspects.
Interview of suspects.

In sum, information can either be 'donated' by a member of the public, in that they come forward of their own volition, or it can be 'generated' through police activities. Many of the officers encountered were quite cynical about public assistance and were of the opinion that people tended not to donate information spontaneously even when it might be relevant, unless they were directly asked.[51] This was captured in the following quote from an officer:

Spent afternoon with officers doing house to house enquiries. One of them said 'People round here, it's not the done thing to be seen helping out the police. They don't like us and we don't like them...I mean there's a few down here who are ok but most of them, how shall I put it, are not best friendly...There's an anti-police culture and the area's well known for it.'

The resistance to co-operating with the police, even in respect of serious crimes, which is often grounded in everyday police–public encounters, provides an explanation as to why resource-intensive activities such as house-to-house enquiries continue to be under-

taken in murder enquiries as a matter of routine. It is also the case
that other techniques, such as media appeals, are increasingly being
used by the police as a cost-effective method of reaching a large
number of potential witnesses (Innes, 1999; Feist, 1999).

Encoding and Communicating Information

The information that is gleaned from these various sources is
encoded by investigators in a variety of formats. These formats
perform several functions. They provide a way of storing the information in a more or less permanent form. This also allows for the
routine communication of the material between members of
the murder squad. At the same time, the formats allow for the
meaning of the information to be stabilized, and the potential for
its revision to be thus reduced. This is significant given that in more
complex enquiries the information held may undergo several interpretations and re-framings as detectives work through a number of
alternative hypotheses as to what happened.

Encoding formats order and organize information to ensure that
it can be processed efficiently and that it will be usable and useful to
the investigation. The ways in which organizations encode the
communication of information is significant, in that it tells us
something about how they view both their environment and
work. In relation to a police murder investigation, information
cannot be entered into the system in any form, as this would not
fit with the rationalistic bureaucratic ethos that underpins the division of investigative labour. The effective and efficient operation of
the system is predicated upon the information that is collected
being fitted into standardized units that can be easily researched,
compared, and cross-referenced at different points throughout the
system.

The particular ways in which the system collects information is
thus a manifest influence in terms of the final product of the
enquiry. Incoming information can be entered into the system via
one of several formats.

● *Statements:* Statements are written formal accounts from witnesses and persons of potential relevance to the enquiry. They
are a central source of information for an enquiry. Statements
tend to be taken only where it is felt that there is substantive

information available that is likely to be of direct relevance to the progress of the investigation.

- *Messages:* Messages are records of verbal communications either from members of the public or between officers. The content of a message may be recorded by the MIR staff, for example, when an officer phones in whilst out on enquiries to relay information that they have uncovered. Messages are a way of getting potentially important information into the system quickly and are often used in this way.
- *Telexes:* A researchable record of all incoming telex communications is maintained.
- *Personal descriptive forms:* A standard form is filled out in respect of the physical characteristics of everybody who, for whatever reason, is involved in an enquiry. This allows that if a witness comes forward to state that they saw a 6-foot male acting suspiciously near to the crime, then the police can use these characteristics as search criteria to identify all the similar individuals that they have had contact with.
- *Questionnaires:* When following a 'trawling' non-directed search strategy to uncover information, questionnaires will be used by officers to identify any potential new witnesses or leads. The information from the questionnaires is entered into the system and is researchable.
- *Officers' reports:* As officers carry out actions they will be required to submit a formal written report if they are a party to any significant developments in the enquiry. The report will detail both the new developments and the circumstances by which they arose. As such, reports may contain 'objective' factual material, or alternatively they can be used to communicate an officer's subjective interpretation of events. For example, if whilst taking a statement, an officer feels that a person was not being totally truthful, then this may be submitted in a report by the officer.
- *House-to-house forms:* A standard form is used to collect the results of house-to-house enquiries.
- *Other documents:* A residual category used for any other written materials collected by the investigation. For example, bank statements or letters belonging to the victim or suspect and also transcripts from any interviews that are conducted will be stored on the system under this heading.

It is not uncommon for there to be a degree of overlap in terms of the content of different document formats. This reflects the fact that these document formats are ordering devices which influence what information is formally recorded and how it is communicated within the investigation. The information recorded in these formats contributes to the maintenance of a number of fully searchable indices.

- *Nominals:* An index is kept of all the names of everyone involved in some way in the enquiry, the idea being that if a new piece of incoming information contains a name from a witness, the police can research their records to see if this person has been mentioned anywhere else in the information collected. If so, then the original document in which their name appears can be easily traced for further examination.
- *Vehicles:* A similar data-set for vehicles is maintained with similar objectives. If several separate mentions of a similar car are made, it may be worth following up this lead.
- *Streets:* Records are kept in relation to all street names that are relevant to the carrying out of the investigation.
- *Houses:* Similar records are kept in relation to houses and their occupants.
- *Telephones:* A list of all the telephone numbers relevant to the enquiry is maintained. Researching telephone numbers is a technique that the police regularly employ on murder enquiries to establish links between particular individuals, or to place particular individuals at certain locations at a set time.

All of the information that is organized through these classifications is fully researchable and can be cross-referenced to build up the enquiry team's knowledge in respect of the incident under investigation. Table 5.1 provides an overview of the amount of different types of information generated and collected in a number of the investigations studied. The case numbers in the left-hand column relate to the case summaries contained in Appendix B.

The contents of this table are significant in that they indicate just how much information is collected and generated by police investigators in a murder enquiry, all of which has to be processed and managed by the members of the enquiry team. In addition, the table also demonstrates the differences of scale for long-running murder

TABLE 5.1. Overview of information collected by investigation

Case	No. of actions	No. of statements	No. of messages	No. of officer's reports	No. of 'other documents'	No. of names	No. of houses	No. of telephones
1	87	70	53	27	67	94	63	68
4	—	86	20	15	72	94	58	55
8	235	267	176	16	180	301	165	145
9	92	75	60	69	122	209	117	81
11	441	181	101	132	227	382	253	199
13	1,420	431	267	408	1,182	1,796	1,717	1,634
14	2,734	1,328	1,084	781	1,651	2,458	1,855	2,084
17	1,987	371	749	374	679	3,613	3,218	1,585
19	4,185	426	519	506	981	6,202	5,194	3,890
20	2,180	116	428	206	509	3,085	2,464	712

investigations (cases 13–20) when compared with those cases where the suspect is identified at the start of the police activity.

Misinformation, Disinformation, and Problems of Reliability and Validity

So far in this chapter I have started to explore how police identify and encode information from an array of sources through their enquiries. In performing this information work, they experience a range of different problems that have to be resolved. One such problem often relates to the sheer volume of material that has to be managed. In addition, if information is received that contradicts already established beliefs as to what happened, then this may provoke uncertainty as to which should be deemed the more credible and plausible. But perhaps the fundamental problem, from which the others emanate, is concerned with issues of reliability and validity, and whether a unit of information should be believed to be valuable or not.

Decision-making by detectives as to which lines of enquiry to follow and how to perform them is often based on incomplete and/or contradictory pieces of information, the reliability of which is not always easy to ascertain. Not all the information that is collected in the course of an enquiry necessarily points to the same conclusion; rather it often suggests a number of possibilities. The ability to resolve the disparities between accounts from different witnesses and sources is then crucial to the ability of the police to construct a solid version of events. A brief example of how the nature of the accounts told to police can differ is provided by the background enquiries that the police conducted with the family and friends of the victim and suspect who had been involved in a domestic homicide. The best friend of the female victim told police how:

... [wife's name] had lost interest in sex with [husband's name] and he threatened to go elsewhere for sex and she had told him he was quite welcome to... On one occasion she said that he'd tried to rape her, he'd climbed on top of her and tried to pull her legs apart, but luckily he was drunk and 'doped up', and she was able to fight him off... [Wife's name] told me of arguments, that he'd grabbed her and shaken her, also on one occasion, at the wine bar [husband] had pushed her down the stairs.

This account contrasts markedly with what the husband's friend recounted to police:

[Wife's name] she was the dominant partner and she changed [husband's name]. She spent money 'like there was no tomorrow' and she could be a very 'cold' person except with other similar 'high achievers'. Image was very important to [wife's name]... Several of her friends at the company she worked at were having affairs, but he was totally faithful to her, although she regularly implied that he was not good enough for her.

These two extracts merely provide an indication of how the information that the police access can be contradictory and provide radically different perspectives on the same situation. In this case, they drew upon elements of both accounts in conducting their subsequent lines of enquiry. From the former, they researched the alleged rape and the assault at the wine bar, which was used to strengthen the case against the suspect. And from the second account, they sought to identify whether the victim was having an affair.

Problems related to reconciling contradictory accounts are symptomatic of a more profound informational issue for detectives. In collecting information from witnesses, they are aware that the person concerned may unwittingly provide them with inaccurate information. Memory, perception, and cognition are fragile and subjective processes and can result in witnesses mistakenly providing inaccurate recollections or impressions to the police. This is *misinformation*. Equally problematic from the police's point of view, though, is that some witnesses, suspects, and informants may deliberately try to mislead them, providing them with *disinformation*.

Misinformation

Misinformation is communicated on the basis that the person relaying it mistakenly believes it to provide an accurate description, when in fact it does not. The problem of misinformation is potentially present for detectives in consulting all information sources. It is especially relevant, though, to understanding the treatment of information from witnesses and informants.

Information and evidence from witnesses presents a number of problems for the police connected to its perceived subjective quality. Before they can act upon it, or rely upon it in building their case, detectives have to try and establish the authenticity of what witnesses tell them. This includes deciding: whether the individual concerned is really telling them all that they know; if what the witness is relaying is an accurate facsimile of what happened; or whether they are mistaken in their recall of important details. The appraisal of the reliability and accuracy of witness testimony is largely achieved through judgements about whether the new information coheres with the police's established understandings of how the event occurred, if it is plausible for a case of this kind, and whether the individual appears to be reliable.

Casting a witness as 'unreliable' was one way in which investigations processed information so as to classify it as non-actionable. In one enquiry, a woman living near the scene of the murder was contacted by officers carrying out house-to-house enquiries. She told the officers that on the night in question she had heard someone cry 'don't, don't'. An action was raised for a detective to visit her in order to collect a full statement. The detective did not take a statement though. He simply filed a report justifying his decision not to pursue the line of enquiry, recording that, 'The witness should be treated as unreliable due to her age and mental condition'. This approach to excluding witnesses reflected the fact that on this investigation the officers felt that they were having to cope with a lot of plainly false information. The organization of the investigative system on major crime enquiries is such that detectives need to distinguish quickly between good and bad information if the investigative process is not to be misdirected. In a different case, similar problems with an unreliable witness were encountered. It was recorded on the HOLMES system that

Information has been received from [name] who is a friend of the witness [name]. She says that she does not believe that [witness name] is telling the police all she knows, because she was involved in a sexual relationship with [victim name] and that [witness name] had [victim name] killed. There are no grounds whatsoever to support this suggestion. The woman is odd!

Of course, not all information can be discounted on the basis that the witness is viewed as unreliable. In some cases, the information provided is believed to be plausible by the police but the witness is viewed as unreliable. On other occasions—and this is a major issue for detectives—members of the public will forward their suspicions to the police. In the absence of any stronger leads, these suggestions from the public have to be followed up, just in case they have some substance.

On one enquiry, a mother rang the police to say that on the night of the murder in question, her daughter had told her that her (the daughter's) boyfriend had come home late that night with blood on his clothing and injuries to his face and hands. A decision was taken to follow this line of enquiry and initially the police viewed it as a good lead because their background checks on this individual revealed he had a previous conviction for 'actual bodily harm'. They arrested the man and interviewed him. As a result of information provided in the interview, the detectives established a line of enquiry to check out the suspect's explanation. A number of witnesses were quickly located who were able to confirm what the suspect said, that the blood on his clothing and his hands was sustained in a pub brawl totally unconnected to the fatality under investigation. False trails of this kind were not uncommon in a significant proportion of the homicide investigations studied.

A related source of misinformation that has to be accounted for is local rumour and gossip. The occasion of a murder often quickly generates rumour and innuendo within local communities. Local knowledge about the victims, crime, and possible suspects tends to feed the 'rumour mill' and in the process gets fed to the police as local people try to assist them in their enquiry. Frequently, such local rumours carry a semblance of plausibility, and as a consequence, on several investigations it was noted that the police enquiries often got involved in following leads emanating from the gossip of the local community.

Information from witnesses is central to investigative work, but it is also viewed as potentially intensely problematic. Counterposed with the apparent 'hard' objective qualities of forensic evidence (which I critique in the next chapter), witness evidence can feel 'soft' and often comparatively ambiguous and vague. It is well established that witness perception and testimony are highly malleable (Ainsworth, 1995; Gudjonsson, 1992). Nevertheless, police construct their interpretations of witness-provided information in such a way that they are able routinely to use it to inform their investigations.

Disinformation

Disinformation is deliberately provided in the hope that it will impede the progress of an investigation. It can result from many different sources. Typically, it was provided by suspects in an attempt to cover their involvement in the crime and to redirect police attention away from themselves. Disinformation was also sometimes provided by people whom the police believed to be witnesses, but who, for whatever reason, did not wish to co-operate with their enquiries. In addition, one of the most significant sources of disinformation in major enquiries were informants.

On several cases, it was noticed that informants apparently wilfully forwarded information which they knew to be false to an enquiry. Such problems were in part caused by the police themselves and the ways in which they sought to task informants. The informants would often come back to their handlers who were not involved in the investigation and tell them rumours, innuendo, and the stories they had 'heard on the underworld grapevine'. The police informant handlers had little knowledge of the investigation and therefore were not in a position to properly evaluate the quality of the informant's data. Overall, it appeared that major investigations often struggled in terms of how to deal with information from informants.

The way in which detectives approached their encounters with suspects and potential witnesses was very much influenced by the understanding that they would lie or 'edit' the accounts that they provide to the police, whilst others make mistakes of memory. In respect of both misinformation and disinformation, detectives used a number of techniques to try and identify false information when it first became available. However, they were not always successful in doing this. In numerous instances, they constructed data from suspects, witnesses, and informants as credible and plausible information, only for their enquiries to subsequently reveal its 'real' status as misinformation or disinformation.

A witness in one of the cases on which ethnographic fieldwork was conducted 'edited' her initial account to the police because she did not want to implicate her boyfriend in the crime. However, it was several weeks later when the investigators compared her statement to those of several other witnesses that a number of inconsistencies were revealed. As a result, two officers went back to re-interview the original witness and through these enquiries it was revealed that the witness had been holding back several items of information because her boyfriend had told her not to tell the police certain key facts.

A more serious example of how these informational problems can impact upon an investigation relates to a case where the police originally accepted the account of the family member who found the body of the victim. This man had provided a plausible account of events and his information was used to orient the investigative strategies around the hunt for a 'stranger' murderer. It was only after two weeks of the investigation following this direction that a number of results from several forensic tests became available which cast doubt on the 'witness's' original story. It was revealed that the supposed 'witness' had been lying to cover up his own involvement in the crime.

In considering the manufacture of knowledge and evidence by police, it is important to be aware of the contingencies involved in the process. Although new information can enhance an investigator's understanding of a particular facet of a crime, at the same time it can promote further uncertainties about other aspects of the case. Similarly, misinterpretations were commonplace, where information was established as knowledge by the police and investigative actions instigated on this basis, only for what was being acted upon as knowledge to be shown to be false.

Information and Action

Information and investigative actions are intimately bound together in the conduct of major crime enquiries. The sorts of problems I have outlined above are indicative of the issues that detectives have to be aware of in their treatment of information. It is in an effort to cope with such problems that they make use of established investigative strategies and familiar evidence-eliciting techniques.

Many investigative actions are products of the information collected, and analysis of this interwoven, complex, mutually productive relationship between information and action is a difficult but necessary task, in terms of understanding the conceptual base of investigative work. Using the data collected, what becomes apparent is the way in which as an enquiry progresses the focus of the information sought shifts, as does the orientation of the investigative actions designed to produce it.

In order to illustrate the nature of this relationship we can make use of two allied analytic techniques that I term diachronic and synchronic tracking.[52]

Diachronic Tracking

Diachronic tracking maps how the information sought by the murder squad through their investigative actions changes and develops over the course of the investigative process. It documents how, over the duration of an investigation, the focus of police activity shifts and changes reflecting different 'information needs'. Therefore, diachronic tracking illustrates the ways in which investigative actions produce different sorts of information about different aspects of the crime, and how this information is used to direct and co-ordinate subsequent actions.

By way of illustration of this point, we can subject a fairly standard domestic homicide to diachronic tracking analysis. The results of this are represented in Figure 5.1. On the vertical axes, it can be observed that the police investigative actions were grouped around a number of lines of enquiry, concerned with establishing information about several key themes: the suspect; the victim; forensic material; and more general information. The horizontal axes divide the progress of the investigation into half-day units. The figure shows at what stage of the investigation individual actions were raised to collect information on these issues. By plotting these over time, we can see how the focus of the attention of the investigation subtly shifts between specific issues as it is progressed.

What is evident from this figure is that the activities of the police remained quite focused and the main elements of the investigation were completed within four days of the crime being reported. It also demonstrates that there was a significant peak in investigative activity on the first day of the enquiry. This reflects the fact that the key sources of information were known to the police and that because of the nature of these types of crime the investigation can follow a fairly standardized procedure.

The next figure provides a similar form of analysis but for a more complex investigation. In this case, the police arrested the suspects quickly, but significant amounts of investigative activity were required to establish a solid case for the prosecution. The tracking of

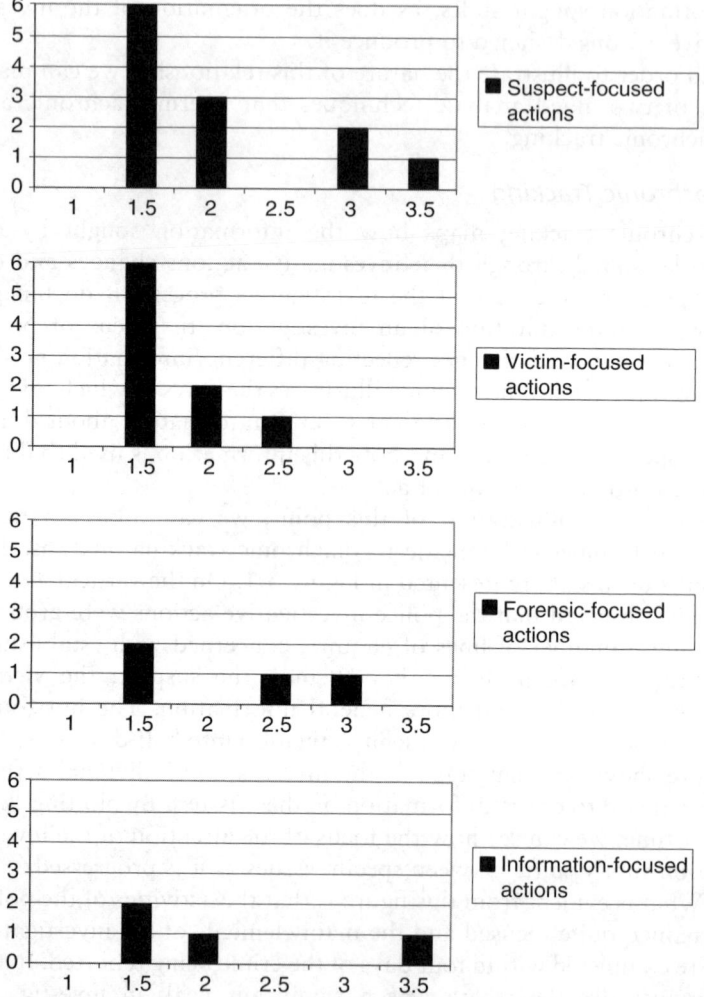

FIG. 5.1.   Diachronic tracking of a self-solver

information activity for this case shows that the process of investigation was somewhat different, lasting for 11 days. In the earliest stages of the investigation, a large number of enquiries were raised in an effort to establish information about the suspects, their backgrounds, and involvement in the crime. The lines of enquiry raised focused upon obtaining information about the victim and the suspects, tracing and interviewing potential witnesses, a significant number of more general information-collection actions, and actions concerned with forensic matters. The figure shows that on the first day of the investigation a total of 27 actions were raised to collect information about the involvement in the crime and the backgrounds of the victim and suspects. Between the mid-point of day 3 and the end of day 6 of the investigation it can be observed that there is a further flurry of police activity focusing upon generating more information about the suspects in custody. This was because up until this point they had not been able to establish a motive for the attack. However, several of the non-co-present witnesses they interviewed had by this point of the investigation provided the police with a suggestion as to why the shootings took place. These actions were following up this important lead.

The diachronic analysis also shows that there were a significant number of actions focused on information, many of which were concerned with the police consulting informants and intelligence databases. In this case, the figure also shows how there were two peaks in the police activity relating to forensic matters. The first of these takes place, as might be expected, on days 1 and 2 of the enquiry. These actions were concerned with analysis of the scene and items seized when the suspects were arrested. The second peak in forensic activity reflects the fact that the police's understanding of the crime had by this point improved. They were therefore able to set up a number of focused forensic enquiries to examine a number of specific items further.

The final application of tracking analysis relates to a complex and protracted investigation that took over 40 days for the police to complete. As has been observed with the other cases above, the early stages of the police activity involved a number of lines of enquiry focusing upon establishing information about the victim. If we examine the pattern of activity in respect of the suspect-focused actions, it can be seen that over the first eight days there are a number of actions raised focusing upon the suspects. Significantly though, these actions were raised as a matter of routine due to the fact that the suspects were members of the victim's family. The fact that it was felt by the detectives conducting these lines of enquiry that this was simply routine led to them lacking a sense of

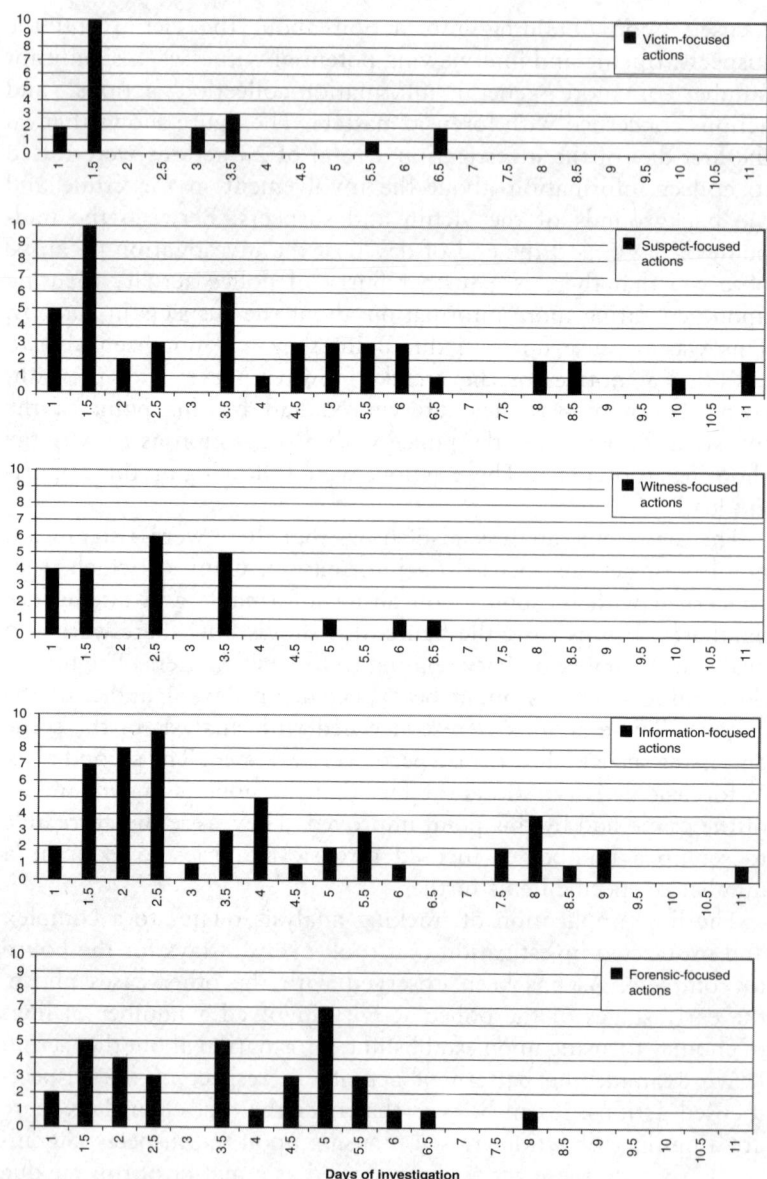

Fig. 5.2.   Diachronic tracking of a criminal cause murder

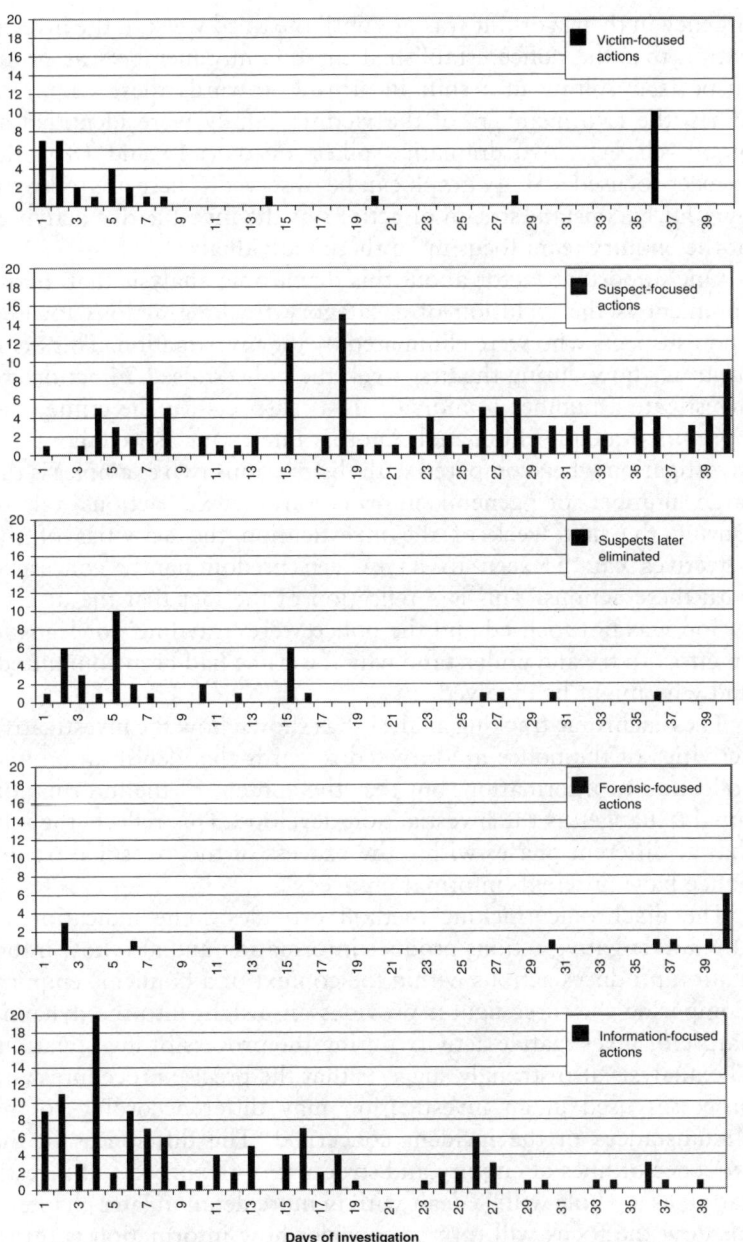

FIG. 5.3.   Diachronic tracking of a hard-to-solve investigation

urgency in their work. It was not until the third week of the investigation that the police established these family members as prime suspects, resulting in a shift in attitude towards these enquiries. When the two members of the victim's family were identified as 'good' suspects, two dramatic 'spikes' on days 15 and 18 in the suspect-focused activity graph can be observed. These are followed by a fairly constant stream of actions as the investigative activities of the enquiry team focus upon these individuals.

One important factor about this diachronic analysis that merits comment is the inclusion of a category tracking actions focused upon suspects who were eliminated by the investigation. This demonstrates how during the first week the police raised 24 actions to investigate a number of individuals as suspects for the crime who were subsequently eliminated. Another interesting aspect about this investigation when compared with the previous two examples is the large number of 'general information'-focused actions raised. During the first week of the investigation the activities of the detectives can be seen to have been predominantly concerned with these actions. This is a reflection of the fact that the investigation was not focused and the police were 'trawling' for leads in an effort to try and understand why the crime had been committed, and who might be involved.

The diachronic tracking analysis has shown how the investigative activities of the police are targeted towards the identification and collection of information, but that the content of the information sought changes as the investigation develops. This reflects the fact that at different phases within the process of the investigation the police have different 'information needs'.

The diachronic tracking method provides some indication of how investigative actions produce information and also how information produces actions within the context of a homicide enquiry. Comparing the three figures provides an insight into the dynamic nature of investigative activity during the process of investigation. The analysis also strongly suggests that the precise procedures and processes used in an investigation may differ according to the circumstances of the incident concerned. The differences in the sequence of lines of enquiry and structure of the process of investigation as a whole will be dealt with in more detail in later chapters, for now the focus will turn to consider how information is transformed as an investigation develops.

What diachronic tracking cannot provide is an analysis of how, as part of these developments in the investigation, the qualitative content or meaning of the information is transformed through the detectives' actions as their understanding of what has taken place improves. In effect, diachronic tracking treats each action as equivalent and cannot indicate their respective levels of importance to the overall objective of the investigation. Such concerns are met through what I term 'synchronic' tracking.

Synchronic Tracking

Diachronic tracking focuses upon the temporal development of information and action within an investigation. Synchronic tracking supplements and complements this analysis by showing how, in such movements, the content or qualities of the information are transformed. It is concerned with mapping out the morphology of information, knowledge, and evidence within the context of a police enquiry. Tracking the morphology of information involves a concern with the network of relations which allows information to be established as knowledge and evidence. In effect, synchronic tracking enables the researcher to construct an 'audit trail' of the major lines of enquiry and the information that results from them in an investigation. It shows how different pieces of information are linked together within an investigation and how investigative actions and 'facts' flow into one another, together with giving an indication of the networks of information that enable the construction of knowledge.[53] Therefore, synchronic tracking helps to convey the complexities of the police task even on apparently 'simple' self-solving cases.

In Figure 5.4, I have mapped out the results of a synchronic tracking analysis for the major lines of enquiry on one of the cases in the sample. As can be seen, this is a complex schematic, which requires a degree of explanation.

On the left of the figure are the seven principal lines of enquiry which were followed during the investigation. These were:

1. to collect information from the witness who called the police;
2. the enquiries directed to the identification and collection of forensic materials;
3. enquiries focusing upon the suspect's account of events, which was obtained over the course of several custodial interviews;

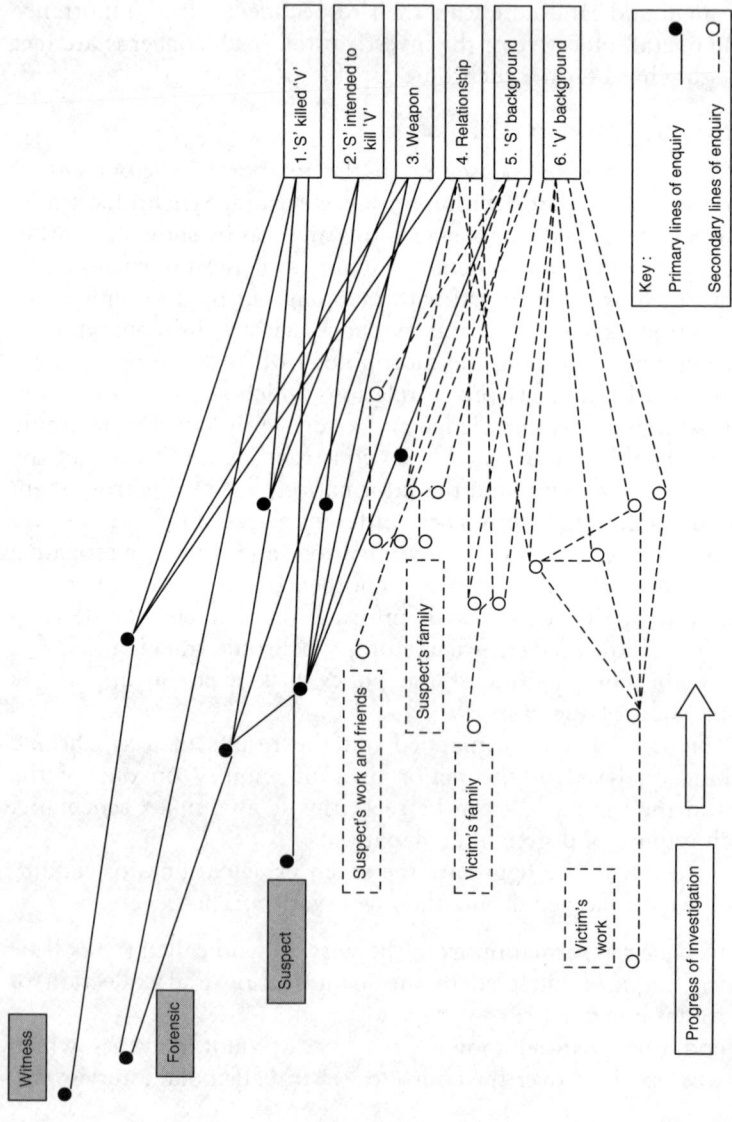

FIG. 5.4. Synchronic tracking analysis of a domestic homicide

4. enquiries with the suspect's work colleagues and friends who were interviewed to get some background material on him;
5. questioning of the suspect's family;
6. the victim's family were also interviewed;
7. a number of the victim's work colleagues were questioned for details on the deceased.

On the far right side of the figure are the six main aspects of the case which the police provided evidence for. They were seeking evidence to prove that the suspect killed the victim and also information on the immediate circumstances surrounding the attack. Another important evidential requirement for the investigators concerned the weapon used and where it came from, as this could have some bearing on whether or not the suspect intended to kill the victim. The other areas upon which the police enquiries concentrated were trying to collect details of the state of the relationship between the suspect and victim, and also background information on both parties.

In-between the left and right sides of the figure are a large number of links and nodes that serve to map out the network of connections that were established between individual lines of enquiry. The nodes (points) on the figure mark where particular lines of enquiry produced pieces of information that substantiated an aspect of the case that was being constructed, or led to new information sources being identified, which in turn made a contribution to the informational development of the police case. As one might expect, a number of the lines of enquiry produced information that was relevant to several of the areas in which the police had a particular interest. The links demonstrate the inferences that the police used to connect pieces of information so as to establish them as knowledge and how in doing so the information was used to generate actions to collect further information and knowledge. In addition to these details, within the figure, a degree of weighting has been included to show the lines of enquiry that appear to have been of greater consequence to the development of the police case. It can be seen that these are a combination of 'primary' and 'secondary' lines of enquiry used by investigators to produce their understanding of the incident.

Synchronic tracking analysis is concerned with mapping out the network of interpretative relations through which information is produced and established as knowledge and evidence within the context of a major crime investigation. In terms of analysing the investigative process, the information audit trail conveys a number of important points. First, it shows the complexities involved in terms of the lines of enquiry managed by even a smallish major investigation. This figure, for the sake of clarity, only features the main lines of enquiry and does not include any of the 'false trails' that were followed. The audit trail also shows how several lines of enquiry were used to provide details on the key issues, as a means of cross-referencing information. For example, in this case it can be seen how the police used evidence from the witness account, from the forensic samples recovered, and from the suspect's own account to establish the facts of how the suspect killed the victim.

Furthermore, the results of the synchronic tracking analysis support those of the diachronic tracking, in suggesting that there may well be a discernible sequence of actions in terms of how homicide enquiries are enacted by detectives. It can be seen that the enquiries made by the police started at the crime scene and, as progress was made, more lines of enquiry were opened up in an effort to collect information from a wider range of sources. Once the basic facts of the police case had been identified and verified, and thus established as knowledge, then the police started to 'legalize' their case, preparing it for trial.

Starting at the left of the figure, it can be seen that the first major line of enquiry that was established by the SIO was to obtain a statement from the witness who had reported the crime. This was quickly followed by a number of actions that were raised to collect forensic evidence from the scene and also from the suspect's clothes, as he had been taken into custody. Because the suspect had been arrested shortly after committing the crime, it meant that the police were able to get an initial account from him as to how events had unfolded. In three further interviews, they developed their enquiries by investigating his background and his relationship with his wife.

These three thematic enquiries were, within the context of the investigation, the main sources of information and were central to the construction of the case (this is why they are identified as 'primary lines of enquiry'). They provided the evidence about the *actus reus* and were the source of the information upon which the police made their judgements concerning the *mens rea* in the attack. It is significant that these themes came 'into play' at a comparatively early stage of the process. Once the basic facts were quickly established, a range of secondary enquiries were introduced in respect of the family and friends of the two participants, collecting background data and providing 'thicker' descriptive details about the circumstances surrounding the incident.

For a more protracted investigation than the example selected, it does seem reasonable to predict, upon the basis of the data collected, that there would be a different structure to the audit trail. Most significantly, a number of the primary lines of enquiry would emerge at a later stage of the investigative process and there would be more false trails within the process as a whole. The synchronic tracking analysis goes some way to capturing the complex nature of the investigative process. It shows how a diverse range of enquiries are used to produce the information that is constructed into the police case.

Conclusion

The discussion in this chapter has focused upon the functions of information in relation to the investigative process. The qualities of information have been considered, as have the primary sources of information in major crime enquiries. Information has been shown to be a product of police actions, and reciprocally used in developing lines of enquiry. The social organization of the murder squad is intended to structure the enquiry as a rationalized information processing system which is appropriate to cope with the central problematic of how to manage, assess, and use the information that is uncovered.

6

Investigative Technologies

Developing the position set out in the previous chapter, I will now turn to examine the investigative technologies that are utilized by detectives to generate information and organize it as knowledge about an incident. As will become apparent, in considering such matters, a key feature of the detective work conducted is the ways in which the acts and actors related to the incident are attributed particular meanings that fold back upon themselves to contribute to the definition of the incident as a murder. I am using the term technology in its more expansive sociological sense, to refer to the range of tools and strategies that police employ in conducting their work.

For the purpose of this analysis, it is possible to identify two principal types of investigative technology. The first are investigative technologies used to generate and collate information from the variety of sources detailed in the previous chapter. The second type are those investigative technologies involved in the interpretation and ordering of information so that it constitutes knowledge and evidence. In the former category, I include the cognitive and perceptual skills possessed by individual officers that are utilized by the enquiry, interviews, media strategies, and house-to-house enquiries. In the latter, forensic analysis, temporal frames, the narrative of the crime, and figuring of moral identities.

Information Producing Technologies

Information producing investigative technologies provide data potentially relevant to the interests of the enquiry team, which can, when interpreted, be enacted as knowledge. This differs from the knowledge producing technologies, because in this latter form, the product of the technology is enacted knowledge, which does not require the second-level translation.

Embodied Skills

As with all social actors, detectives, as they seek to navigate their social worlds, recursively utilize themselves as a form of technology. The physical presence of the individual's body and the cognitive faculties of their mind are deployed in the accomplishment of particular tasks. In a murder investigation, the detectives in the outside enquiry team are effectively enacted as an investigative technology. They are assigned particular actions or lines of enquiry and are tasked to produce information that relates to their instructions. In a sense, then, detectives are the pre-eminent investigative technology.

In undertaking the tasks assigned to them, detectives draw upon a range of subtle (and not so subtle) embodied skills to manage the interactions and encounters they have with various individuals cast in different roles by the investigation. Detectives were frequently observed to engage in strategic forms of 'face work' and impression management to try and encourage people to provide information to them.[54] The following observation provides one example of this:

Spent the morning with two of the detectives who have been key players in the investigation. At one point they encountered three men who have been connected with the enquiry, providing background information on the relationship between the victims and suspects in particular. [Name of detective] called out to one of them something like '[name] a word please' he then led the other man off about 15 yards from where we were standing. Couldn't hear all of what was said, but the detective was really 'in the face' of the man talking quite forcefully but in a low voice. In the mean-time the other detective talked to the remaining two men in a more relaxed manner. After five minutes the other detective came back and the three of us left. As we walked away the detective explained—'Someone's told us that matey back there knows more about this than he is letting on, I just reminded him that he'd better not be holding back. Anyway it turns out that he has heard that [name] has been telling various people about [suspect] involvement in drugs.'

This is one example of where detectives used their physical presence to assist them in their work of producing information relevant to understanding the crime. The control of their body language and emotional display was used in an attempt to prevail upon this individual to co-operate with the police. As shown above, the manipulation of personal space in an interaction is one way of increasing the sense of pressure upon the other party to comply with the detective's wishes. In other contexts, when dealing with individuals cast in different roles, the police utilize different 'front-management' tactics.

In a related manner, detectives also utilize embodied skills in providing an initial interpretation of the information that they glean from their interactions. Officers make provisional evaluations of the validity and reliability of the information and its source as an intrinsic part of the work that they perform. The use of these types of skills is exemplified in one case in the fieldwork, where a detective felt that the actions of the victim's wife were not quite appropriate, given the circumstances. The officer recorded their suspicions in a report, which was passed to the SIO:

At this stage it struck me that she was not as upset as perhaps she should have been. Throughout the next couple of hours with [wife's name] her emotions were not what I would expect from a lady whose husband has just been shot to death. She did shed some tears but I found it rather disconcerting that she was easily comforted.

It was eventually established by detectives that the wife had hired someone to kill her husband, but it was the initial suspicions of this officer that gave the enquiry the initial direction and enabled them to uncover the wife's involvement in a protracted and difficult investigation.

Detectives as investigative technologies do not simply follow the instructions generated by the other parts of the investigative system. They are creative in the conduct of their work, drawing upon various embodied skills involving the perception of small interactional or environmental cues which, based upon experience and knowledge, are identified as being either appropriate or out of place.

Interviews

The control of space and monitoring the reactions of others are also key features of certain types of interviews that detectives conduct. As a general information producing technology, interviews are possibly the most important method for the police in terms of collecting information from co-present and non-co-present witnesses, and suspects. The style of interview conducted by police, whether it be with a suspect or witness, will be governed by the interviewer's assessment of the person's level of co-operation, an evaluation of the plausibility of what is being relayed, and a belief, based upon these factors, about what interview strategy (i.e. more or less coercive) is likely to be the most effective. Some suspects and witnesses interviewed elect to co-operate with the police, others, though, choose to provide either partial or more wholesale forms of resistance to the enquiries put to them. The police utilize various interview strategies and tactics in an attempt to overcome any such recalcitrance.

Our understanding of the conduct of police interviews can be enriched by Goffman's (1969) model of strategic interaction. The detective will seek to anticipate how the suspect will react to their interview tactics and thereby steer the interaction towards an established objective. In so doing the interviewer tries to manage the interview interaction in order to extract relevant information from the interviewee, making use of an array of moves and counter-moves to overcome any conscious or unconscious 'blocking moves' that may restrict the exchange. These interview tactics regularly include: 'misdirections' designed to mask their true intentions (see Chapter 3); persuasion and threats to encourage co-operation; impression management; appeals to the conscience and morals of the other person, and so forth. Therefore, as Leo (1996) comments, although the interview is fundamentally an information gathering activity, in action it resembles the process, sequence, and structure of a confidence game, although, in adopting this imagery, the implicit coercion and manipulation available to the police should not be overlooked (Gudjonssen, 1992).

A range of interrogatory tactics are available to the interviewer; their skill is in 'reading' and 'manipulating' the subject's vulnerabilities and deceit, and selecting the right approach to persuade the interviewees to provide information that advances the police enquiries. Importantly though, the moves and counter-moves made by interviewer and respondent should not be understood as solely based upon cool strategic logic. The situation and the nature of the interaction frequently evoke and demand emotive responses from both parties, which have an important impact upon determining both the process and outcome.

A custodial interview provides the opportunity for the police to test out their hypothesized suspicions and to gauge the reactions of the suspect when confronted with them (Stockdale, 1993). This can occur on a subjective level, in that the interviewing officers may form the impression that the suspect is guilty, or it may be more objectively based, in that new evidence is forthcoming. The interview may either (a) confirm the police suspicions; (b) result in new leads to be followed up; (c) cast doubt on their suspicions; or (d) refute them. In the latter instance, the police will release the suspect and return to re-examine their evidence. If the result of the interview is more equivocal, then they may decide to try and check any alibis that the suspect may have offered, and attempt to strengthen their case. An interview may result in new evidence coming to light, or it may produce information which can be cross-referenced with other facts established by the enquiry, to validate and support that aspect of the police case. Although officers are increasingly being encouraged to view the custodial interview as an information gathering exercise, there is little doubt that encouraging suspects to make self-incriminatory or confession statements remains an important objective for investigating officers (Hobbs, 1988; Gudjonssen, 1992; Ainsworth, 1995).

The custodial interview is then a central event in the progress of the investigation and the police are advantageously situated within the interview, in respect of their control over the suspect and the situation, to advance their case (McConville et al., 1991). Contemporary interrogation strategies are based upon a notion that the best way to uncover a suspect's deception and to test the integrity of any account is to question them repeatedly over time about their claims. If ambiguities and discrepancies can be shown between different accounts, then the interviewing officer will seek to follow these up and exploit them.[55]

A key facet of the interview interaction relates to the interviewers' structurally enhanced powers to legitimately manipulate and deceive the suspect into (often unwittingly) assisting the police enquiry (Leo, 1996). After listening to the tape-recordings from the interviews with a suspect in one case in the fieldwork, I questioned the two interviewers about how they had approached the task.[56]

R   I was quite surprised you know, by the tone and the low-level way in which you did the questioning.

DS   What do you mean by that?

R Well I just thought, that what with everything and the way in which you've been talking about him, you would have gone in and started shouting at him and what have you. I just seemed to expect something a bit more confrontational.

DS Well we did talk about that didn't we, before we started.

DC Yeah, we thought about it quite hard.

DS Mmm. But after talking to the boss we came to the conclusion that if we just walked in and started banging the table and shouting and pushing him, he might just close off from us. So we decided to see if we couldn't play it a bit more 'softly softly'.

DC The thing is, what you're looking for is how can I get this person talking to me. You've got to think, 'what is it that I've got that I can use to my advantage over this person?' Sometimes you might decide to go in and hit 'em with it straight off and try to simply confront them with it. On other occasions, like in this case, we went in there with a 'Yeah, look we understand, we know it must be difficult for you' approach because that's what we thought would work.

DS I mean although he didn't 'cough the job', I think in what he said, he gave us a few things to follow up and a few pieces that might confirm other details.

This is supportive of my earlier comments concerning the strategic nature of the interview interaction and how detectives try to exert control over the encounter. Gudjonsson (1992) identifies that when suspects confess, it tends to result from a combination of internal and external pressures together with a belief that the police have a strong case against them. The skill of an interviewer is in part based upon their ability to manipulate the suspect's perception of such factors.

In the force studied, it was established practice that only those officers who had received 'advanced interview training' would be permitted to conduct interviews with murder suspects. The murder suspects in the cases studied were often interviewed on three or more separate occasions. Partly this was in order to comply with the requirements of PACE, but a break between interviews also allowed investigators to study the suspect's account, to compare it with the other evidence that had been collected, and also to work out how all 'the pieces' were fitting together. More importantly though, getting suspects to repeat their account of events several times over an extended period was believed to be a good tactic for revealing any lies or discrepancies.

The following extracts taken from police interviews with a man who had killed his wife after an argument further support many of the points already made. Of particular relevance to this discussion is the way in which the production of an authoritative account of events is negotiated between police and suspect. The questions used by the police are concerned with trying to construct the charge against the suspect. The suspect tells how early in the evening he and his wife had been bathing their baby son:[57]

S   When we were bathing [the baby] she said 'Oh I don't want to be in the same room with you'... She just made another snide comment... I just had... it was an unbelievable, uncontrollable urge to hurt her.

P1   I don't wish to dwell on it but do you remember anything about the comments she made to you and why it makes you so angry... what the content of that comment was?

S   The content wasn't important... just the way she said it. I had the knife in my right hand and I just turned round and pushed it in her.

In the above, the officers were obviously trying to establish whether the comments made by his wife could be construed as constituting sufficient provocation to warrant a temporary loss of control. At this point, the interview was suspended for a 15-minute break. When they returned, the interviewee was encouraged to continue and in the following extract they move on to cover the actual attack itself:

S   The, I was just out of control, I mean the next 30 seconds were just a mad... I just went mad and we were just fighting... I was just stabbing her repeatedly... I remember stabbing her in the chest and back. She was fighting back trying to protect herself... blood everywhere.

P1   You had one knife did you at any time stab her with the knife she was using?

P2   There are indications that both knives were used in the fight, can you recall how they were used?

[...]

P2   Were you threatened at all?

S   Not in the normal sense of the word.

P1   With regards the cannabis, had you smoked any that day? We're not interested in the cannabis *per se* but its relation to the murder.[58]

S   No I smoked some the night before. I had two pints at lunch time.

[...]

The police here were trying to establish that the suspect was not intoxicated to such a degree that he was not aware of his actions, which goes to the *mens rea* of the offence. A short time later in the course of the interview the detectives shifted the focus of the questioning in an attempt to obtain more details on the background to why the attack took place:

P2 Why is your marriage breaking up?
S   She doesn't love me ... I'm just one of those wasters at the bar.
P2 Having been through a broken marriage myself I know how difficult it can be.
S   I didn't want it to end, she wanted to. There's been a lot of problems this year for me ... When we married I was the one who had to do all the changing.

The answers that he provided here are indicative of his sense of him losing 'ownership' of his wife. In the next exchanges the police directly questioned the suspect about his intentions. This line of questioning was obviously connected to the decision as to whether he should be charged with manslaughter or murder:

P1 What was your intention whilst you were stabbing her?
S   To hurt her.
P2 Ultimately did you have an intention?
S   I didn't have any conscious intentions.
P1 Was it your intention to kill her?
S   No, not to kill her. I didn't think she was dead when I left. I'm not making any excuses for what I did. There's no reason for it.

If we examine the two themes within the interview interaction, which are of primary interest to this discussion, it can be seen that the killer was trying to explain his actions to himself as much as the police. Variously he refers to his intention 'to hurt her', that he was in the grip of a temporary 'madness', and that 'there's no reason for it'. In other parts of his speech, he seemed to imply that he was provoked. As such, these extracts support some of the comments raised in Chapter 2 concerning the role of emotion and its influence upon how homicides occur. In terms of the police role in the interaction, we can see how they were skilfully probing the suspect's account to test particular evidentiary requirements of their case. The man was charged with murder by the police and convicted of manslaughter at his trial.

This extract serves to illustrate how, in some interactions, the police are actively engaged in negotiating with the suspect to assemble a plausible definition of the situation. In doing so, they draw upon a range of resources in an effort to establish a definition that coheres with their objectives. The interviewing officers in the above can be seen to be deploying 'uncovering moves' (Goffman, 1969) intended to undermine the possible excuses, alibis, or mitigating claims offered by the suspect. As discussed in an earlier chapter, such tactics may be accompanied by 'misdirections' used to mask the intentions of the interviewer and to trick the suspect or witness into revealing more information than they might otherwise have done.

Media Strategy

One way in which police often try and access information from members of the public is through co-operating with journalists.[59] The mass communication that media organizations provide represents a comparatively cost-efficient and quick mechanism through which the police can make contact with a large number of potential witnesses. For their part, journalists are often interested in murder investigations because such stories fulfil the institutionally maintained criterion of what is 'newsworthy' and what the public is interested in. Consequently, on major crimes, SIOs use press conferences, family appeals, reconstructions, and interviews to encourage members of the public to forward information which may be of potential relevance to the enquiry.

The use of media as an investigative resource requires careful impression management by an SIO and their team. They have to be careful about what information they reveal through the media, but they are also aware of what is required in order for the story to receive the right amount of media coverage. The next field note illustrates some of the concerns involved.

This morning a big press conference was held, at which members of the victim's family made a public appeal. The conference was held in the bar area of the police station with blue logo screens placed behind the desk where some chairs were arranged for them to sit. There was a fair degree of milling around and the room was fairly full of journalists, including two camera crews and a lot of photographers as well as several radio stations. Just before the family came out the woman from the Press Relations Office who had been involved in setting up this event came in with the SIO. She said to the assembled journalists 'The running order is going to be that the family [she then read out their names] will make a short appeal for information and for people to contact the police, they will then be led out and will not be taking any questions, then Superintendent [name] will make a

short statement after which he will answer a few of your questions, ok.'
After which the SIO said 'Now obviously, they are very upset and it has
taken a lot for us to persuade them to do this so I would appreciate it if the
level of disruption can be kept to a minimum . . . not too many flash pictures
and what have you, as it may take them a bit of time to settle down'. Both
of them then briefly left by the door at the back of the room and shortly
afterwards reappeared leading in four members of the victim's family, two
women, one older than the other and two men. When they walked in their
was a flurry of activity amongst the journalists and a lot of flashes of camera
bulbs. They sat down at the desk where there were a number of micro-
phones. The SIO then introduced the family members to the press audience.
After which, the younger woman began to read out the statement that had
been prepared with the police the day before. As she started describing her
mother, her voice started to falter and she began crying, although she kept
trying to read she couldn't manage it, and the older woman took over from
her. One of the men put a comforting arm around the younger woman's
shoulders. Once the older woman had finished reading the statement one of
the men added what I think was an impromptu remark saying '[Victim's
name] was a lovely woman, someone's got to help us, if they know
anything, please tell the police, please.' There was then a frantic burst of
flash photography which had been more intermittent whilst the statement
was being read out. The family got up to leave and as they did so several
journalists began trying to ask them questions, but the police ushered them
out. As they left I was very aware of how emotionally intense it had been
and the whole atmosphere had been charged whilst the statement was
being read. The SIO returned and recited a statement and took a few
questions about various details of the case many of which he answered to
the effect of 'no comment'. . . . Afterwards, a few of the officers were
discussing the conference in the Incident Room. One said 'Well that was
a result, a few tears, bit of emotion that should get us on the one o'clock
news', to which another replied 'Yep, they gave us just what we needed,
couldn't have done it better if we asked 'em'.

These latter comments are indicative of the sense of compromise
that is intrinsic in police–media relations. The police know what
factors make a story attractive to journalists and they are aware
that they may have to exploit certain aspects of the crime and those
connected to it, if the media's effectiveness in helping them to
investigate the incident is to be realized. Such co-operation is also
seen as a way of managing media interest, although as will be
discussed in more detail in Chapter 10, this is not always done
successfully.

House-to-House Enquiries

House-to-house enquiries are a routine investigative strategy, conducted in the area around the crime scene, in order to generate
information. The routine use of house-to-house enquiries as part of
the investigative methodology is a reflection of the police belief that
'local knowledge' is crucial in solving and understanding crimes.
The actual work of doing the house-to-house enquiries will usually
be given to a team of officers. They will be directed to visit all the
premises in a specified area surrounding the scene and to speak to
all the residents in case they noticed anything suspicious or can
enhance the police's understanding in terms of what has occurred.
The following extract from the policy file on a whodunit enquiry
shows how the police attempt to use information from the house-
to-house enquiries to identify people in the vicinity of the crime
who should be made the subject of more extensive contact:

> The SIO or deputy SIO will examine all the house to house forms
> according to the following criteria:
>
> 1.   Knows or has knowledge of the victims or has visited the scene.
> 2.   Unverified alibi for the material times.
> 3.   Persons within the house to house area [the evening and night on
>   which the victims were killed].

These lines of enquiry did in fact result in an important witness
being located, who up until the police spoke to him had not realized
the importance of what he had seen. House-to-house offers an
initial sweep of a locale to establish potential leads which can
then be the subject of further actions to follow them up.

It should be acknowledged, though, that house-to-house is a
fairly 'blunt' investigative tool. Whilst in several enquiries it did
produce useful information that advanced the investigation, on all
occasions it generated a lot of irrelevant or unreliable data.

Intelligence Work

Developing my comments from the previous chapter concerning the
role and functions of intelligence sources, two main forms of 'intelligence work' are conducted by police on major crime enquiries.
The following directions from an SIO provide some indication of
how informants and intelligence databases are used in combination:

Force Intelligence Unit to establish list of MO suspects for offence... all MO suspects raised by research by FIU to be entered on the system immediately, Further research to be carried out to determine the priority given to their elimination... Priority made contact all informants West Division, Central Division, Drug Unit, Antique Unit and Regional Crime Squad. Officers to see in an effort to elicit intelligence on this enquiry.

The use of intelligence sources in this way is particularly important for those cases where the incident is related to ongoing criminal activities.

Especially in those cases where a suspect was not immediately identified, one of the first directions regularly issued by an SIO was to research the police intelligence databases for possible *modus operandi* suspects. The following excerpt from a policy file provides an example of this, 'FIU [Force Intelligence Unit] to research files for possible M.O. suspects, these to be entered on HOLMES and prioritised for raising actions in order to T/I/E [Trace/Interview/ Eliminate] particular individuals'. Similarly, it was established practice to research the local crime reports to see if there are any potential links to other incidents in the area. Consulting informants and interrogating intelligence databases is one way in which police can start to get an enquiry moving, using these tactics to identify possible suspects and sometimes to find out background information on the victim.

Knowledge Producing Technologies

Whereas the investigative technologies detailed above were implemented by detectives on the understanding that they would in some way contribute to the production of information, the second set of technologies that are a constitutive part of the investigative methodology are concerned with the analysis, interpretation, and organization of this information and thus its translation into knowledge and evidence.

Forensic Work

Within the crime investigation process, forensic evidence, derived from the 'scientific' analysis of the physical detritus of the crime, is routinely attributed the status of providing objective proof. Indeed, it is this rhetoric of 'hard science' that has manifestly contributed to the power of forensic techniques in modern crime investigations. It shapes how detectives and other actors within the criminal justice system respond to and seek to use physical evidence.

However, drawing upon the anti-foundationalist critique of scientific practice found in the literature on the sociology of scientific knowledge (SSK), we can develop a more critical understanding of how physical materials are enacted as evidence in crime investigations. Authors writing from a constructionist SSK position have shown that laboratory science is a creative, interpretative practice (Latour, 1985; Knorr-Cetina, 1980). It is normal in experimental science for the 'local' environmental conditions to be carefully manipulated to make the procedure in question work and for the results to be subject to interpretation, in order that they are meaningful within an 'epistemic culture' (Knorr-Cetina, 1999; Lynch, 1994).

Compared with the more standard forms of laboratory science, from which it appropriates many disciplinary principles, forensic science is even more subject to environmental contingencies and reliant upon the interpretative skills of the scientist. The crime scene examiners work in the messy and chaotic conditions of the crime scene which contrast with the artificially sanitized and ordered social worlds of laboratory work. As a consequence crime scene examiners and forensic scientists are routinely confronted with problems in terms of how to identify, extract, and process potential evidence, and great care has to be taken in this work. The search for contact trace materials is framed by the existing knowledge held by an investigation, but in turn, the analysis of these traces often causes alterations in the details of the narrative that is being constructed. Because evidence based upon contact trace materials is often held to be more objective than alternative sources of evidence, it is frequently pivotal in the narrative, establishing and warranting some of the key facts of the police account.

The identification of forensic evidence is thus an involved and complex process. Frequently, police would remove hundreds of different items and exhibits from the crime scene in order that they can be subject to different types of testing. This massive extraction of evidence from a scene obviously creates problems in relation to the potential for cross-contamination of evidence, which have to be carefully managed. Relatedly, on several occasions, the recovery of samples for DNA testing was shown to be problematic in that the investigators were dealing with small amounts of very sensitive material. In a couple of cases, DNA testing could not be carried out because the samples submitted were not of a sufficient quality. Such issues were often compounded by the fact that investigators were not always fully aware of what could be tested and what precisely was required to conduct different types of test.

In common with most other types of criminal investigation, the two main sources of physical evidence on murder enquiries are the crime scene and once a suspect is identified. Identifying and collecting contact trace materials from the crime scene was based around a methodical and ordered set of actions, combined with a degree of 'improvised practice' to account for the particular circumstances of the incident concerned (Williams, 2001). The crime scene examiners would first seek to identify the obvious 'contact points' where physical materials relating to the crime were evident and collect these. Then, on the basis of the distribution of this material, read in conjunction with the detectives' early understandings of what sort of crime it is and the likely actions and interactions that have occurred, the examiners would seek to identify whereabouts further evidence is likely to be and direct their searches accordingly. When a piece of physical material was identified, then its presence was carefully documented, prior to its careful extraction to facilitate analysis at the crime laboratory.

A matter of particular consequence in understanding the practice of forensic science is the relationship between the police investigator and the scientific expert. The specialist nature of the scientist's knowledge, whether this be in ballistics, toxicology, serology, or some other area, means that their contribution to the police's developing understanding of the case is specific to a particular facet of the crime. However, in order to produce results that are meaningful for the police in relation to this facet, forensic scientists often require some degree of contextual understanding of how the crime happened. In order for them to have this understanding, they are briefed by detectives as to what is believed to have happened and how, on the basis of this understanding, the artefact concerned is important to the police case. This briefing is significant, because it effectively provides a hypothesis to be tested and imbues the procedure of testing itself with a certain logic and purpose. A sense of this is provided in a statement made by a scientist reporting their findings on one of the cases studied:

I was asked to examine photos of the scene and to compare the boot's sole pattern...I cannot confirm that injuries on the face result from the boots concerned although there is moderate support for the allegation that the wearer of the boots was present at the scene of the murder.

Although the scientist qualifies the results of their analysis, they do provide implicit backing for the hypothesis that the police have asked them to test. Similarly, in the same case, 'The presence of heavy bloodstaining on boots in heavy quantity was probably made by contact with a wet bloodstained surface. Therefore it is possible that [suspect] kicked [victim] with right foot.' From these comments we can see how the significance of much forensic evidence for the police relies upon a situationally justified rationality, with the scientist providing an interpretation that takes account of the 'local' conditions.

The expertise and interpretative skills of the scientist are often used by police to validate the opinions they have already formed, and to further enhance their understanding of what happened. In this next case, the ballistics expert plotted the trajectory of the bullets fired to draw the following conclusion, 'At the time of the shooting [victim name] was most probably crouched down on the landing floor near to the foot of the stairs—firer would have been positioned above her at the moment of firing'. It is important to acknowledge, though, that this is the expert's opinion. Based upon a corpus of knowledge concerning the behaviour of bullets when travelling through the human body, together with the details provided to him by the police concerning the distribution of evidence at the scene, the expert reconstructs a plausible story of the fatal interaction, which accounts for the pattern of injuries and the final resting places of the bullets.

As in other forms of scientific practice, forensic scientists make use of particular techniques of representation that seek to enhance the perceived objectivity of the results.[60] As the previous examples suggest, a degree of equivocation is not unusual in the findings, although this is mitigated by the use of a clinical and technical style of description in reports. In the next extract from a report of a forensic expert who was tasked to analyse the blood at the scene, four key facets of the work conducted are illustrated. First, it gives a sense of the 'messy' conditions that the scientist is working in and has to account for. Secondly, it illustrates the ordered yet improvised practices used in doing forensic work.

Thirdly, the use of inference to develop a preliminary theory concerning the fatal interaction that accounts for the distribution of evidence is notable. And fourthly, the ways in which scientists use language to frame opinions in an 'objective' fashion is suggested:

There was bloodstaining on the walls and doors, and a partial footprint in blood on the floor. Also bloodstaining on the taps and washbasin. The soap dispenser also bore a light smear of blood. The telephone and one earring were found on the floor... The blood spray patterns indicate that [victim name] was lying on or at least near the area where her throat was cut. The lack of extensive blood splashing and spray suggests she was face down. My findings therefore indicate that [victim name] had her throat cut approximately in the position she was found... The extensive blood smearing on the floor is the result of actions taken by the ambulance personnel at the scene...

Samples of bloodstaining were grouped. The results obtained showed that the blood on the right side of the door frame to toilet and 2 spots of blood from hallway floor near the front of the stairs could have come from [suspect name]. This bloodstaining could not have come from [victim name] or any of the 101 other persons from whom blood samples were received. The combination of blood groups occurs in approximately 1.4% of the British population...

The denim shirt and T-shirt of [suspect name] gave a positive reaction to the presence of blood, but the size was too small for conventional grouping purposes.

There was an observed tendency for detectives to treat forensic evidence in an objective and factual fashion. Under pressure to progress an enquiry, what for detectives were the elliptical subtleties and extraneous equivocations expressed in the reports of scientists could for all practical intents and purposes be glossed over. The results of forensic analyses were treated by detectives as 'hard evidence', and not seen to be plagued by the vagaries associated with 'softer' forms such as witness statements. This pragmatic treatment, though, ignores the subjective components involved in the production of the physical residues of the crime as evidence. Whether it be fingerprints, DNA, or some other substance, the establishment of a sample as evidence is dependent upon the interpolative role played by a scientific expert in translating the results of a scientific processing into something meaningful in the context of the police's wider investigation. Ignoring or overlooking the subtleties of forensic analyses sometimes led detectives to misunderstand the weight of interpretation that could be placed upon a particular finding.

Temporal Ordering

Temporal ordering, involving organizing the actions known to have contributed to the fatal interaction in a chronological sequence, is a crucial aspect of how detectives start to assemble a sense of how the crime being investigated occurred.[61] This work is effectively an inflection of how time and space as phenomenological properties provide a sense of order to the lived realities of individuals as physical and social beings.[62] Detectives use the basic properties of time and space to ascertain who had the physical opportunity to commit the crime and thus can be potentially considered as a suspect. Mapping time was regularly used as a way of identifying suspects and destroying or substantiating the alibis that they provided.

The conduct of this temporal ordering work by detectives is captured in the ways in which all the investigations studied maintained up-to-date 'sequence of events' charts. These provided a 'temporal map' of the police's knowledge of the order in which specific actions and happenings related to the crime took place, as well as the gaps present in their knowledge. A field note from one of the investigations observed provides a sense of how sequence of events charts were used and updated.

Observations in the major incident room . . . Alongside the left hand wall of the room is the sequence of events chart. It is a long strip of several pieces of paper joined together and must run for about 10 ft. along the wall. Along the centre of the paper is a thin red line, off of which are plotted the points at which the police have 'knowledge' of something or other that has happened. Each entry has a time and a brief description of the relevant information and its source e.g. 12.40 victim got on bus—source ticket and witness (bus driver). During the morning [the analyst] removed a couple of sheets of paper from the chart and replaced them with new sheets upon which additional information had now been added. New information is only added when it has been confirmed and they are reasonably confident that it is reliable. Although I did notice that at several points where there were conjectures between information it was added with a question mark signalling the potential conflict.

The act of murder involves a form of interaction between a victim and offender at a particular location, at a particular time.

For police investigators tasked to try and establish what happened in such an interaction, they are confronted by the fact that it is something that has occurred in the past. It is also something that they are unlikely to have observed directly and consequently any understanding that they are to have of the incident has to be reconstructed from a variety of sources of information. Thus, from the perspective of a police investigator, a murder can be seen to possess many of the qualities of Mead's (1932) notion of an 'event', that is, a past happening interpreted according to the concerns of the present and a way of marking time, thus ordering the temporal aspect of existence.

As an event, the police reconstruct an understanding of the incident through the use of a number of tacitly based 'temporal frames'. These enable them to both organize the lines of enquiry that will be undertaken and also to order the information that results from their activities. These temporal frames place the act of murder at the centre of the police concerns and thereby allow officers to plot how various incidents and actions can be seen to relate to the central event.

From the police's point of view, a murder is conceived of as an episode, with a beginning, middle, and end, and the action that pertains to it as having a sequence. The role of each of the elements potentially connected to the event (e.g. victim, offender, witnesses, weapons, locations) is analysed in terms of what each one did or the state of it:

- previous to the crime;
- immediately prior to the crime;
- during the crime;
- after the crime.

This approach to their work assists officers in constructing a coherent and orderly narrative account of what happened.

The police organized their tasks and the resultant information through these tacitly maintained temporal frames. Throughout their enquiries, actions and policy directives were set up to detail how all the individual actions that were relevant to the incident related to each other. The following passages taken from a policy file give an indication of how an SIO used a set of temporal frames to structure the lines of enquiry followed by the investigating officers. The estimated time of death for the two victims was

07.40 a.m. Enquiries were established to 'Trace and interview all the users of the car park at the rear of the scene in order to establish if any unusual vehicles or persons were seen at the relevant time'. A press release was issued and the SIO gave a direction that it should '...concentrate on witnesses who were in [town name] at about 08:45 on [date of offence] in view of neighbours [sic] evidence of loud bangs heard about this time'.

As more information was collected by the investigators, we can see how time continued to play an important part in directing the investigative effort, 'Priority Lines of Enquiry: In view of the sightings of a Ford Escort at 6.30 a.m. on [date] in the car park behind Scene 1, all actions relating to sightings of any persons or vehicles between 6 am and 10 am on [date] will become high priority'. The next day a further instruction was issued to investigators, 'Movement of Witnesses: Statements taken from all associates and relatives of the deceased should include their full movements between 12 noon [day before offence] and 12 noon [day of the offence]. Vehicle details and movements will be included in these statements.' Further to this, the SIO stated that efforts should be directed to 'Fully establish the movements of the deceased between midnight [two days prior to the offence] and the time of death'. In addition, a more general instruction was included to research the financial background of the deceased. Once the prime suspect was identified, he was interviewed on a number of occasions, and again the police enquiries concentrated around issues of time in their attempts to link the suspect to the crime. The questions that were posed during the interview sought to establish his movements after the time of death, in an effort to locate a number of items of evidence to further incriminate him.

An excerpt from the policy file on a different case shows how a set of temporal frames were established at an early stage of the investigation in relation to the collection of information about the victim and the scene. The victim was discovered in his flat above his business premises at approximately 20.30. The next day at the first briefing of the enquiry team, the SIO issued these instructions:

The following sequence of events charts are to be created.
(a) Victim from 08.00 [day before he died] until 20.20 [night the body found].
(b) Victim's background.

(c) Sequence of events for scene covering times listed in (a) above. Enquiries are to cover all the movements of the deceased and all movements and sightings in the vicinity of the scene.

In a sense then, the information collected by the police is used to establish the plot of the event, within which are contained a number of 'event biographies' detailing the relationship between the significant actors and the incident. The information that is collected is slotted into place in terms of its contribution to the police understanding of how the event unfolded.

The Case Narrative

Temporal ordering as an investigative technology contributes to the methods by which police assemble an understanding of the sequence in which various actions took place and thereby contributed to the fatal event. Such work is also central to how the police construct a narrative of the crime.

Narrative is a social technology that enacts the communication of complex forms of information in a structured and meaningful form (Maines, 1993; Plummer, 1995; Couch, 1996). As Maines (2001) notes, narratives are 'dominant stories' that perform and dramaturgically display a moral message within a given cultural context. It is in this sense that the police produce their account of what happened as a narrative. It is a story of the circumstances and interactions pertaining to a particular incident, sharing similar conventions of emplotment and casting of roles for the participants with other similar stories of similar events.

The use of temporal frames by investigators implicitly recognizes the fact that the actions and permutations of experience of an event are in some sense held to be organized and causally related. Constructing a narrative imputes a certain sense of flow, impetus, and chronology to the various actions, establishing contextually situated sense-making connections between the actors, settings, objects, and actions that are constitutive of the event. The case narrative abstracts from the phenomenology of an incident and provides an edited, sequenced, formalized, and authoritative account of how it can be interpreted and thus understood.

Police case files that result from investigative activity frequently consist of thousands of documents and records, which in turn contain many items of information. In order to make sense of all the data contained within the file, police seek to produce a story, which connects the key facts of the crime and the evidence that the police have to warrant these facts. The narrative of the crime event is then an artful construction, a selective interpretation that is both a product and transcendence of the competing and contested accounts provided by the participants and witnesses to the crime.

The following police narrative, which was used at a pre-trial hearing, gives a sense of how the constructed narrative provides an edited and organized version of the event.

[Suspect's name], a known offender, beat the head of the victim with a number of objects including an electric fire, frying pan and saucepans causing severe head wounds. The offender then appears to have taken a shower in the victim's premises and then returned to the bedroom where the attack took place. He then started a fire at the foot of the victim's bed and left premises. At some stage the offender hand washed clothing that it is believed he had been wearing at the time of the offence.

This short overview of the crime sets out the sequence of key actions and in so doing connects evidence derived from a range of sources. It can therefore be seen to be central to what Cicourel (1968) described as the 'creation of a history'.

Importantly though, in the context of major crime investigations, such narratives are not simply the product of investigative actions, they are also enacted by officers as investigative heuristics to organize the information collected. This ongoing ordering of information that takes place throughout the investigation provides for an enhanced understanding of what has probably taken place and thereby assists the police in the development of investigative actions and plans for the conduct of further lines of enquiry. Detectives on a murder squad informally produce a shared narrative of the crime, which they update regularly to guide their ongoing work. On occasions, particularly on large-scale protracted investigations, the construction of a case narrative was used more formally by the SIO to establish the state of the enquiry's knowledge to date. This in turn could be used to identify what wasn't known. In one case, the investigation had conducted over 4,000 enquiries when the SIO produced the following:[63]

The belief... has been throughout that the motive for this attack upon [victim name] was one of robbery. Indications are he had been alive at least until 20.10 [date] because he had received a call up until this time from a friend. Evidence suggests he died sometime within a few hours of this call. Known from the outset that [victim name] was a practising homosexual. He had lived for many years with a partner called [name] until his death in [date]. During that relationship they'd accumulated a great number of friends and acquaintances. After the death of [partner's name] there is considerable evidence that [victim name] became very depressed... The fairly complicated lifestyle which [victim name] led, caused us to have to trace a large number of people who knew him to a greater or lesser extent and eliminate them from this enquiry.

This was used by the team members to establish at that point of the investigation what was known about the crime and consequently those areas where some further development was required.

During the fieldwork, a number of officers described the mechanics of a murder enquiry in a similar way as this detective did:

The best way I can describe it is like doing a jigsaw puzzle, but without knowing what the picture is, or sometimes what the pieces are. But just like doing a jigsaw, the more pieces you can slot into place, the easier it becomes to work out what you're looking at and what's missing.

This seems to be a useful metaphor, which captures the incremental dynamics of how enquiries often progressed. But as this officer pointed out, we should not follow the analogy too far, as an important aspect of the police task relates to the fact that they are also having to identify which 'pieces' are relevant to the narrative and which should be discarded. In discussing the relationship between investigative activity and the assembling of a narrative, I am examining the processes by which 'the picture' is constructed.

The assembling of a case narrative involves individual pieces of information, drawn from various sources, being combined and inter-leaved through the interpretative agency of the detectives concerned. The 'facts' of the case are 'fitted' together, with certain pieces of information acting as warrants for others. In a sense then, the original material of the incident is imbued with the characteristics of a 'story of a murder', involving principal and supporting actors, scenes, cues, and plot-lines. Detectives have established conceptions of what murder narratives should be like, and through their work, they act to produce their account of an incident in a way that is commensurate with these established conceptions. As such, there is a certain dramaturgical quality to the product of the police investigation.

The process of narrative construction is recursively directed by detectives through the use of a set of basic questions. These are:[64]

1. Who is the Offender?
2. Where is the Offender?
3. When did the crime occur?
4. What evidence is there available?
5. Why did the Offender commit the crime?
6. How did the crime take place?

These questions split the case into a number of specific issues, thereby making the whole task of providing a coherent account of what happened more manageable. They identify the key elements of 'the story', which will have to be evidenced if the police account is to be probative and meet the requirements set out in law.

Case narratives selectively focus upon the key actions and the array of factors that can in some sense be understood as impacting upon the event. As part of this focusing, the police narrative excludes other extraneous material that does not contribute to making sense of the crime, and would otherwise obfuscate the issues being attended to. It is important to remain aware that the process of constructing event narratives is not clear-cut and unproblematic. Information that is irrelevant to the enquiry is collected by the police and acted upon. Lines of enquiry that prove to be unproductive are carried out and false leads followed, although within the narrative such matters can be edited out. The production of a narrative is a persuasive form of representation that recursively influences the work that detectives perform.[65]

It can be seen, then, that the temporal ordering work performed by detectives is intimately connected to their role in manufacturing a narrative. In sequencing the key actions and identifying their chronology, the detectives represent the event as a process, with a beginning, middle, and end. If temporal ordering equates to the structuring of the narrative, then there is a second aspect of detective work that is equivalent to the poetics and polemical qualities of narrative construction. As part of the work performed in the production of the narrative, police figuratively produce moral identities for victims and suspects which reflect the broader adversarial nature of the criminal justice system (Bennet and Feldman, 1981) and its politics of knowledge. The 'factual' status of knowledge is always underpinned by established structuring relationships of power and authority. The moral identities produced as part of the case narratives are based upon extant 'scripts' that govern the manufacture of homicide stories; the deceased tends to be portrayed as the innocent and 'undeserving' victim, and the suspect as a malevolent predator.

Victims, Suspects, and Moral Careers

As part of constructing a narrative that explains and connects actors, actions, and their causes and effects, the police assign individuals to particular roles within the story. These roles have specific 'legal identities', in that through the interpretative work of the police, a certain individual will be cast as the victim, another as the perpetrator, and still others as witnesses. There are, though, allied to the production of these legal identities, particular moral characteristics that are routinely attached to them.

These moral roles are deliberately 'worked up' by police as a reflection of the politics of the adversarial legal system. Such roles seek to provide further moral clarity to the narrative by portraying the victim as an innocent party, or at least not deserving of being murdered, and the suspect as an embodiment of 'the bad guy' or 'symbolic assailant' (Herbert, 1996; Skolnick, 1994). As such, in constructing a narrative of a crime, the police dramaturgically construct victim roles and suspect roles to which they assign participants. It is a process similar to Troy Duster's (1971) notion of 'total moral identities', whereby the individual's public identity is figured around their role in the crime. For the purposes of this discussion though, I am particularly interested in the process of 'moral tainting' as a form of stigmatization,[66] which impacts upon how detectives aim to re-figure the moral identities of some victims and suspects.

As the following example illustrates, for those victims who were drawn from respectable groups in society, the portrayal of the victim as the innocent party by police was comparatively unproblematic. The case involved the killing of a middle-aged female in her flat and the police investigation had been running for a couple of weeks without much progress being made. At the morning briefing, in an effort to try and maintain the morale and effort of the team, the SIO summarized the state of the enquiry thus:

As you all know, by all accounts [victim's name] was a nice lady, she did a lot of work for charity, she comes from a nice family. There are no obvious indications as to why she should have been targeted for this attack . . . We need to find whoever was responsible for doing this to her.

When people from these sorts of groups are killed, they are effectively 'good' or 'worthy' victims for the police. They are 'respectable' people who cannot in any sense be blamed for their victimization. There are, though, another group of victims that I term 'tainted victims'. These people previously had what police culture (and perhaps other mainstream groups also) maintains to be a 'deviant' lifestyle and/or were involved in criminality. From the police point of view, they would usually constitute 'police property' (Reiner, 1992). When these people are the victims of homicide, we might predict that for the police there is effectively a sense of tension surrounding the degree of effort to be put into the investigation. Ordinarily, these people would be treated with disdain according to the values of police culture. However, as victims of a serious crime, they are viewed as deserving of a high level of investigative effort by police.

The fieldwork suggests that in the majority of cases involving 'morally tainted' victims, their victimization was viewed as more important by police than their everyday former lifestyle. The fact that someone has been murdered is generally felt to be of greater moral and political significance than any equivocation that might be felt about their behaviour or status. The moral ambiguities and contradictions of a case will tend to be subsumed under the primary political consideration of unlawful death.

One episode drawn from the fieldwork may help to illustrate the relevant issues in this process of moral construction. The victim was a local businessman who was known to the police for his criminal business activities and his propensity to swindle money from people. In a conversation with one of the officers on the investigation, a number of themes were brought up that are illustrative of these concerns:

As we investigated his background, gradually we got to quite like him. You just saw this larger than life bloke never done anybody any real harm, just took money from the people who were stupid enough to believe him. You listen to the stories he used to spin these people and you think well if you're stupid enough to give him money you basically deserve to be conned. He never deserved what he got.

The assigning of participants in a homicidal interaction to moral identities was part of how the police sought to establish a degree of moral clarity for a potentially complex narrative.

The moral identities used by the police are part of the narrative structure, and the particular details associated with an individual's imputed identity will be embedded in and constitutive of the wider story that is progressively refined and worked up. And as the incident itself is understandable as a process, so too can the moral identities which are related to the narrative. These identities are not stable and constant, rather they are altered and built up as the investigation progresses. They can therefore be seen to share a number of characteristics with Everett Hughes's (1958) concept of 'career'.[67]

The Moral Career of the Murder Victim

As a result of their enquiries the police would typically obtain a considerable amount of information about the victim. The sorts of information that they concentrated upon tended to alter as the investigation progressed. From the point of view of the police, the victim's career can be seen to be formed of three key stages.

1. The victim as 'physical object'

The first encounter that the police are likely to have with a victim is as 'a body on the floor'. In this state, the victim is in effect a 'physical object' for investigators, where the wounds and patterns of injury are interpreted and 'read' in order to suggest a cause of death, a possible weapon, likely suspects, and so forth.

2. The victim as 'individual subject'

As the police enquiries commence, the type of person the victim was, their habits, likes and dislikes are assiduously detailed by the police. Here, from the police perspective, the victim in a sense becomes 'an individual subject'. That is, the police get some sense of the type of person the victim was, their biography and social identity. From this, they may start to develop some conception about why this person should have been killed.

3. The victim as 'moral object'

The third stage in the career of the murder victim is where they are transformed into a 'moral object', with the police, as part of the construction of their case, stressing the fact that the individual is a 'worthy victim' or at least not deserving of this fate. In this stage of the career, the individual details of the deceased's identity are of less consequence than the way in which they can be shaped to further support the case against the suspect. The identity of the murder victim is essentialized and poetically reconstructed in the terms of the politics of adversarial justice.

The Moral Career of the Murder Suspect

In dealing with 'tainted victims' the police seek to neutralize the perceived 'impurity' that may be attributed to the person. In contrast, though, as part of their work related to incriminating the suspect and detailing their involvement in the crime, detectives will seek to taint and impugn the character of that individual. A number of the enquiries that the police conduct in respect of a suspect are concerned with examining aspects of his/her life and their relationship to the crime that they are alleged to have committed. In addition, then, to the careful detailing of the suspect's physical and mental engagement in conducting the crime, the suspect's past is documented in terms of whether there are any factors that could in a sense have 'caused' this individual to become a murderer, or, alternatively, whether there are any past behaviours that could be used to infer that this person is the type of individual who is likely to commit murder. In particular, past involvement in deviant and criminal activities is used by the police to substantiate and reinforce their case.

As the police collect increased amounts of information about the crime and their suspect, the suspect is increasingly exposed to a range of more coercive police powers that assist in the investigation, and a variety of increasingly stigmatizing labels are attached to them. The legal identity of the suspect shifts from suspect to prime suspect, where the police enquiries will centre upon detailing their involvement in the crime and any other material that might support their suspicions. Following on from this, if there is sufficient evidence, then the suspect will be *charged* with the offence and may become a *defendant*. If the prosecution case is proven, then they will be convicted of a form of homicide. At each stage, the individual's legal career can be terminated for a variety of reasons.

More significantly though, attached to this legal career we can identify that, from the investigation's point of view, there is a moral career of the murder suspect composed of three stages:

1. *Unknown assailant:* In the early stages of those investigations where a suspect is not identified, the police attempt to infer aspects of the unknown assailant's physical and psychological make-up from the crime scene.

2. *The personified adversary:*[68] Once an individual is identified as a suspect, then effectively there is a transformation in their status for the police. Knowing the identity of a suspect makes available a lot of biographical and social information that the police can use in developing their case against them. Importantly though, as part of this work, the police have to attempt to counter, neutralize, and debunk any mitigations or excuses that the suspect may offer to exculpate themselves from suspicion. It is only if these alibis cannot be overturned that the suspect is likely to be conclusively eliminated from further consideration.

3. *The criminal author:* The concluding stage of the suspect's moral career is when they have been charged and the majority of police enquiries have been concluded. Here the very 'self' of the suspect is viewed as having been tainted by the act, they are accused of being 'a murderer', and their moral identity is intermingled with the act. The story that the police case tells is how this person came to kill another human being.

As part of this process of incrimination, the past identity and life of the suspect is examined and interpreted in relation to the commission of the murderous act:

The individuals subject to police attention are also transformed, as they become first suspects, then prisoners, then defendants...Elements of the person's identity are identified and emphasised (and possibly supplemented by imputed characteristics of the person's group, race or type) while others are omitted as irrelevant. These processes involve the construction of the person in a shape suitable for legal processing, a translation into an appropriate subject of legal discourse. (Dixon, 1997: 270)

In particular, examples of past violence and deviance were used by the police as indicators that this might be the sort of person who commits murder. The police, through their investigations of the suspect's past, construct a biography of the suspect that is selective and edited, in an attempt to produce an image of the 'pathological' individual who commits murder. Such actions reflect the politics of the adversarial legal system and the role of the police in the construction of knowledge about the crime. But such information is not merely explanatory; within the context of the adversarial legal environment it is justificatory. As was discussed, proving criminal intent is often problematic for investigators. 'Tainting' suspects on the basis of their past behaviours is a way in which juries can be encouraged to infer subjective intent for the criminal act.

Where possible, the police like to be able to establish a motive for the crime or supporting evidence against a suspect, as this is felt to be an important factor in persuading a jury to accept the prosecution case. A detective inspector explained why this is:

The trick is to start by assuming that the jury are stupid, well not stupid, but that they are going to know very little about the law and even less about what murder is like in real life. Juries can do some very strange things, but what they do like, is to be able to understand why this person could have done what we say they've done. If you can show them why this person grabbed a knife or whatever, then many of the other things can be shown to follow on from this.

This type of understanding underpins much of the case-construction work performed by the police. In particular it appears to be of especial significance in the more pathological crimes where what we might term 'rational' explanations for the murder are absent.

The construction of the moral careers of victims and suspects by detectives is implicitly related to the more general symbolic content of this type of investigative work. In the construction of their narrative, the police focus their work towards certain 'cues' and elements of 'the plot', which cohere around various facts that have to be proven to meet the requirements and definitions established in law.

Conclusion

Within the context of an investigation, the various information and knowledge producing technologies that I have identified tend to be used collaboratively and in concert. The products of their use are combined, overlapped, and inter-woven by detectives as they attempt to construct a detailed, evidenced narrative of the crime. The use of these investigative technologies is underpinned by and co-ordinated by an investigative methodology, the details of which will be the subject of the next chapter.

7

Investigative Methodology

The information work performed by detectives through the use of a combination of investigative technologies is informed and structured by the presence of an investigative methodology that is produced and reproduced through investigative actions. The investigative methodology binds together the various methods employed by detectives to generate knowledge about a crime, providing them with a grounding and unifying logic. It governs how the various investigative technologies are used both individually and in combination, and why particular investigative methods are selected from those available, in order to accomplish particular objectives. But it also shapes and guides the ways in which detectives interpret information and understand the involvement of people, places, and objects in crimes.

Investigative Practices

The discussion of investigative technologies detailed how they are used by detectives to produce information and knowledge. The enactment or performance of these technologies establishes them as practices. The precise nature, style, and conduct of these investigative practices, and the particular combination of technologies that are collaboratively enacted by them, will depend upon the situated issue or problem being addressed, as well as the investigative methodology deployed by the SIO. Nevertheless, most major investigations will involve some version of the following practices: crime scene analysis; victimology; suspect identification and incrimination; witness identification and assessment; and intelligence-based enquiries. In addition, they will also tend to include family liaison, media management, and community impact assessment practices which, although they are perhaps less directly concerned with identifying and prosecuting a suspect, are none the less important to the police's role.

Crime scene analysis practices are composed of all the technologies that are deployed in order to interpret and process the crime scene, and thereby render it in a form that contributes in some way to the investigators' understanding of the incident, how it happened, and who was involved. Typically this will involve a variety of technologies for locating and analysing contact trace materials, as well as accounts from co-present and/or non-co-present witnesses. As discussed previously, a particularly important element of such practices is their role in contributing to the definition of the incident as a crime or otherwise. Victimology practices relate to the work done to identify and collect a range of details about the victim (or victims). Due to the nature of homicide these are often closely connected to the crime scene analysis practices. The investigative practices directed towards identifying and subsequently incriminating potential suspects vary considerably according to the situation concerned and the circumstances of the crime. In a similar fashion to what happens to the family and friends of the victim, in the earlier phases of an enquiry, the last person to see the victim alive is often the subject of police suspicion until such time as they can be eliminated. Once a suspect is identified then the focus of the investigation becomes more targeted and the investigative practices shift towards trying to substantiate the case against the individual (or individuals) concerned, often by trying to connect them in some way with the crime, the victim, or the scene. The enactment of investigative technologies also routinely focuses upon identifying and extracting information from potential witnesses and evaluating the usefulness and reliability of these data in light of the police's developing understanding of the case. A further commonly performed set of investigative practices are those that focus upon developing the intelligence base of the enquiry and using intelligence to inform the lines of enquiry that are being performed.

In addition to these investigative practices that manifestly contribute to advancing the passage of an investigation, some of the police's actions seek to address several wider concerns. For example, family liaison work has become an increasingly important function in murder squads. Close contact between the victim's family and the police whilst an investigation is ongoing allows the

vide a degree of emotional support for the family, but
have the benefit of improving the flow of information to
rs in respect of the sort of person the victim was, who he
w, and so forth. Equally pragmatically, from the police
point of view, performing this caring role is likely to reduce the
probability of the family voicing their criticisms of the police via
journalists, should the investigation fail to progress satisfactorily.
The increased use of professional news management techniques as
part of major investigations is a topic that I will address in further
detail later, but it is worth reiterating that news management strategies can be used as a positive way of trying to advance the state of
an investigation, but equally frequently, such tactics are used by
police as a defensive measure to try and offset any criticism that
may be made. Allied to these ancillary practices, particularly on
high-profile cases, several of the practices performed by the police
are designed to try and manage the impact of the crime on the local
community and to reassure local people about their safety.

Contemporary major crime enquiries are complex processes routinely involving multiple and concurrent lines of enquiry, where the
various practices performed by detectives overlap and are inter-
twined, frequently addressing multiple coexisting objectives. An
appreciation of the complexity of investigative work is important
in terms of understanding the articulating dynamics of the organizational systems, and the investigative processes and sub-processes
that are enacted.

On Investigative Methodology

Crime investigations are composed of a number of discrete yet
linked investigative actions, which are directed towards the production of knowledge about how and why the crime occurred.
These actions, which are informed by, and part of, the investigative
practices take place both sequentially and concurrently, with the
information that they produce used to make sense of the crime, but
also to inform the ongoing investigative work. Many of the individual investigative actions are organized and related through 'lines
of enquiry', which are akin to thematic areas to be researched by
the detectives. A line of enquiry is comprised of a number of inter-
linked and inter-dependent actions, which have the potential to
collectively promote an enhanced understanding of a particular

aspect of the crime. Therefore a line of enquiry often incorporates several different types of investigative practice. Within a major crime investigation, typically there will be a number of lines of enquiry running at the same time. They are co-ordinated and structured through a more general investigative methodology.

The investigative methodology is comprised of the combination of practices, procedures, processes, routines, conventions, theories, and techniques through which police respond to a crime. It informs the methods which police officers employ to acquire and interpret information when investigating different types of crime, accounting for the situational factors pertaining to the specific incident. Thus the investigative methodology utilized when responding to a major crime may differ, for example, from that used in respect of a burglary or drug offences. In effect, the investigative methodology represents an adaptive, police-relevant, practical epistemology, which takes account both of the social and legal functions of investigative work, and the problems that inhere in performing such a role. It reflects the fact that the police have at their disposal a range of strategies and theories which act to structure and direct their activities in developing an objectified narrative account of the crime.

The concept of investigative methodology is informed by the sense that in the majority of enquiries a number of fairly standardized, but adaptable, practices, procedures, and strategies are utilized by police in their investigation. As such, the methodology that the police draw on needs to be understood as being both structured and sequenced, and adaptive and malleable. This 'plastic' quality ensures that the methodology, broadly conceived, is relevant and effective in respect of a number of different settings, investigative problems, and crimes. Therefore the investigative methodology should not be understood as deterministic and prescriptive; rather it is responsive and flexible, and can be shaped according to the situated investigative problematics that are involved in different cases.

The investigative methodology shapes how information is produced, interpreted, and constructed as knowledge and evidence in the process of investigation. In turn, the investigative methodology is itself shaped by the legal environment and the particular circumstances of the incident under investigation. From the police point of view, whilst each murder is phenomenologically unique, the investigative function is organized to establish certain 'facts' and overcome certain core investigative problems relevant to the concerns of the legal frame. The shape, style, and focus of the police response to an individual incident is thus constructed from an array of potential investigative strategies and tactics, according to their predicted probability in enabling the crime to be solved. As such, the investigative methodology implemented for a particular murder can be said to have a situated rationality informed by a set of established general principles of crime investigation work and the specific circumstances of the offence.

Some lines of enquiry are routinely applied by police in all murder enquiries. These include analysis of the crime scene, house-to-house enquiries, and the questioning of the victim's family and friends. Once a suspect is identified, then at some stage it is usual to conduct an interview with them as a means of collecting further information about that individual's participation in the crime. Other strategies are more selectively employed, according to the particular situational circumstances of the crime.

Signs of Crime

Underpinning the investigative methodology and the use of investigative technologies as practices to generate information and knowledge is the sense that detectives are essentially engaged in trying to determine what particular objects and acts tell them about how and why the crime subject to investigation happened. Conceptually, these objects and acts, which in police parlance are termed clues or leads, can be thought of as 'signs'. These signs encode information (and therefore potential knowledge) about the passage of the fatal interaction and those involved in it. If properly decoded, these signs become signifiers, providing enhanced understanding about some aspect of the crime and/or its participants (the 'signified').

Broadly speaking, five types of investigative signifier can be identified:

- 'signifiers of crime' connotatively and denotatively encode meanings related to understanding some aspect of the circumstances of the crime event;

- '*signifiers of intent*' are objects or behaviours that can be construed as indicative of the motivational state of the suspect at the time of committing the offence (see Chapter 3);
- '*signifiers of criminality*' are those items or behaviours that can, from the police's point of view, be used in an inceptive fashion to suggest that a particular individual is probably involved either in crime generally, or in a particular offence;
- '*signifiers of guilt*' are stronger versions of the signifiers of criminality, which, if decoded, can be used by detectives to either objectively or subjectively incriminate or implicate a suspect in the commission of the crime under investigation;
- '*exculpatory signifiers*' are items or behaviours that suggest that an individual either cannot or may not have been involved in the offence under investigation.

Each of the signifiers can be either a 'behavioural' or 'material' signifier. Behavioural signifiers are based upon interpreting actions, whereas material signifiers are developed from the interpretation of physical objects. Sometimes the two are linked in that a material signifier can be used to construct an inference about the actions of a participant in the crime.

The processes of identifying and interpreting signifiers are informed by the construction of abductive inferences.[69] Abduction involves inferring to the best explanation. It is a creative form of sense-making interpretive inference, wherein the presence of a fact is used to generate an explanation for its causes. Abductions are thus 'ampliative inferences', in that the result of the process of abduction is that the detective will be possessed of a better understanding of the situation than they had prior to producing the inference (Josephson and Josephson, 1996). In a sense, then, crime investigation practice is founded upon the abductive interpretation of various signifiers and can thus be construed as a situated and stylized form of applied semiotic analysis.[70]

Whether at an autopsy, attending the crime scene, or in an encounter with a suspect or witness, what typifies the detectives' role is that they are engaged in trying to identify and read the available signifiers to enhance the state of their knowledge about the crime. For example, the analysis and processing of a corpse is a form of semiotic work. The violence inscribed onto the body in the form of wounds is interpreted as indices or symptoms of the fatal interaction, which if decoded correctly will become signifiers allowing the investigators to know much about the interactional dynamics of the fatal assault and possibly the identity of the author. The following extract demonstrates how, by reading the signifiers inscribed into the body of the victim, the pathologist can provide suggestions about the 'howdunit' of the crime and suggest a sense of how the physical aspects of the fatal interaction developed. Such details are used to focus the lines of enquiry involved in the identification of the murder weapon.

Died of asphyxia and sustained severe facial injuries. His coronary disease did not cause death but could have accelerated the death once injuries caused. Appearance of body suggested been dead at least 24–36 hours prior to the examination . . . Injuries to deceased's face are consistent with heavy blows to this area by blunt weapon(s). Difficult to estimate exact number of blows, but minimum of 7–10 blows and other more minor injuries caused by head being struck against the floor. . . Some of the injuries to forehead and right side of face suggest use of a hammer. Lacerations around eyebrows could have resulted from blows by the base of the brass table lamp found at the scene. Hard punches could have been responsible for some of his injuries, particularly those around the mouth and nose. . . . Distribution of blood suggests first attacked at the front door, blood dripping from broken nose . . . Bruises on deceased's arms consistent with restraint by firm gripping . . . Injuries to the deep structures of the neck indicate single handed manual compression of upper part of neck. Appearances indicate firm gripping by fingers just below angles of jaw with a degree of pressure applied to left side of voicebox.
Injuries to rib cage and the transverse processes of lumbar vertebrae suggest assailant knelt violently onto the small of his back or stamped on his back, whilst deceased was lying face down on the floor.
The ligatures to deceased's arms and legs were very tightly applied with resulting bruising in the underlying skin and subcutaneous tissues. This can restrict respiratory movement and contribute to asphyxia.

Similar themes can be identified in an extract from the report of a post-mortem examination on a second case:

She was a female infant of medium build. There were numerous bruises over her trunk, face, scalp and limbs indicative of severe physical abuse which has taken place during a period of up to 3–4 days prior to death. Many of the injuries appear to have been caused during the period of 24 hours leading up to death. The others have been caused in the preceding day. She had suffered two episodes of violent blunt trauma to her abdomen... The appearances are those of injuries caused by not only beatings but by forceful gripping by an adult or adults.

In 'reading' the body and interpreting the patterns of the wounds, the pathologist contributes to the police's understanding of the fatal interaction and how the violence was performed within the setting. Similarly, during interrogations or interviews with witnesses and suspects, detectives carefully monitor the verbal and proxemic communications made by the subject of the encounter, in an effort to ascertain whether there are any signifiers of guilt evident in their conduct. In the extracts that follow, drawn from the case file on an extremely complicated investigation into a double shooting, we can see how the police interviewers infer from the suspect's failure to adequately answer their questions that he was involved in the commission of the offence. As the encounter develops, the police progressively reveal the extent of their incriminating knowledge to the suspect. In so doing, they persuade him to continually try and explain away the increasingly incriminatory evidence. By his own admission, the suspect places himself at the crime scene at the time when the victims were killed. In terms of constructing the case for the prosecution, this confirmation greatly assists the police.

The male and female victims were found shot dead in their house. The police searched the scene recovering a vast amount of material, all of which had to be researched in case it contained a potential lead. One thing they found was that the male victim, who had a reputation for his somewhat dubious business dealings, was in the habit of recording all his telephone conversations. It would turn out that the killer was unaware of this fact. As hundreds of lines of enquiry were pursued and a number of suspects eliminated, one tape-recording of a telephone conversation between an unknown man called 'Dave'[71] and the victim, arranging a meeting for the morning on which the victims died, was identified as potentially important by the police.

This tape was played on the BBC's *Crimewatch UK* programme with an appeal to anyone recognizing the voice of 'Dave' to contact the police. No one did, but unbeknown to the police, several people had recognized the voice and had confronted 'Dave' about it, telling him to go to the police. In order to try and avert the mounting suspicion, 'Dave' prepared a statement and voluntarily presented himself at the police station. At this point, a 90-minute taped interview was made, at the start of which he was reminded that he was not under arrest and was free to leave at any time. The interview was used gradually to reveal the extent of the police evidence and suspicion, and the interviewer sought to persuade 'Dave' that his proffered explanations did not sufficiently counter the police evidence. The extracts from the interview reproduced below show how the police managed the interaction in such a way as to gradually persuade the suspect to reveal more and more information. In the process of doing so, the suspect is, perhaps without realizing it, further incriminating himself.

Q   This would've been easier six weeks ago—we've been trying to locate Dave who arranges a meeting for 8.00 a.m. Dave doesn't put his hand up saying 'well it was me' so we're thinking 'Well the reason Dave hasn't put his hand up is because he's involved.' The reason we've not made it public is because we want to try and find him without him knowing we've taped his call . . . it's a last resort . . . once you know it's taped and you're connected you're gonna start tidying things up. So it's probably taken 20 officers nine weeks to find you . . . You can see how important to the enquiry this is.

This marks a pivotal point in the exchange; prior to this the interviewee has been encouraged to provide an explanatory account as to his movements, but here the previously veiled accusations become explicit. The sentence, 'once *you* know it's taped and *you're* connected, *you're* gonna start tidying things up', establishes the accusations directly. It demands an adequate justification from the suspect as to why he didn't come forward. The suspect is thus persuaded to progressively extend his explanations of why he made the phone call, why he didn't seek to eliminate himself, and why he was in the vicinity of the scene at the material time? This in turn results in a number of inconsistencies being revealed. The interview continues:

Q   If that tape hadn't been played on *Crimewatch* you'd never have told us would you?
A   Well probably not no.
Q   Yet *you* were at the same time at er . . . you are the most vital witness possibly.

The interviewers then get the suspect to describe the times of his various activities that morning and to describe the clothes he was wearing. This section of the interview is interesting because it shows how detectives can manipulate the suspect, through the information he provides, in order to strengthen the prosecution case. The suspect tells them that he drove his car to the victim's house on the morning concerned and he describes his car. This was to prove to be a vital piece of evidence. He also states that he was wearing a grey suit (this also was to prove important). The suspect says he went to the house twice that morning between 8.20 and 8.40 a.m., receiving no reply and that between these two times he walked up the high street, past the bank and back. The interviewers then question him about the exact details of his movements:

Q Is it [the suspect's suit] light grey?
A Yeh.
Q So it might ... so it's a black and white film, it might be a white suit then?

Here for the first time, the police alluded to the fact that they had recovered CCTV film from a bank in the high street, near to the scene of the crime. The film contradicted 'Dave's' account on a number of important points. At this point in the interaction, the presence and nature of the misdirection that has been used by police is starting to be revealed. They secured their suspect's initial co-operation by persuading him that they just needed to eliminate him from enquiries. As they reveal the extent of their knowledge though, the suspect is, in his attempts to explain different aspects of the police case, further incriminating himself. The exchange continued:

Q So you go back to the cottage about 8.25 to 8.30 and try again on the door. So you've walked up the high street past [the newsagent], past [the bank], back to the cottage and knocked on the front door, no reply, so you've got into your car.
A Yep.
Q Well at 8.32 [victim's name] was buying cigarettes in the newsagents.
A So ... I was sitting in the car.
Q Well he was up and dressed at 8.32 'cos we've actually ... on film going into the shop. At 8.34 he returns from the shop. So at 8.34 [victim] is alive and well and under no restraints. So ... right ... you've gone to the car and you saw nobody approach the cottage or hanging around outside?

The interviewee then goes on to describe for the first time going round to the back entrance to the cottage and tapping on the kitchen door.

Q So at 8.35 you're at the back door tapping on the glass panel... [victim] at 8.35 is walking in the front door from the shop... We've got a facility you see which gives us, which will enable us to tell you what time you arrived and what time you went away.

In this interview, the police read the suspect's reactions to their questioning and his failure to adequately 'neutralize' the evidence they have as signifiers indicative of his involvement in the offence. They mask their real intentions and get the suspect to incriminate himself. After the 90-minute interview had finished, the suspect was arrested on suspicion of murder.

In a second example from an interview with a suspect, similar processes can be observed. But in this case, the suspect's past criminal activities were retrospectively interpreted by the police as a potential signifier of involvement in a new episode of violence. Questioning the suspect the police said:

P Would you say that you were a violent man?
S No. I'm no worse than anyone else.
P Is that so. Well you see [suspect's name], we've spoken to a number of people who know you, who seem to think that you can be very violent. They say if something touches a nerve with you, you can respond very violently, very violently indeed. They say you have a history of this sort of behaviour and I have to say, many of them didn't seem surprised that you could be involved in this sort of thing.

Constructing and interpreting signifiers in order to develop an enhanced state of knowledge about a crime and who was involved lies at the core of the detective role. The construal of objects and actions as signs of crime in this manner is informed by the use of three kinds of ratiocinative logic. These logics are introduced by detectives according to the current state of the enquiry's knowledge about the crime and the situation concerned.

By far the most commonly deployed form of investigative logic on murder enquiries is the previously mentioned abductive inference. Abduction moves from the consequent to the antecedent, and involves detectives in constructing a synthetic inference, wherein signs of crime or criminality are interpreted according to what else is known or hypothesized about how and why the crime took place.[72] The inference drawn is that the acts or objects on display support the established understanding of the crime and that this interpretative framework occasions the reading of the act or object in this particular way. As such, drawing upon their established understandings about the crime, detectives infer the circumstances that produced the object or behaviour concerned. The particular difficulty of abductive reasoning in detective work is the slight tendency for consequent factors to be interpreted in such a way that their inferred antecedents are assimilated by the current dominant hypothesis held by the police about the crime. There is in effect a degree of bias that gravitates towards interpreting new material in such a way as to support the established theory about the crime. This is particularly so in relation to incidents that appear to possess traits associated with the police's archetypes of murder. This bias explains why, on some investigations, detectives were observed to continue to follow a line of enquiry even though they were in possession of material suggesting the defunct nature of the guiding theory. For each unit of information and indeed potential fact, there are often several possible interpretations available and the interpretation selected at a particular point in the progress of an enquiry is framed by the established understanding of the crime, which in turn 'keys' the interpretation. Of course, faced with 'new facts' it is not unusual for an enquiry team to have to re-frame their understanding of an incident and thus to re-key their interpretations of the information and facts they have marshalled together. Sometimes this re-framing and re-keying will occur several times during the passage of a major investigation as alternative hypotheses about the crime are worked up and then discounted.

On occasions, detectives engaged in what Eco (1983) terms 'undercoded abduction'. This occurs when the inference drawn still leaves several plausible alternative explanations for events, and thus selection between the alternatives has to be based upon other criteria. In such conditions, detectives will often make use of their experience in order to decide how to proceed. The ability of detectives to engage in fabricating abductive inferences is shaped by four modes of investigative reasoning that will be discussed in more detail presently.

Although in fictional accounts of crime investigation, detectives are frequently presupposed to use deductive methods, in reality, the use of deduction is fairly limited. For the most part deductive inferences only become useful and feasible when the narrative of the crime is fairly well established. It is only then that deduction can be used to fill in any gaps in the story. Similarly, the use of a 'pure' inductively based logic by detectives tends to be restricted, for the most part, to a small number of cases, where in the early stages of the enquiry they struggle to infer a sense of the causes of a crime.

Investigative Reasoning: From Information to Knowledge

Constructing inferences was an important way in which investigators advanced their understandings of how and why a crime happened. The ability of detectives to identify signifiers of various kinds and to decide upon what they might mean in terms of further understanding the crime was an important part of how they developed a hypothesis about the dynamics of the incident and who might be involved. It was then a method of starting to translate the available information into knowledge. My use of the term abduction also echoes Dewey's (1933) comments that information is established as having a 'factual' status through a double interpretative movement of induction and deduction. A fact is so constructed as a result of a piece of information making a contribution to a suggested comprehensive account of what happened, within which the various fragmentary data make sense. But at the same time, the general account substantiates the particular interpretation placed upon the individual fact.

The ability of detectives to construct inferences in this fashion, and to identify and interpret signifiers of crime and criminality more generally, was informed by the presence of four distinct investigative reasoning styles. An investigative reasoning style is a particular cognitive method employed by detectives (and other police officers) in order to make sense of information and problematic situations.[73] For the purposes of analysis, it is useful to separate out the four different reasoning styles, although it should be noted that in practice they are inter-woven and enacted collaboratively.

Common-Sense Reasoning

Detectives as social actors make use of a pragmatically based, experientially grounded form of knowledge about the world around them to navigate the various arenas of social life that they encounter. It is a form of 'practical consciousness'[74] that is shared with the majority of other members of a society, and provides a set of normative expectations about how people normally act in different situations and the motives that will underpin various kinds of social action. Therefore, in terms of understanding detective work, the notion of common-sense reasoning is important in two ways. First, although detectives do employ more esoteric and specialist reasoning styles in their work, much of what they do in making sense of a crime uses the same knowledge and modes of rationality that we all employ in problematic everyday life situations. Secondly, detectives themselves believe that, in making sense of a crime, common-sense standards have to apply, if members of a jury are to believe and be persuaded by the prosecution case when it is presented in court. As such, common sense constitutes a base standard in investigative work.

The use of common-sense reasoning by detectives was particularly evident in their attempts to infer motives for different crimes. In the following observation, we can see the detectives drawing upon socially accepted 'scripts' concerning why an otherwise apparently 'normal' man would kill his wife.

Over lunch in the canteen, the five detectives discussed the interviews with the suspect from this morning. [Detective's name] said 'Well from what he's saying things have been bad between them, she was on the verge of leaving him and he couldn't let that happen. And more or less that's all there is to it.'

Here sexual jealousy and possessiveness are identified as being the motivation for the suspect becoming emotionally over-wrought and thus committing a crime of passion. In reaching this verdict, the detective made use of his understandings about 'normal' human nature and motives, derived from everyday experience, to make sense of the incident. A further way in which detectives sometimes used 'common-sense' reasoning to validate the information or knowledge available to them was by trying to disprove the reliability of a proposed 'fact'. If it could not be disproved, then it might be viewed as more reliable by detectives. Thus it should be noted that although detectives do make use of specialist skills and knowledge, they also employ similar cognitive faculties to those that we all use in everyday life.

Indexical Reasoning

In addition to their use of common sense, detectives employed what can be termed an indexical reasoning style. Indexical reasoning is based upon the interpretation of information accounting for the 'local' context in which it is situated. Thus meaning is ascribed on the basis of the relationships that can be identified between a selected item and that which is situationally connected to it. This notion of indexicality informs the contingent, occasioned, and opportunistic character of much detective work, and a feeling that what counts is the ability to make things work in problematic situations.

The use of an indexical reasoning style by detectives was frequently exemplified in terms of how they defined crime scenes. The following field note illustrates the nature of the interpretative work conducted.

The morning briefing and the SIO went over the state of the investigation, which had been commenced two days ago. He projected a series of photographs of the crime scene and talked over them ... 'This is the kitchen, as you can see someone has had a good go through the cupboards and drawers as if they were looking for something ... The lounge, where the body was found, again in some disarray. It looks like some of this could have been caused during a struggle, but most of it is as a result of someone looking for something ... Last slide ... the bathroom. As you can see there is some blood on the hand basin and around the taps. So it looks like they've gone into the bathroom after attacking [victim's name] and tried to tidy themselves up a bit.' There then followed a brief discussion amongst the team about the scene. The SIO summed this exchange up saying 'Anyway, from what's gone on at the scene and from what we've got on the victim so far, it looks as if we are dealing with a burglary that has gone wrong.'

In the above, it can be seen that the disarray of the scene is interpreted by the detectives to infer a cause for the killing.

Analogical Reasoning

The ability of detectives to engage in indexical reasoning is to a degree founded upon experience and a familiarity with particular kinds of circumstance. The role of experience is even more pronounced in relation to their use of analogical reasoning. Analogical reasoning is based upon associating a present problem or situation with the qualities of past problems or situations, and using the knowledge about these past cases to develop a solution to the current one.

Analogical reasoning was often employed by detectives, but it was particularly important in relation to the less common forms of homicide, where individual detectives are likely to have little personal experience of investigating crimes of this type. In such circumstances, detectives would have to interpret their previous investigative experiences in light of the particular problems posed by the current case, to see in what ways they could draw upon the past to assist them in the present.

At a more general and abstract level, a form of analogical reasoning underpins the development of organizational procedures and processes, where particular working practices are developed by the police as they provide an expeditious way of solving commonly experienced problems in detective work. However, a form of analogical reasoning can also be identified at the level of individuals, where detectives draw upon their own experience, or the experiences of others, to construct innovative solutions to particular problems.

Analogical reasoning was used in one case to identify the motives for a robbery-homicide:

Talked with officers in MIR about case. They were talking in particular about the son-in-law of the victim as a possible suspect for the crime. In the course of the conversation [name of an officer] said 'I reckon we need to take another look at [son-in-law's name]. We know he's a druggie and his habit is pretty big, plus he's got form for burglary. There's no real money coming in and he finds out she's got some cash. He gets desperate and decides to do her over, not necessarily kill her, but get her money. Anyway he's at her flat trying to find where she's stashed the money, she comes back and things go wrong.'

Here the officers are drawing upon their experiences of dealing with other cases of this type to identify a possible motive to link a suspect to the crime.

Legal Reasoning

Investigators also use a legal reasoning style to ensure that their case meets evidential standards and requirements as specified in law, and that their investigative actions are lawful. Law suffuses and structures investigative decision-making, but because I have addressed such issues in more detail in an earlier chapter, I will only briefly reprise such concerns here. Law is a significant influence upon what detectives do and how they do it. It informs how they interpret events, people, and accounts, and it provides a set of standards to which they work. In a practical sense, though, it also frames the interpretative work they perform. They evaluate whether the account they have constructed or are constructing 'works' in a legal sense, and whether the account and evidence appear to have sufficient probative value.

The sense-making work that detectives perform in constructing an investigation's knowledge of a crime is informed by a 'fuzzy logic' that incorporates these several different styles of reasoning. The detectives studied often talked in terms of 'hunches' and the possession of a particular intuitive insight to explain how they had resolved a particular issue. For example, 'It's very hard to explain what it is, but it's almost like a sixth sense working, you don't necessarily know what it is . . . you can't pin it down specifically, but you just feel that something isn't quite as it should be'.

This notion of an almost intuitive 'feel for the game' emphasizes the 'craft' basis of detective work suggested in the opening chapter. However, the development of the four investigative reasoning styles begins to unpack the key interpretative and inferential skills involved in developing accurate hunches. Hunches are based upon a combination of experience and perceptual acuity that allows detectives to identify ambiguities, and to inferentially extrapolate causes for them.

Suspicious Minds

At the level of practice, the implementation of an investigative methodology by individual detectives is guided by their use of a pervasive 'institutionalized suspicion' concerning the motives and actions of others. In turn, this suspicion is grounded in a culturally figured, fairly pessimistic view of human nature. It is established that suspicion is a key feature of the police personality (Skolnick, 1994). But if it is to assist detectives in the conduct of their enquiries, it has to be employed skilfully. The following example shows how suspicion was employed by detectives to establish a suspect who was subsequently eliminated from the enquiry. The police established this individual as a prime suspect because he was a member of the victim's family, because he could not provide an alibi for his movements, and because he had previous convictions. An officer serving on the enquiry explained why they had identified this man as a suspect:

Looking at the scene there's no sign of forced entry, which suggests that she answered the door to the killer and let him in, which again suggests that she knew her killer. Over and above this, you know as well as I do by now, that it's most likely to be someone who knows her that's gone and done her in. Plus the bloke's got a bit of form [a police record]. Looking at the scene together with what we know about him, at the moment 'matey' looks like our best bet.

Although subsequently eliminated from suspicion, this person had rapidly been identified as a suspect for the police, because of his proximity to the victim and the fact of his previous convictions.

The identification of potential suspects by the police is intimately connected to the way in which investigative suspicion is invoked. Reflecting the aetiology of homicide, in the absence of any leads to the contrary, there was an established tendency for the police to focus upon people known to the deceased as suspects in the early stages of the enquiry. Once these groups were eliminated, then the enquiry would more obviously consider other suspects.[75]

It should be stressed that this focus upon the victim's family, friends, and acquaintances and the more loosely bounded open-ended suspicion are not exclusive but are operationalized in a manner whereby each complements the other. The background consideration of anyone as a potential suspect is necessary because, at any point in the investigation, the possibility remains that new information may arise which will establish a new suspect, thus contradicting the previously hypothesized suspicions and requiring all the information collected to be re-evaluated.

A tendency amongst detectives to be suspicious about the motives of everyone encountered is, to a degree, a correlate of the uncertainty and the problems of establishing trust in information that they experience. In this respect three different types of police suspicion can be identified. Matza (1969) distinguished between 'methodical' and 'incidental' suspicion, the former referring to a tendency amongst police to search for suspects for a crime from a pool of 'the usual suspects', the latter invoked on the basis that the person concerned had a relationship with the victim and/or a physical opportunity to commit the offence. In addition to which,

Marx (1988) identifies a form of 'categorical suspicion', which is based upon the suspect's possession of certain characteristics. This research suggests that, in those cases where a suspect is not rapidly identified, police tend to use these three forms of suspicion as complementary strategies.

The three forms of investigative suspicion were used to identify those people who knew the victim and known offenders who had either the physical opportunity or a motive to commit the crime. If suspects were identified on the basis of one aspect, then investigators would tend to look for further evidence relating to the second aspect. That is, if a known offender was identified as being in the locale of a major crime, then research would be conducted as to whether he or she had any associational or motivational connection to the deceased and vice versa.

Working Rules

The uses of suspicion and indeed the wider investigative methodology employed on homicide enquiries are informed by a stock of pragmatically oriented police knowledge about how and why murders happen, and relatedly how and why investigations succeed, encapsulated in a number of working rules. They influence how incidents are investigated, suspects produced, and cases constructed. These informally based rules of 'how to get the job done' draw upon individual and organizational knowledge and experience of crime investigation, and the various problems that are regularly encountered and have to be resolved. Consequently, these working rules should not be seen as simply blueprints for social action, they also provide a way of viewing and interpreting the environment external to the police organization in a manner that coheres with the organization's social functions and perspective.

Experience, as encapsulated in these working rules, allows investigators to achieve 'cognitive economy' in selecting courses of action, inasmuch as whilst details may change between incidents, the fundamental problems to be overcome remain similar (Lloyd-Bostock, 1992). As such, the organization and the individuals within the organization who carry out its work develop strategies, procedures, and modes of operation appropriate to these problems. Individual police detectives and their activities on a murder enquiry can be understood in this manner. The detective is a member of a larger organization from which they absorb certain knowledge, expectations, and standards (individuals contribute to the repro- duction of these elements of organizations through their actions), which guide their conduct and imbue it with a contextual propriety.

These working rules, in concert with the police typologies of murder, constitute a pragmatic, experientially grounded lexicon of tacitly based police theory about murder, how and why it occurs, and consequently how it should be investigated. These investigative theories serve to rationalize the complex and unpredictable nature of the environment and construct it in a manner appropriate to the objectives of police work. They guide the interpretative practices of the police, and establish precedents in terms of how information and social actors should be viewed and treated.

Conclusion

Over the last three chapters, I have sought to develop a conceptual framework that sets out the key premises involved in homicide investigation work. I have argued that the work of investigators can be conceived as being concerned with the identification, inter- pretation, and ordering of a range of signifiers which are used to construct an evidenced narrative of the case. The evolving narrative is used by detectives as an investigative heuristic, providing a con- text in which newly identified signifiers and the information they encode can be situated and thus made sense of.

The concept of the investigative methodology captures how the police order their practices when investigating criminal homicides. Homicides are not investigated in an ad-hoc manner. There are both implicit and explicit controls present in the design and con- duct of investigative actions which shape how an investigation progresses and how the information work that is central to the investigation is performed. Detectives make use of a number of specific investigative technologies which enable them to generate information from an array of sources and to organize these data so as to progressively enhance their understandings of how the inci- dent unfolded and who was involved. The introduction of particu- lar investigative technologies at particular points of the investigative process is governed by a combination of pragmatically oriented theories about murder and its protagonists that are held by detectives. Some of these theories are organizationally and culturally embedded, sustained by the precedents of the investigative systems and detective culture respectively. Others, though, are more intuitive theories which are invoked by individual detectives to overcome certain situational problematics.

Although there is a fair degree of variation in the circumstances and details of different crimes, as mentioned elsewhere, there are certain basic issues that have to be dealt with by investigators, if they are to fulfil their social and legal functions. These core themes, such as the need to establish the identities of the participants and the mode of death, are used by detectives to order their work as they attempt to establish the significant details of the crime under investigation.

PART III

The Process of Investigation

8

Self-Solvers

A police murder investigation is a process of enquiry, the passage of which involves a number of stages of investigative work being conducted if a suspect is to be identified and charged. As such, the structure of the enquiry is dynamic, with the focus of police activities shifting between different tasks, requirements, and problems as the enquiry progresses. Having mapped out some of the key aspects of the methodology and technologies utilized in murder enquiries, I will now explore how these are involved in the investigative process.

In earlier chapters in this book, I have noted that police distinguish between different types of murder and that due to the circumstances in which they occur, the majority of homicides are comparatively easy for the police to solve. These elements informed how officers thought about and conceptualized murder investigations. They differentiated between 'self-solving' investigations and 'whodunits' or 'runners'.[76] The former label referred to those cases where the suspect was identified comparatively easily and thus police investigative activities were more focused and directed towards substantiating their involvement in 'causing' the fatal interaction, whereas in whodunits, there was a more problematic and extended search conducted in order to establish the identity of the suspect. In the following two chapters, my analysis of investigative processes utilizes these notions as a means by which to order and frame the discussion. There are, I argue, two main sequential models of the investigative process which relate to 'whodunit' and 'self-solving' cases respectively, and these will be the focus of the following discussion.

Self-solvers and Whodunits

The strategies that the police employ in order to establish and interpret information, where they look for it and the problems they encounter, are influenced by the particular circumstances of the incidents subject to investigation. Nevertheless, as will be shown in the ensuing discussion, at a meso-level of analysis, the majority of investigations broadly conform to a model of either the self-solving or the whodunit process. Such a finding is in accord with the sociological literature on organizations which has shown that the primary function of an organization is to order social actions so that problems and tasks are dealt with in familiar and established ways (Weick, 1995; Manning, 1992).

To argue in favour of understanding the homicide investigation process in one of two forms is not to deny that there are significant differences between individual investigations and the circumstances of the incidents that are the subject of enquiry. However, abstracting from situational details, we can start to uncover and identify the patterned conventions, routines, and common practices that are involved in investigative work, which is crucial in terms of enhancing our understanding of how murder enquiries are conducted.

Whether an investigation is adjudged to be a self-solver or a whodunit is in effect dependent upon two related concerns. First, the nature of the incident can make a case either harder or easier for the police to solve. Connected to which is the fact that the quantity and quality of knowledge available to detectives at an early stage of an enquiry is crucial in terms of how quickly they will be able to begin to progress the investigation. For the most part, self-solvers are solved comparatively easily by police because there is sufficient evidence at the crime scene for them to identify a likely suspect. This may occur due to the suspect being present at the scene when the police arrive, a witness who is able to tell the police what happened, or there being significant forensic evidence available.

As the following officer makes clear, there is a general adage maintained by the police that most murders are solved fairly quickly, 'I mean it's difficult to say for sure but I would guess that for about 70–75% of cases you're gonna have a pretty good idea of who you're after within 24–48 hours. If you haven't by then, then you know you're in for the long haul.' It is orthodox police practice to make a lot of resources available in the early stages of an investigation in order to ensure that as much information, knowledge, and evidence as possible is collected before it starts to decay in quality, for example, before witnesses' memories fade and forensic materials are contaminated.

In terms of conceptualizing how various situational factors relating to the incident under investigation impact upon the work of the enquiry team and the 'solvability' of the case, it may then, for the purposes of analysis, be useful to think of different sets of circumstances as existing on a continuum. At either end are the two 'strong ideal types' of the self-solving and whodunit models. The ideal type self-solvers are those cases where the suspect calls the police to the scene, where they then confess to the crime, and where there are substantial amounts of forensic evidence, as well as witnesses of some kind who can confirm elements of the suspect's story. Basically then, the necessary evidence is presented to the police during their preliminary investigation. At the other extreme is the 'pure' whodunit model, which would be typified by those cases where there is little or no forensic evidence available and there are no witnesses to the crime. In such situations, the police could not definitively interpret the situation so as to establish a clear sense of what had taken place and who was likely to have been involved.

In Figure 8.1, I have constructed a continuum, featuring the 20 cases that I studied in depth during the fieldwork. A brief outline of the main details of each of the cases is provided in Appendix B. The notion of the cases being part of a continuum between the two 'strong ideal types' provides an indication of how variations in the circumstances of the incident impacted on the 'solvability' of the individual cases. It also avoids the sense that there is a categorical distinction that can be drawn between self-solving and whodunit cases.

The cases are divided into three groups; those linked by a single line can be classified as self-solvers. In these cases, the police investigation identified a suspect at an early stage and there was abundant evidence to support this identification. The suspect was often identified either due to a witness observing the incident, or seeing the suspect in the vicinity of the crime around the material time (cases 1, 3, 8), or due to the fact that the police enquiries quickly established that the suspect had the physical opportunity to commit the crime (cases 2, 4, 7, 9, 10). In a number of these cases, the suspect was the last one to see or be seen with the victim alive, which

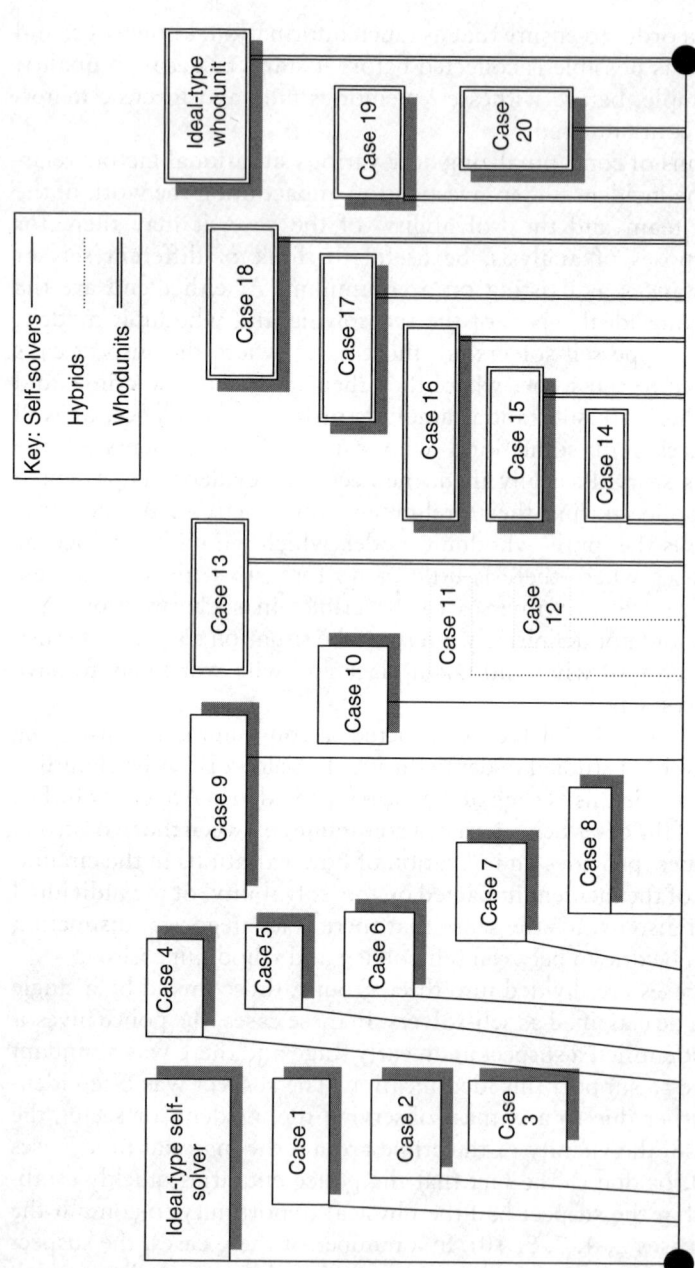

FIG. 8.1.   Continuum of case effects

immediately brought them to the attention of the police. It was also often the case that there was good quality forensic evidence which could be used to support the police's early suspicions.

Another important feature of these cases was that once arrested, the suspect made self-incriminating or confession statements which aided the police (cases 1, 3, 4, 5, 9). Finally, in a number of the cases identified in the sample as self-solvers, an important source of information were those people who were able to tell the police of a previous dispute between the victim and a suspect.

At the other end of the continuum, and linked by a double line, are those cases which were more typical of the whodunit model of investigation. Where these cases were solved, it was only as a result of extensive investigative efforts on the part of the police and a more detailed discussion of the features of whodunit investigations will be provided in the next chapter. As can be seen, four of these cases were 'stranger' murders (14, 15, 16, 17). Case 13 involved members of the victim's family hiring someone to kill him, and in cases 18 and 19 the police felt that they had identified strong suspects, but they were unable to establish sufficient evidence to support a prosecution.

In the middle of the scale are two cases linked by a broken line, that can be identified as 'hybrids'. They share features from both the self-solving and whodunit ideal types. These cases in the sample are important because they show that although for the purposes of analysis, it is useful to focus upon the two basic categories of whodunits and self-solvers, in reality, there is not some absolute distinction between the enquiries that fall into either of the classifications. Rather these hybrid cases exemplify the need to recognize the complexities involved in the situational aspects of different incidents and how these impact upon the police investigation. In case 11, the circumstances of the crime bore all the hallmarks of a whodunit and yet the suspect was identified rapidly by alert police officers because he was 'overly interested' in their investigation. One officer who was a member of the enquiry team on this case commented: 'You know we would never have got him if he hadn't made himself so obvious. If he'd just kept his head down and faded into the background, realistically it was very unlikely that we would have made the link.'

In fact, this candid quote makes a very important point about the police investigative process. The police are not in control of all the factors which will determine the success or otherwise of an investigation. Indeed, the whole notion of a continuum captures the central notion that the investigative process is negotiated and contextual, that the outcome is by no means certain, and the structure of an individual enquiry is the result of the interplay of several key variables. There are a range of factors external to the police actions, which are likely to impact upon their work.

In case 12, as in cases 13 and 14, the police investigation had quickly become focused on the idea that the offender was most likely to have been a stranger to the victim. However, after extensive enquiries it was revealed that the killer was in fact a family member. It was also noticeable that in these cases there was only a small amount of forensic evidence recovered from the scene, which made the police task more difficult. I have mentioned these three cases because they illustrate a couple of key points that are important for understanding the investigative system used by police. First, they show that the process may not lead directly to the offender; false trails are followed and these impact upon the overall structure of the individual enquiry. Secondly, these cases demonstrate that the police do not necessarily get it right first time. In cases 12, 13, and 14, they interpreted the available information at an early stage of the enquiry in such a way as to suggest that the offender was unlikely to have been known to the victim. As a result, they concentrated their enquiries on locating suspects who were not drawn from the victim's immediate circle. It was only at a later stage, when new information became available, that they returned to consider family members as potential suspects and thereby identified the killers.

By constructing a continuum in this way, it is possible to see that the range of issues involved in analysing the content of murder investigations is complex. Cases are not easily comparable; different crimes will establish both unique and common problems for the police enquiry. Furthermore, the continuum shows how the broad headings of self-solver and whodunits used by police actually cover a diverse variety of situational factors.

Process Mapping

Drawing upon the diachronic tracking analysis in Chapter 5 and combining it with more qualitative data derived from the field observations, it is possible to see how the structure of the investigative process differs according to whether a case is a self-solver or whodunit. Furthermore, mapping the process in this way demonstrates how there are a number of fundamental stages of investigative activity that are passed through on the way to a suspect being identified and prosecuted. In order to illustrate the significance of these patterns, Figure 8.2 allows for a comparison of the results of the diachronic tracking analyses for the three cases featured in Chapter 5.

The three graphs illustrate the basic activity patterns of detectives on the three cases analysed. They show that the number of

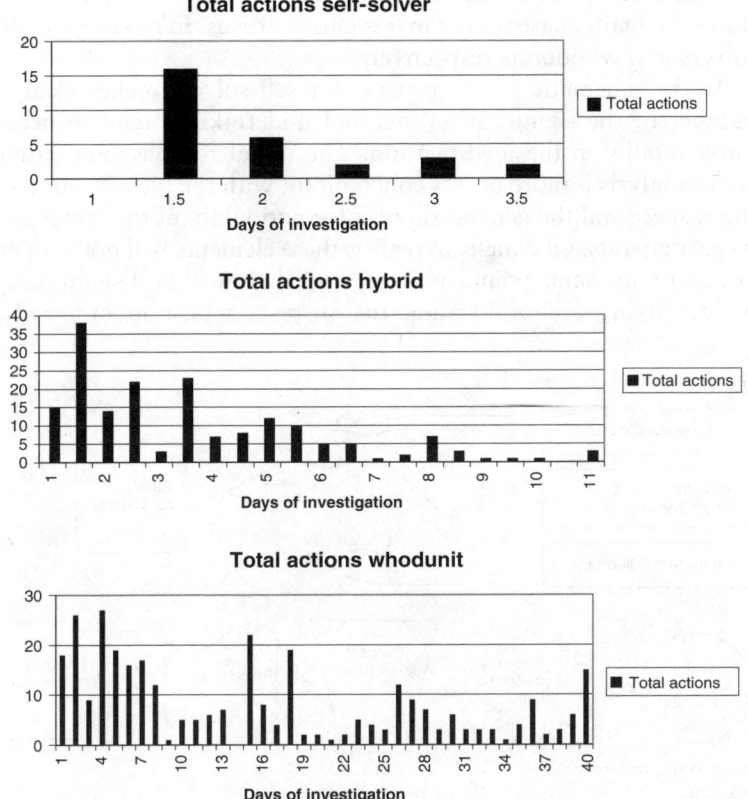

FIG. 8.2. Diachronic tracking comparison

investigative actions and the time period over which they are conducted differs greatly between cases. By combining the results of the tracking analyses with data obtained from ethnographic observation, two analytic 'maps' of the investigative process can be constructed. The maps are obviously archetypes that set out the principal phases that are common to the majority of cases, rather than reflections of the intricacies and complexities associated with particular incidents. Nevertheless, they are useful because they demonstrate how the focus of investigative actions changes over the course of an enquiry as it progresses.

Within the two models of the investigative process, there are a number of common elements and themes, but there are also important differences between them. Figure 8.3 comparatively illustrates the main phases of the investigative process in relation to self-solvers and whodunits respectively.

As the schematic of the process for self-solvers makes clear, a number of the significant events and undertakings tend to occur fairly rapidly in the investigation. The initial response and crime scene analysis is more or less concomitant with the identification of the suspect and the generation of information about the crime and its participants. Of course, in reality, these elements will not happen at exactly the same point. In some cases there will be a slight delay in identifying and/or locating the suspect, whilst in others the

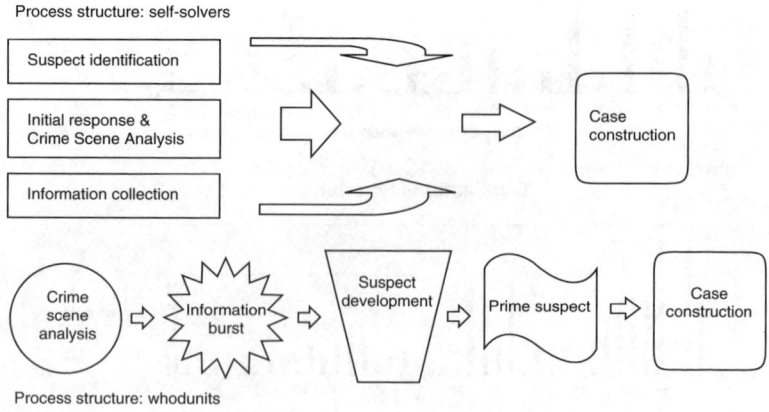

FIG. 8.3.   Comparative outline of the structure of the models of the investigative process

suspect may be arrested prior to the initial response and crime scene analysis occurring. Nevertheless, the figure captures the key facet of these types of homicide investigation, that very early on the police will have identified a suspect and established important details about how the crime happened. Importantly, because in self-solvers the identity of the suspect is established, the lines of enquiry followed by detectives tend to be more tightly focused in terms of what new information needs to be identified and collected. After the initial flurry of activity, the investigators can then progress to develop the case for the prosecution, establishing a more detailed 'legalized' narrative of the crime.

Comparing the model of self-solving investigations with that of whodunits, there are a number of obvious differences. Whodunits commence with the initial response followed by extensive crime scene analysis, the aim being to identify any material and behavioural signifiers that can be used to develop some understanding of how the crime was committed and who might possibly have been involved. The second phase of the passage of whodunit enquiries is what I have termed the 'information burst', where the lines of enquiry undertaken by the investigators begin to produce a large amount of information (of varying degrees of relevance) from an array of sources.

As information starts to become available, it is used by detectives to infer the components of the suspect's profile and thus identify those individuals who might possibly have been involved in the crime. Those people who meet the increasingly refined criteria of the suspect population will be subject to more focused research in order to ascertain whether there is any evidence that further incriminates them. Once a prime suspect is identified, then the focus of investigative activities turns to detailing their involvement in the offence and case construction. Self-solving investigations are addressed in the rest of this chapter. Whodunits are the subject of Chapter 9.

Self-Solvers

I will start my discussion of self-solving enquiries with a narrative of an incident based on a police case file before going on to 'deconstruct' it in order to discuss the various stages of the investigative process.

Two young men were enjoying an after-hours drink in a village pub. Also present were three men who were related (two older, one younger) and the manager of the pub. Throughout the evening, the three younger men had been giving each other 'looks' and 'words' had been exchanged. At the end of the evening one of the older men produced a gun and shot the two younger men in the head. The manager saw this happen. The man who had shot the two victims then gave instructions to the other three persons present (his two colleagues and the manager) to move the bodies outside, which was done. Whilst this tidying up was under way, the manager escaped and ran to a nearby house where the police were called. The witness identified the suspects to the police and sometime later they were arrested.

From the start of this enquiry, the police's actions were informed by the details provided to them by the eyewitness (manager). Although traumatized and in shock, in the first interview with police he was able to provide a detailed account:

...As I walked around the open door, I saw [suspect 1 name] produce a gun, he raised it pointing at [victim 1 name]'s head...he was about an arm's length away from him. There was a loud bang from the gun and [victim 1 name] threw up as he fell to the floor... As this happened [victim 2 name] turned around and [suspect 1 name] pointed the gun at his head and shot him.

The witness was thus able to name the suspects and to provide extensive details about how the incident had taken place. Consequently, the early stages of the investigation centred upon analysis of the crime scene and acting upon and developing lines of enquiry derived from the eyewitness's information. The suspects were quickly arrested and forensic evidence was secured to connect them to the crime.

The police investigation then shifted into a different phase of activity where it was focused upon conducting background enquiries concerning both the victims and the suspects. These revealed that there had been a low intensity, simmering feud between the two younger men and the youngest member of the family group. Although the suspects were arrested and charged quickly, it took the police a further two months of fairly hard work to carry out all the lines of enquiry and to collect sufficient evidence to construct their case to a standard with which they were satisfied. Considerable effort was expended by the police in researching a whole range of leads and combining lots of little pieces of incriminatory evidence and drawing strong inferences from them, in order to construct the narrative of the incident. Through painstaking and methodical investigation of the various leads, the police were able to construct a strong case for the prosecution. The investigators experienced a number of problems in this case relating to establishing the reliability and validity of the information they collected surrounding the background to the killings. They were never able to establish strong evidence of a motive for the crime.

This case outline illustrates how the work involved in self-solving murder investigations occurs in practice and how the different elements of it blend into each other. As an example, it also demonstrates an important point, in that whilst the suspect(s) may be comparatively easy to identify for the police, this does not automatically equate with the presumption that the resultant investigation will be a simple matter. There is often considerable work and skill involved in constructing cases, which on the surface appear ostensibly to be solved. The successful resolution of this case required the police to conduct a complex enquiry in which there was a prolonged information collection stage and a considerable degree of effort expended in relation to the construction of the case. The police had to try to understand and cope with a number of contradictions in the evidence and an intricate array of potentially linked events. At least part of this complexity was obviously related to the fact that there were three suspects and two victims, all of whom had to be fully researched. Despite the fact that the suspects were in custody within 12 hours of the shooting, in the course of the investigation 267 statements were taken from various witnesses; 235 individual actions raised by the major incident room; and 180 'other documents' entered as evidence.

Having provided a brief discussion of the key stages involved in the self-solving investigative process, I will now provide a more detailed examination of the nature of the work performed in each of the stages.

Initial Response and Crime Scene Analysis

In self-solving investigations, much of the early work conducted by police is focused in and around the scene of the crime. It is here that the majority of forensic evidence is likely to be recovered. And due to the circumstances of these types of crimes, it is not unusual to identify eyewitnesses or for the suspect to be present at the scene when police arrive.

Self-solving homicides are typically reported to the police either by the offender or by witnesses to the incident. Standard call-out procedures (as detailed in Chapter 4) tend to be followed and once the SIO has been appointed and appraised the scene, the investigation proper will commence.

A crucial concern in the initial response stage is protecting the scene of the crime, so as to minimize the potential for disturbing or contaminating the available evidence. Access to the scene should be carefully controlled and detailed records are supposed to be kept explaining precisely what actions were taken. The level of micro-management involved at this stage is illustrated by this extract taken from a scene log, which is used by police in all investigations to make a record of all movements at the scene:

19.45 DC [name] into corridor.
19.49–19.52 [name] access to corridor to private area.
19.52 DS [name] into corridor.
19.55 [name] collects coat and out.
19.56 Corridor clear.
21.10 DC [name]/ photographer/ DS [name] on scene.
21.37 DI [name] on scene.

The early stages of an investigation are frequently chaotic and confused, and from the ethnographic fieldwork conducted it was evident that problems were often experienced in exerting control over the scene in the earliest stages. It was frequently the case that the continuity of records such as that above was not maintained, as officers became distracted by more urgent and pressing tasks.

Once the investigators arrive on site, the crime scene will be subjected to a thorough and meticulous search and it is often a significant source of forensic and behavioural evidence for an enquiry. As one detective described it,

The forensic teams go over it with a 'fine-tooth comb', but if they're going to be able to do their job the last thing they need is for the local plod who found the body to have gone round with their size 12 boots on, leaving their prints over everything. It's not as big a problem as it used to be, because I think officers are more aware, but one of the problems we still have is protecting the scene until a forensic team can get in to do their thing.

The scene, the victim, and all the objects that fall within the specified area will be examined in respect of connections to the crime and the evidence they provide to the police.

A case from the fieldwork shows how at the scene the search for forensic evidence is directed by the SIO. The victim was a young woman who was found in her house where she lived alone. The extent of her injuries revealed that she died from severe blows to the skull. There were no signs of forced entry to the property. The first actions raised related to the analysis of the crime scene by a specialist team. The specific directions issued for the team were to:

1. Fingerprint everything possible in the bedroom where the victim was found.
2. Quasar bedroom.[77]
3. No fingerprint examination in the second bedroom or of the deceased's car.
4. In the kitchen and lounge only fingerprint near where blood marks are found or where objects that are likely to have been handled by the offender are located, e.g. glass mug etc.

With this list of directions, the SIO takes care to direct the forensic searches to particular areas of the scene. It represents an attempt to avoid swamping the investigation with too many marks, all of which have to be processed and researched. As such, it provides an example of how past experience and a particular form of investigative logic are employed by detectives in order to direct the investigative methodology.

The suspect was quickly identified by the police because he was the boyfriend of the deceased and he was the last known person to see her alive. In addition, the police suspicions were heightened when background checks revealed that he had previous convictions for offences involving inter-personal violence. Based on these circumstances, a decision was taken to arrest the boyfriend. Up to this stage, it can be seen that the investigation developed in line with the principles of the structural model outlined previously. In particular, the first lines of enquiry centred upon analysis of the crime scene and the suspect was identified because he was close to the victim, a factor supported by both incidental and methodical police suspicion. Furthermore, the forensic searches of the scene had revealed a direct physical link between the suspect and the crime, which appeared to be supported by a range of circumstantial evidence.

During the early stages of an investigation, the pathologist will usually try to study the body of the victim *in situ*, documenting the patterns and extent of the wounds and interpreting them to draw inferences about the intentions and identity of the assailant. The location of the crime is an issue of considerable importance to the investigative strategies employed by the police, especially in the early phases of an enquiry. It influences what forensic evidence is likely to be available, as well as the likelihood of there being witnesses. If the crime scene is inside a building or structure then the potential for physical evidence being destroyed by the natural elements is obviously reduced. The physical boundaries of an environment can also guide the search for evidence in terms of the hypotheses that can be drawn by detectives, in respect of how the offender entered, moved around, and exited the scene and so forth. As seen in the previous example, it can also be used by an SIO to direct the forensic searches to particular areas of the scene.

Officers will analyse how the situated details of the incident contribute to their understanding of the crime and their search for the offender. Questions such as 'what takes place at the location usually?' can be used to trace people who are familiar with the area and who may be able to tell the police about whether the victim or offender have ever been there before. Similar considerations are also important for identifying potential witnesses.

Overall, then, the analysis and processing of the crime scene and the victim's body form the basis of a process of ideation by detectives, whereby they establish a provisional definition of the situation, which in turn provides them with a sense of what happened. This sense-making work informs the early lines of enquiry conducted by the police and is refined, developed, and reformulated as the pool of knowledge available to investigators expands. The distribution of evidence at the scene, the extent of the injuries suffered by the victim, and the physical environment of the scene itself will all be used by investigators to gain some sense of what happened, which can inform their investigative strategies accordingly.

Suspect Identification

Perhaps the key characteristic that separates self-solving cases from whodunits is the rapid identification of a suspect. As a consequence, the police are more concerned with evidencing their suspicions, and the interview with a suspect may provide police with a lot of details about how the crime happened.

Sharon[78] told me that dinner was in the kitchen. I went and got it and then we went and sat in the lounge. I tried to make conversation with Sharon but she wouldn't answer. Then she said something I couldn't quite hear... she repeated it and I lost all control and I just stabbed her and I heard her say 'oh!' and then we just attacked each other and I still had the knife in my hand and I keep repeatedly stabbing her[79] and we tossed and turned and the next thing I know we're on the floor near the fire and then she said 'you're killing me' and then she said 'sorry' and I stopped after... and I just couldn't... she held my arm and I was holding a knife towards her and I then just ran off. I leapt into the car and drove to a telephone kiosk at [town name] and phoned for an ambulance. [...][80]

In this domestic homicide, where the partners' relationship had been deteriorating over time, the suspect's account was in accord with the evidence at the scene of the crime.

The identification of the suspect is frequently closely allied with the other information generation strategies. Lines of enquiry will usually be set to research the backgrounds of both the victim and suspect, to trace and collect information from potential witnesses, and to document in detail the nature of the suspect's involvement in the fatal interaction. Analysis of the HOLMES list of actions on the following case provides a good insight into the type of enquiries being pursued:

A10 Mother of D/P[81] to be seen.
A11 T/St[82] brother of D/P.
A12 T/St sister of D/P.
A14 T/St [name] neighbour of deceased—intimated to PC on guard duty that there were 'mitigating circumstances'...
A20 Pre-cons. Check on D/P...
A25 T/St [name]—[suspect's name] long-term friend.

A29 T/St Mother of deceased . . .
A37 T/St [name] previous boyfriend of deceased.

Obviously investigators will attempt to comprehensively catalogue the suspect's actions in the commission of the crime. They
will also, though, be interested in their activities after the offence.
In particular, the police will want to trace where they went and who
they talked to after the crime. In one case in particular from the
sample, the importance of such attention to detail was demonstrated. Under interview, the police got the suspect to describe his
actions the morning after he was suspected of having been involved
in a murder. The suspect claimed that he had gone out for a walk
that morning to exercise his dog as he usually did. This confirmed
the account of an independent witness whom the police had identified, but the witness had stated that they had seen the suspect on the
morning in question carrying a bag. The police were interested in
the contents of this bag, because they believed that the suspect had
been attempting to dispose of a number of incriminating items,
although at this point in the interview they did not reveal to the
suspect that they had this witness, or that they knew about the bag.
Instead, they got the suspect to describe his walk that morning,
getting him to provide as much detail as possible. In doing this, the
objective was to identify whereabouts on his walk the suspect could
have disposed of the bag. Following up the information that the
suspect had provided to them, the police became interested in one
particular location that seemed a particularly good place to dispose
of the bag. As a result of this line of enquiry, the police recovered
the bag and in it they found a pair of recently washed trousers,
which when subjected to forensic testing linked the suspect to the
crime. In the bag were also a number of items of correspondence,
which effectively linked the bag and its contents to the suspect.

Information Collection

What is apparent from the discussion of the initial response and
crime scene analysis, and the identification of suspects, is that
police rapidly tend to acquire significant and detailed information
about the incident concerned in self-solving enquiries. This information is used to generate follow-up enquiries and develop major
lines of enquiry that assist in the production of a case narrative.

In cases such as the one above and indeed many self-solving and whodunit investigations, the family and friends of the victim and offender are often important information sources for the police in terms of understanding the motivation for the offence. Particularly because self-solving type crimes are rarely 'out of the blue' occurrences, it is likely that the family and friends will be able to provide important details of the pre-history to the fatal assault.

The following extract provides an idea of how a number of lines of enquiry are set to run concurrently and how they are co-ordinated. The main lines of enquiry that were followed, in an effort to collect more details, were set out in the policy file as follows:

1. A formal interview to be conducted with the suspect.
2. Trace and interview the customers in the pub in which both the suspect and victim were seen drinking together, a few hours before the estimated time of death.
3. Enquiries with the neighbours either side of the deceased's house in case they saw or heard anything suspicious.
4. Family background enquiries on victim.
5. Family background enquiries on suspect.

These details show how the police used a combination of focused and 'trawling' lines of enquiry to collect detailed information relating to the circumstances of the attack and the possible motivations for it. In this particular case, the enquiries carried out with the family and friends of the victim revealed that the victim thought she was pregnant. However, the various friends of the victim and suspect who were interviewed were able to tell the police that there was some degree of doubt over the identity of the father, due to the fact that the victim had had a sexual relationship with a number of men over recent months. This information was interpreted by the police as providing a possible motive for their suspect, whom they had already arrested.[83]

In cases where the victim and offender were intimately related, such as domestic murders, the families are potentially important information sources. It is, however, important to acknowledge that in such cases the relationship between the police and the family is often complex. The surviving family are often a major source of information about the victim's background for the police, but at the same time they are profoundly distressed and as such the police may actually have difficulty in accessing the information in which they have an interest. Matters are further complicated by the fact that a member or members of the family may have been established as a suspect(s) by the police. Whilst the police need to obtain information from the family, the family will also want to find out from the police the various circumstances of the murder and as Rock argues from the family's point of view, 'It is a consequence that, just at the time that a family is trying to assimilate the unassimilable, they may find themselves under suspicion, stripped of control, kept at a distance and subject to repeated, intense and often aggressive interrogation' (Rock, 1998a: 75).

There is, then, within the police/family relationship, the potential for substantial conflicts of interest, particularly in view of the fact that one or more of them may be a suspect. Furthermore, the breadth and depth of the police enquiries will often result in hitherto hidden information that 'discredits' the victim or other members of the family coming to light with implications for the surviving relatives and friends.[84] Similar enquiries and problems may be encountered with the friends of the victim.

Case Construction

Case construction is where the police 'legalize' (Dixon, 1997) the information they have collected and organize it so as to form a coherent, legally valid, structured narrative account of what they believe took place in the incident that they have investigated (McConville et al., 1991). This is where officers make sure that they have collected all the necessary evidence to show in detail how the suspect was involved in the commission of the crime.

Throughout the process of investigation the police are constructing their case, testing the various 'pieces' to see how they fit into the overall narrative that is being created. Once they are satisfied that they have identified the suspect and they have charged him or her in conjunction with the offence, and after seeking advice from a representative of the Crown Prosecution Service (CPS), then the focus of the investigative effort shifts to making sure that the police account of the incident is comprehensive and fully evidenced. Detectives are engaged in constructive work throughout an enquiry, but it is a particularly pronounced focus of their work in the latter stages of the passage of the investigation. It is therefore useful in analytic terms to conceptualize this as the last phase of the process.

The work performed in the case construction stage is not, though, simply about incriminating the identified suspect. An important element is concerned with thinking strategically about the impending prosecution, and trying to predict and neutralize any alternative accounts or mitigating factors that defence counsel may choose to offer. An example of this anticipatory work is provided by the case cited previously, of the pregnant woman who was killed by her boyfriend. In this self-solving investigation, the case construction stage was focused around two key tasks. First, the police had to co-ordinate all the various pieces of incriminating evidence and construct them into a coherent narrative meeting the requirements of legal discourse. Secondly, a number of their activities at this stage of the enquiry were directed towards demonstrating that the crime could not have been committed by another of the victim's lovers. The following thematic line of enquiry was issued by the SIO on the case, four days after the female victim was found: 'Trace, interview and eliminate all the former boyfriends. Enquiries are to include fingerprints, blood and DNA for all those persons believed to have had sexual intercourse with the victim in the past three months.' Here the police enquiries were undertaken in preparation for the adversarial court trial, in order to try and ensure that defence counsel could not undermine their case against the suspect with a fairly obvious suggestion.

A key element of case construction is taking decisions about what should be included in the narrative and how this should be evidentially substantiated. This involves trying to anticipate any lines of attack that the defence may employ at trial, but also selectively editing the material so that it contributes to the overall case. The conduct of this work was observed:

The detective sergeant who has been a key player throughout the investigation has been tasked with preparing the case file. He is working in a room in a small hut away from the main police station. In the room there are piles of papers stacked at various heights on the desk. His job is to go through checking all the information, identifying what contributes to the narrative and what doesn't. As he described it he is also meant to 'pick up any loose ends that need resolving'.

Whilst a further process of editing and construction is made by counsel, it is important to recognize that the police in concert with CPS to a large extent define the relevant issues of the case.

Due to the nature of the established relations between victims and their killers that are typical of self-solving investigations, there is often a complex pre-history to the fatal assault that has to be unpicked by investigators. Untangling the complex webs of action, reaction, and interaction that are often involved in these emotionally charged and traumatic events and the attribution of legal culpability on the basis of this is a complex task. As a consequence, an important element of the case construction stage is deciding upon an appropriate charge. That is, do the circumstances of the crime warrant and support a charge of murder, or should the suspect be properly charged with manslaughter or some other form of homicide? This is often a contentious matter that is further complicated by considerations of how any such decision will be interpreted in a court by a jury.

Over lunch in the pub with 6 officers from the murder squad they discussed the morning's proceedings in court. There was a concern that one of the three suspects was not going to be convicted of murder although having been so charged. Similar concerns had been expressed about what he should be charged with throughout the investigation and evidently some time had been taken in persuading the CPS to support a charge of murder against him. The mood at the table was fairly pessimistic. Walking back to the court one of the detective sergeants said to me in a quiet voice 'You know, I never thought we should have charged him with murder. I did the interviews with him and I just don't think he knew what was going to happen that night when they went to the pub ... But that's the game we play. I mean I can understand why we charged him with murder but whether he's factually guilty on that point I guess I disagree with the others.'

This is an important extract because it signals some of the difficulties in the decisions taken in respect of charging a suspect with a crime. Furthermore, it is indicative of the fact that, within a murder squad, officers may to varying degrees contest the public narrative of the crime that is assembled.

Case construction work and assembling an evidenced narrative often constitute a significant proportion of the overall investigative effort on self-solving cases. As one detective constable who was interviewed noted, 'It's a mistake to think in terms of investigative work as being just about identifying an offender. Very often that's the easy part and it's once you've got them that the real work starts.'

Case Study: A 'Criminal-Cause' Murder

The following investigation is provided as a brief case study to illustrate how in practice the investigative process in self-solving cases is enacted. It also demonstrates how the police are sometimes able to identify a suspect or suspects comparatively easily, but there is considerable effort involved in actually physically locating them. In this case, the only motivation for the crime that the police could establish was robbery.

The body of the victim was found in a local beauty spot, mid-evening, out in the open. In the first morning briefing, the enquiry team were brought up to date about the progress that had been made since the body had been found the previous evening:

The SIO led the meeting he said 'The body of [victim name] was found at [location] with multiple stab wounds by the witness [name] who said that he heard two or three raised voices then silence. Another male [name] then arrives on scene and between them they manage to call an ambulance. So far we have managed to trace that the victim was a resident at [hostel name] and was last seen there by his mother on [six days earlier].' The deputy SIO was asked about what the pathologist had said to which he replied 'There are no apparent defence wounds'. The briefing was then told that 2 men had been arrested but released as they are not believed connected. The SIO did though say that 'There are two other residents from the hostel [name 1] and [name 2] who are being sought for interview, because they have not been seen since the discovery of the body'... one Sergeant who has been following up an intelligence lead told how there is a report of 'a suspect in Bethnal Green who apparently told a friend that he'd stabbed someone in [place name]'.

By this stage then the police had already identified two suspects for the crime on the basis that they were unexpectedly absent from the hostel. That day further enquiries were conducted and by the evening briefing significant further progress had been made.

The SOCO reported about the various scenes that are connected to the crime. The two suspects mentioned this morning are evidently being viewed as connected and a search of their rooms has been conducted. Then a detective constable told how he had identified a new witness and that 'He says that he saw 2 youths in the hostel matching the descriptions of the suspects and that one of them appeared to have blood on his hands. The other was in possession of a ghetto blaster similar to that which is believed missing from the victim's room. He also says that in the course of their conversation they boasted of "having done someone over" and asking him about possible outlets to sell the ghetto blaster.' To which the SIO said 'Ok on the basis of this info. tomorrow I want to have some idea of how accurate his timings are and I want some actions to try and trace whether there was any attempt to sell the items at the place suggested.'

As a result of the developing suspicions, a decision was taken to apply for a warrant to search the rooms of the two prime suspects in addition to that of the victim. The police were also able to trace the person who had purchased the ghetto blaster. After several days where the police enquiries were focused upon trying to trace the whereabouts of the two suspects, they were eventually tracked down and arrested in different parts of the country.

The sequence of events provided below shows how the significant events in the investigation relate to each other, how they relate to the sequential model of the investigative process, and the time scale involved for their completion.[85]

Sequence of Events

Day 1	*Initial Response*
0	Body found. Murder enquiry launched. SIO and Home Office pathologist visited the scene. Detailed search of the crime scene. Lines of enquiry relate to identity of the victim.
+5 hours	Press release stating that a body of a young male has been found, the cause of death is not yet known and a post-mortem to be carried out.
+1/2 hour	Identity of the victim is established.
	Information Collection and Suspect Identification
	Over the next 24 hours a picture began to emerge as a number of witnesses were able to place the victim and two suspects together and their suspicious behaviour marked them out as appropriate for police suspicion. Whilst the forensic searches continued, the information collection stages of the enquiry become more significant.
Day 2	The police enquiries shift to an intelligence gathering type of operation focusing on the identified suspects. In the policy file the SIO establishes that the priority lines of enquiry were as follows:

(1) Research [suspect 1] and [suspect 2] in order to locate.

(2) Trace witnesses who saw the victim on the afternoon before he died.[86]

(3) Issue a press release appealing for witnesses to come forward. A nationwide alert was issued and locations where the suspects were known to have contacts are placed under observation.

+44 hours 92 hours after the discovery of the victim's body a report is received from another force that [suspect 1] has been arrested. The lines of enquiry at this point relate to researching his recent movements.

+41 hours *Case Construction*

[Suspect 2] is arrested in another jurisdiction. Upon their arrest both suspects were found to be in possession of property belonging to the deceased. Once more lines of enquiry are established to investigate this suspect's movements. In the intervening period [suspect 1] has been interviewed on a number of occasions. He has suggested that [suspect 2] was responsible for the murder. Upon his arrest [suspect 2] is interviewed.

+3 hours As a result of the interviews and after consulting with a representative of the Crown Prosecution Service, a decision to charge both men jointly with murder was taken.

The total time between the body being discovered and both men being charged was 137 hours.

As part of the case construction stage, research into the movements of suspect 1 after the crime revealed that, whilst he had been on the run, he had tried on several occasions to get himself admitted to hospital. He was voluntarily admitted on one occasion due to the fact that he was showing signs of schizophrenia. As such, the police enquiries were particularly concerned with trying to establish whether the victim was really mentally ill to such a degree that he could not be held legally responsible for his actions. In pursuing this strand of the case development, expert psychiatric opinion was sought, which concluded that the suspect was not delusional or mentally ill. The police enquiries were also interested in the clothes that the two men were wearing because it was felt that there might be important forensic evidence on them.

This enquiry conformed quite closely to the model of the self-solving murder investigation. It started with an analysis of the crime scene where important evidence was recovered and the early lines of enquiry established several witnesses, whose information was used by the police to identify two prime suspects within 24 hours of the body being discovered. By this point, we can see that the investigation had shifted more to a concern with information collection. Several detectives were conducting research into the victim's background and family, and as the extract from the SIO's policy file on Day 2 shows, lines of enquiry were also established in relation to the two suspects. The final phase of the process model commenced when the suspects were arrested. Here the police enquiries were concerned to establish precisely who did what in relation to the assault, as well as preparing the case for prosecution and anticipating any potential legal problems. The sequence of events also shows that whilst there are separate stages that can be identified in terms of the investigative activities, in practice the boundaries between them are blurred as might be expected in relation to a complex sequential and concurrent process.

Conclusion

In this chapter, I have examined the investigative process as it relates particularly to self-solving murders. Self-solvers are marked out by the fact that at an early stage of the police enquiry there is a sufficient quantity of high quality evidence to enable the police to identify a suspect. It was shown, though, that an important element of the work that is done in these enquiries relates to the construction of the case in preparation for the prosecution. Although the rhetoric of law portrays itself as a 'truth'-finding mechanism, police practices and the interactions between police and suspects contribute to the construction of a 'legal reality' for a case and in a broader sense the moral identities of those involved. In the next chapter, the process of investigation as it relates to whodunit murders will be discussed.

9

Whodunits

In the previous chapter, it was identified that the investigative process on protracted hard-to-solve murders shares elements with that utilized on self-solving enquiries, but that in a number of areas there are important differences between them. Whodunit investigations tend to be concerned with those comparatively rare instances of fatal violence where there is no established relationship between the participants and the suspect is not identified quickly. Generally, whodunits are perceived as more serious by the police and public, they are likely to receive more media attention, and will often require a considerable investment of police resources to solve them. In this chapter, I will explore how these complex cases are investigated. The following summary of one case in the sample provides an indication of some of the key issues involved in these types of investigation.

The victim, a middle-class, middle-aged woman, was found dead in the hallway of her house with multiple stab wounds. Analysis of the crime scene suggested that the offender had been cut in the attack, as a fingerprint in blood other than the victim's was found on the front doorframe. There was no sign of forced entry to the property and the victim had not been sexually assaulted. There appeared to have been no property removed from the house. This presented the police with a major problem; there was no apparent motive for the offence upon which to base their early enquiries. The police research into the victim's movements prior to her death revealed that she had followed her normal daily routine.

There were three principal theories used by the police to orient the investigative methodology. The first of these centred upon the husband of the victim. He worked away from home for long periods of time and whilst he was alibied from direct involvement, the police officers who spoke to him felt that his reactions were not appropriate to the situation. This heightened their suspicion towards him.

Due to the fact that the crime was apparently motiveless and given the high level of violence in the assault, the SIO elected that a number of enquiries should be launched to examine the possible involvement of people with mental disorders. The problem for the police was that although it was a prosperous neighbourhood, in surrounding areas there were a large number of community re-settlement centres and hostels for the homeless.

A third line of enquiry developed as a result of the media publicity that the crime had received and was more promising. A woman living near to the victim phoned the police to report that about an hour before the murder she had answered her door to a young man who behaved suspiciously. The man was acting strangely and only left when confronted by the woman's male neighbour. Both the woman and her neighbour were able to provide descriptions of the man. At a later stage of the enquiry, it was to prove important that the woman told the police that during their conversation the young man had asked for directions to a particular street.

A photo-fit picture of the man seen by the two witnesses was composed and publicized through the media. Unbeknown to the police at this time, whenever he saw this picture the offender became agitated and would comment to family and friends about the likeness between him and the picture. His family and friends found this behaviour somewhat strange as they could see only a very vague likeness, but they did not report it to police.

Elsewhere, though, the police were making little progress. Several suspects were identified and eliminated. As they reached the point where all the possible leads had been exhausted, a decision was taken to try a house-to-house canvass in the area which the young man had asked the woman for directions to, over a mile away from the crime scene. As a direct result of this strategy, several of the suspect's friends were questioned during routine enquiries. They happened to mention their friend's strange behaviour and this led to him being interviewed and eventually arrested. A DNA and fingerprint match with the marks found on the doorframe was obtained, as was additional forensic evidence, and the suspect was charged. Prior to the suspect's arrest and subsequent to it, the police established that the suspect was perhaps slightly mentally unbalanced and that there was a possibility that he had exhibited violent behaviours in the past.

This was an extremely large enquiry; the 'trawling' actions of the house-to-house team resulted in 3,613 names being entered on the HOLMES system and 3,218 houses being canvassed. 371 statements from witnesses were recorded on the system, as were 374 reports from police officers. 1,987 separate actions were administered by the major incident room. The suspect was arrested 137 days after the murder was committed. The example above provides a very brief outline of a case that can be classified as constituting a 'whodunit' investigation. The victim was killed by a complete stranger and the police investigation was a complex and long-drawn-out affair.

Investigating 'Whodunit' Murders

Cases were defined by the police as whodunits where a suspect was not identified in the course of the preliminary investigation. The majority of the cases that can be classified as whodunits involved victims and suspects who were not acquainted or had only a loose acquaintance prior to the crime. Thus the process of enquiry can be seen to be concerned with two key inter-linked objectives: first, the need to identify the offender and secondly, to develop a case to support prosecution. As a result, the 'mechanics' of the investigative process differ somewhat from that on self-solving cases.

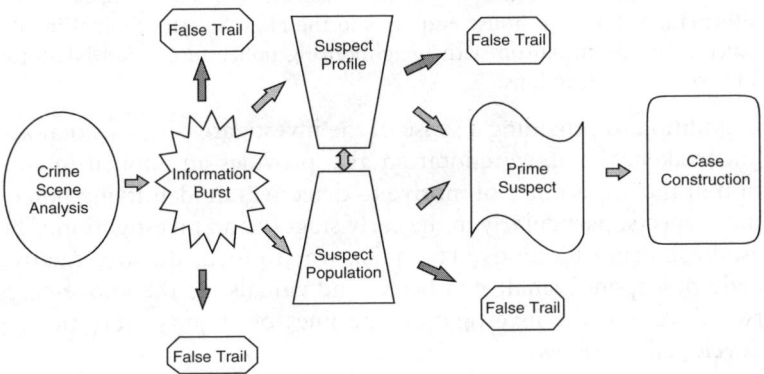

FIG. 9.1.   Process model 'whodunit' murders

Initial Response and Crime Scene Analysis

The initial response stage in whodunit enquiries shares much with that already discussed in relation to self-solving investigations, revolving around identification, interpretation, and collection of information and evidence at the crime scene, so as to establish a definition of the situation. Such material is used by detectives to assemble an idea of what happened and to develop 'leads', which provide them with a sense of 'how to go on' with their investigation. Therefore, I will not repeat my previous comments here, merely seek to develop them as appropriate.

Characteristic of the crime scenes of whodunit murders is that there is no clear indication of a potential suspect. In such circumstances, and in the absence of any substantive leads, detectives draw upon their experience and the available 'cues' to infer what sort of homicide this might be and thereby implement a fairly standardized set of enquiries. These standard lines of enquiry are used on the basis that they are likely to generate the sorts of information that police need to develop their understandings of what has taken place and who may have been involved. Typically, these enquiries would include crime scene searches, house-to-house, researching the victim, and considering the family and friends of the deceased as potential suspects. The following extract from an SIO's policy file provides some indication of the approach used:

At this stage, because there is no obvious motive for this crime the lines of enquiry will be as follows: close family of the deceased including ex-wives for background information; business associates, again for background information; house to house enquiries in the High Street; criminal intelligence enquiries in liaison with [neighbouring police force] and NCIS for any criminal connections.

In addition to providing a sense of the investigative actions that are undertaken, the above quotation also provides an implicit indication of the importance of motive to detectives in identifying potential suspects, particularly in the early stages of an investigation. The establishment of a motive is a quick way to focus the investigative activities upon a small number of individuals. In the above case, two days into the investigation the lines of enquiry were further developed as follows:

Existing lines of enquiry will continue and will be extended to cover the following: Evaluation and necessary action on information being supplied by officers from [neighbouring force] concerning [suspect 1 name] and [suspect 2 name]; elimination of white Fiesta seen outside the scene at relevant time. Enquiries at School for potential witnesses; T/I all users of the car park at the rear of scene to establish any unusual vehicles or persons being seen at relevant time.

Victimology

Researching the victim is one way in which police on difficult cases attempt to start to identify relevant information which might suggest why this person was selected by the assailant, and thus who might be responsible. One SIO described the reasons for a concentration upon researching the victim thus:

> In the absence of any firm leads, at the start of an enquiry you are going to get the investigation moving by looking at the victim. You want to quickly get an idea about who they knew, what were their habits, routines, likes and dislikes, and vices. Basically, you're looking for that thing that makes you think, 'I need to look at that person's involvement a bit more closely'.

The police will construct a highly detailed biography of the victim. The extent of the detail into which these enquiries sometimes go is illustrated by the following report, compiled by officers tasked to conduct background enquiries for a female victim who, the police enquiry eventually revealed, was killed by someone unknown to her:

> Victim married, but prior to marriage she'd had a relationship from which there was a son... Victim had 3 sisters and 2 brothers... Both parents still alive but divorced... She worked as a secretary at [firm name]... Her hours of work were 9am to 1pm Monday to Friday and she travelled to and from work via the bus as she couldn't drive and did not own a car... Victim and husband owned the home where she lived and was killed—no mortgage outstanding and no apparent financial worries... Nothing to suggest heavy drinking although both she and her husband were treated for a drink problem 20 years ago, apparently successfully... She had a very small circle of friends, mainly female. She was variously described by different people (not her friends) as aloof, shy and quiet—neither of her neighbours knew her Christian name... The victim led an unremarkable lifestyle... she doted on her young daughter... She enjoyed her part-time job and worked more for pleasure than for income. Regularly had a group of female friends every Monday afternoon for a coffee party. Did main shopping Wednesdays... Appeared never to employ a babysitter and spent every evening watching TV with her daughter... She was in touch with most of her relatives and they visited

each other often. We were unable to find any suggestion of marital infidelity by either the victim or her husband.

The above extracts convey a sense of just how thorough the police research into the victim's background can be. But they also give an indication about what aspects of the deceased's past are considered particularly important by the police. It can be seen that the police have examined the possibility of the husband's and other relatives' involvement. Further to this, though, the content of the report also provides an illustration of some of the points that I made previously in Chapter 6, relating to how the actions of the police can in a sense be seen to be involved in the construction of a moral identity for the victim. Although the report itself was compiled for the purposes of the investigation, the sorts of issues that are highlighted stress the 'moral worth' of the victim. The sense that she was a 'good wife' and in particular a 'good mother' runs throughout the report and this may have implications for the degree of effort made by the police.

Detectives will treat the scene of the crime as a range of signifiers to be decoded, in order to manufacture some sense of the interactional dynamics of the crime and how it took place. As can be seen from the previous example, an important source of information that is available to officers at the crime scene is behavioural. Investigators will examine the scene in an attempt to reconstruct the *modus operandi* of the offender. They will seek to analyse what the distribution of evidence tells them about the attack. Did the offender bring the murder weapon to the scene or take it with them when they left? Does the offence appear to be planned or unplanned? How much violence was used in the assault? These types of questions will all contribute to the construction of the suspect profile. For example, in one of the investigations in the sample, the victim had been found dead in her house and the post-mortem revealed she had been sexually assaulted. Further analysis of the crime scene had revealed that entry to the property had been gained via a downstairs window. The police used this information about particular facets of the crime to direct and target their offender search strategies.

Attention is also directed to what (if anything) is done to the victim by the offender after the death, any witnesses, and then by any law enforcement personnel at the scene. Consideration of such issues is important in terms of the identification and collection of physical evidence. If the body or the scene is disturbed in any way this can have profound implications for the evidence that will be found and the interpretations that can be drawn from the crime scene.[87]

In whodunits, a relevant consideration is whether the victim was found at the same location as they were killed. The crime scene is often one of the most important sites for the location of forensic evidence. But if the victim's body has been moved after death, having been attacked elsewhere, this fact obviously has important repercussions for the search for evidence. In sum then, the physical examination of the corpse has to be conducted with great care and the police have to consider a whole range of possibilities relating to whether the victim was in contact with anything or anyone else between their death and the corpse being secured by police. If they were, then the police must attempt to identify who or what did it, how and why this happened, and how does this affect the evidence? In order to preserve the integrity of the chain of evidence, great care has to be taken in relation to how the victim and the assorted artefacts are handled throughout the investigation.

As the police investigation becomes established, lines of enquiry will be set to track the victim's movements immediately prior to the crime, as part of the work to identify persons who might have had the physical opportunity to assault them. In the case involving the female victim earlier in this chapter, just this sort of information was collected by a team of officers. Their research established that the last-known movements of the victim were

08.45 Dropped her daughter off at school.
09.05 Caught bus from nearby shop to work (1 mile journey).
09.20 Arrived at work.
13.10 Left work.
13.15 Met sister-in-law for lunch at a nearby café (a regular meeting).
13.40 Left café and went shopping locally.
13.48 In Woolworths.
14.00 Brentford Nylons.
14.12 Icelands.
       The above times are based on till receipts from the shops—no positive sightings following above, but probably caught bus home. Earliest arrival home 14.30.

15.20   Failed to collect daughter from school.
16.05   Body found.

In all murders the police will seek to establish who the victim was with and what they were doing in the hours and minutes before the assault. They will attempt to trace the victim's movements prior to the attack, making a careful note of the timings involved, as this may provide them with an indication as to who had the physical opportunity to commit the crime.

The Victim's Family

Once the identity of the victim is established, then their family have to be informed of the death. The relationship between the family and the police differs slightly when compared with the self-solving model and there are different problems to be overcome. As was indicated in the previous chapter, it is often the case that the police will, in the early stages of the enquiry, view members of the family as the most likely suspects for the crime. In several of the cases studied, the first lines of enquiry concentrated upon trying to prove the involvement of a family member, only for it to be shown that this individual could not have committed the offence. Nevertheless, the very fact of the police's research can stigmatize the family and increase the stress they are under. This was exemplified in one enquiry where the wife of the victim requested to see the officer leading the investigation to complain that the lines of enquiry that the police were following were causing malicious gossip about her in the local community. In an attempt to 'cool her out'[88] but not denying the police's view of her as a suspect she was told that, '...the investigation is currently following a number of lines of enquiry. None to the exclusion of any other.'

This is an important point, though: part of the investigative process is about eliminating potential suspects as well as incriminating them. Once relatives have been eliminated from suspicion, the relationship between police and family is likely to become more supportive (Rock, 1998a, 1998b).[89]

As well as the family, police enquiries will seek to identify the victim's close friends, acquaintances, and work colleagues. As is the case with immediate relations, in the absence of an identified suspect the police's motives for contact with these groups are twofold. They are looking to increase their general pool of knowledge about the victim and their background, but they are also looking to see if any of these individuals conform to the characteristics of the suspect profile that is being constructed.

The early stages of whodunit enquiries are thus mainly concerned with analysing the crime scene and establishing the various dynamics of the assault in an effort to construct a definition of the situation. Enquiries will also focus upon the victim and those persons known to the victim. From the commencement of an enquiry, then, the police are using the available information to contribute to a profile of the suspect and the type of person they are looking for. Informed interpretations of what occurred in the fatal interaction can be used by police to draw abductive inferences about the type of murder it is and consequently identify potential suspects.

Information Burst

Whereas with self-solvers the lines of enquiry are usually fairly tightly focused, in whodunits the information collection strategies tend to be more widely dispersed. As the investigation becomes established and lines of enquiry are set up, the police rapidly begin to collect and generate a lot of information potentially relevant to the case. Some of this material will contribute to the police's understanding of the crime, whilst much of it will prove to be of no real consequence. Nevertheless, crucial to the management of this process is how all the data are produced, interpreted, recorded, and used. The principle guiding the process is that through the collection of a lot of information the police should be able to validate some of this material as knowledge about the crime and as their knowledge increases, their enquiries should become progressively more focused.

In the early stages of this filtering process, though, where detectives are often 'trawling' for potential leads, the structure of the process is defined by the mass of information that rapidly starts to flow into the system as a result of a range of different enquiries. I have termed this phase the 'information burst' in an attempt to capture how in a short space of time the police go from knowing almost nothing about the circumstances of the incident, to being in possession of lots of information about many of the people, places, and objects related to the object of enquiry. There is then, in the information burst stage, a build-up of investigative actions as these are generated in response to the in-flows of information that have to be worked through by officers on the outside enquiry team.

As Figure 9.1 makes clear, the structural dynamics of whodunit enquiries as a whole are very much influenced by the fact that a lot of the enquiries that are undertaken turn out to be false trails that are not relevant to the eventual outcome of the investigation. One of the SIOs I interviewed described how these problems could impact upon an enquiry:

On the last job I was on we were inundated with 'red herring' lines of enquiry, they were coming from everywhere... You finish up with hundreds of lines of enquiry that don't go anywhere and I had to take quite a hard-nosed decision and say we will not be pursuing those ones.

Sometimes false trails consist of just going to interview a potential witness who turns out not to hold any valuable information. Others, though, constitute major themes within the progress of an enquiry. For example, on one investigation, the police had received information that the male victim had been having an affair with a woman and her adult son had been very unhappy about this. As a result of the information they had received, the investigators spent the first week of the investigation focusing on the son as a prime suspect. But through their enquiries it was shown that he could not have committed the crime and neither was he involved in its commission. The police later identified a different suspect who was convicted of the offence. False trails occur in all murder enquiries to a greater or lesser extent. But as a result of the circumstances in which whodunit murders take place and the types of investigative problems that have to be resolved by detectives on them, false trails tend to be more numerous and have a more direct impact upon the overall structure of the enquiry in whodunit murders when compared with self-solving murders.

Through the various lines of enquiry that are enacted, the team start to generate a lot of information that can be developed by the officers in the major incident room into further leads and enquiries. As such, the information management function of the MIR is particularly important. It should be restated, though, that on occasions potential witnesses or suspects refused to co-operate.

Using the Media

One investigative technology that was used by the police when they were being met with resistance or when the enquiry was not progressing was to employ the media as an investigative resource in the hope of encouraging people with relevant information to come forward. Typically, at the start of an enquiry, the police will only release a limited amount of detail about the incident to the media. If, however, after a few days, the usual lines of enquiry do not appear to be successful, then there may be a shift in the police policy. This change in the management of the media in such investigations is typified by the entries made by one SIO in his policy file. In the early stages of this enquiry the policy was to restrict the level of information provided to the media:

Press conference to be held, to state that the police are investigating the death of two persons in suspicious circumstances. Identity of the deceased, the sexual nature of the attack, the method of entry, position of the bodies and description of the weapon are not to be given.

The initial press publicity led to a lot of information being forwarded by members of the public, but no really good leads were produced. As a result, two days later, the SIO elected to release more information via the media in the hope of getting an improved response:

The sexual nature of the attack is to be released to the press and mention is also to be made of the possible connection with offences in other parts of the country. The latter is to be downplayed though, in view of the press likelihood to portray a positive connection. No further information is to be released to the press at this stage.

Local media organizations in particular may act as a conduit for police communication with the local public, which can result in the police receiving a lot of calls from people who wish to assist them. Much of the information that results from such media appeals tends to be of little consequence to the progress of the investigation, but the use of such tactics can be seen as another example of the unfocused 'trawling' techniques that the police use. They are undertaken with the view that they may result in important information being discovered.

The information that results from the various lines of enquiry is used by the MIR staff to develop more focused lines of enquiry which will trace and focus upon potential suspects for the crime. They are seeking to maximize the number of actions that make a positive contribution to the development of the enquiry, while minimizing the number of irrelevant false trails that are carried out, in order to identify the offender as quickly as possible and run the enquiry in an effective and efficient manner.

The Suspect Profile and Population

From the outset of the investigation, the thinking of investigators is attuned to interpreting information in line with the need to answer the question 'who did this?' In the absence of a 'smoking gun' suspect, the investigators attempt to collect knowledge about the crime and through a dualistic process of incrimination and elimination construct a chain of evidence that identifies one individual (or group of individuals) as a suspect. In whodunit cases it is not unusual for several suspects to be identified and eliminated, prior to a prime suspect being identified.

As all the information flows into the investigative system, particular leads are identified by the staff in the major incident room as being sufficiently interesting and potentially relevant to warrant further investigation, and 'actions' will be raised for research on these matters. If the defining characteristic of the opening phases of the investigation is the collection and management of a large amount of information, then the middle section is about sifting, juggling, and working through the information, refining and interpreting it in relation to a broader hypothesis of how the crime occurred, all as part of constructing the suspect profile.[90] By this I mean building up an increasingly detailed picture of the suspect and the crime, so as to limit the numbers of people who can be included within the scope of the suspect population. As was illustrated in Figure 9.1, these two elements of the process work in concert and are mutually determining, in that the more detailed the information in the suspect profile, the more tightly defined the boundaries of the suspect population.

The police use the information in the suspect profile to build up a list of known characteristics about the offender (e.g. white/male/6-foot-tall etc.), which in turn is used to construct the membership of the suspect population. The suspect population is composed of those persons who share characteristics known to be possessed by the killer. Typically, they would be further refined on the basis of known offenders and being acquainted with the victim. The focusing of the suspect population is achieved through the addition of details to the suspect profile. From the start of an enquiry, the investigator is looking at all the information in terms of what inferences and interpretations can be made about the identity and characteristics (physical, moral, and cognitive) of the offender from the available data. They are trying to collect sufficient information in order that a single individual (or where appropriate several persons) can be identified as a prime suspect.

Information or evidence can therefore advance the state of the investigation if it either further incriminates a particular individual or group of individuals, or if it eliminates persons from further suspicion. As a senior detective described, there are several criteria for elimination from police suspicion:

> Basically you tend to eliminate suspects either through forensic evidence; through them not matching an eyewitness description; or they might have an alibi from an independent witness; or maybe sometimes an alibi of a relative, friend or spouse. Of course you have to be particularly cautious about an alibi provided by someone who knows 'chummy', but you also have to be aware that eyewitnesses can be wrong, sometimes spectacularly wrong, and that's always in the back of your mind.

As the above quote indicates, the reliability of any alibi provided should be subjected to considerable scrutiny, although in several of the cases in the sample, suspects were able to provide an alibi that was initially accepted by police, only for it later to be shown to be false.

The above process is indicative of how many suspects were identified on whodunit investigations. Through a progressive refinement of the knowledge about the crime possessed by the investigation, detectives were able to focus in upon particular individuals. On other occasions, though, the 'break' in the investigation was far more sudden. Sometimes, luck and good fortune, as an ancillary of persistence, plays a role in solving cases.

Prime Suspect

A number of officers commented that a problem they regularly encountered when investigating whodunit murders was that they collected a lot of information about the various characteristics of the killer, but this did not necessarily mean that they could identify a particular individual as a suspect. As one officer commented, 'It can happen that you know a lot about your suspect, almost everything, except their name and when this happens there's little that you can do except hope that you get the break'.

Another officer described similar problems in a somewhat more prosaic fashion, 'We've reached a stage on this case where we know almost all we can know about how they actually killed him, but we're buggered in terms of actually pinning it down to one single identifiable person'.

Once a 'strong' link between an aspect of the crime and a particular individual is established, then they may become a prime suspect. The identification of a prime suspect is obviously an important development, and it tends to be accompanied by a shift in the style and focus of the investigation. Rather than focusing on the investigation of the crime, the police focused upon investigating a suspect. This often includes shifting to a more intelligence-oriented style of investigation, such as researching databases to see if the person has any 'history' or 'form', or talking to people who know the suspect in case they are aware of anything which could be inferentially used to connect the subject to the crime in some way. The following, taken from the SIO's policy file, provides a sense of this shift:

The arrest of [suspect name] is a significant development. As a result the principal lines of enquiry will be:-

a.　Test explanation he's given and attempt to disprove his account of his contact with the deceased.

b.　Interview all persons who may be able to establish the truth or otherwise of the account [suspect name] has given so far.

c.　Research fully all material and other exhibits [suspect name] has so far given.

d.　Research and fully collate all crime reports relating to the documents traced to [suspect name]'s possession.

e.　Prepare ANACAPA charts (i) whilst [suspect name] on day release from prison (ii) from [date] to present time.

As the above documents, rather than the more general information collection and construction of the suspect profile, with the establishment of a *de facto* suspect, the investigators' attention becomes a more 'positive' search, directed towards exploring any substantive links between the suspect and the victim or the crime.[91] An example from a briefing observed in the fieldwork further details the nature of this shift in direction. The SIO was talking to his team and said, 'From this point on, we are treating [suspect's name] as our man. I want to know anything that might even remotely link him in with this crime.' A similar logic was evident in the decision-making of an SIO on a different case, where in his policy file he recorded,

After discussion with CPS about the evidence in this case at [time] on [date] decision made to charge [suspect name] with 2 murders. In view of this a full assessment to be carried out on outstanding actions. In view of charging [suspect name] priority lines of enquiry will be to fully investigate the background of [suspect name] and to continue gathering evidence of his involvement.

Once a prime suspect has been identified then, in addition to the enquiries seeking to link them to the crime, the police will also conduct background enquiries in order to establish if their past behaviour can be used to support the view that this person is a killer.[92] The police are searching for any potential evidence that might further incriminate their suspect. Of course, these enquiries sometimes eliminate the suspect. When this happens, detectives have to return to a further consideration of the members of the suspect population and the details in the suspect profile. As briefly mentioned previously, it is a commonplace occurrence for the police to establish and eliminate several 'prime suspects' in the course of an enquiry. On one investigation, a total of 21 suspects were arrested in connection with the offence and then later released once the police had eliminated them from their enquiries. In each of the whodunit cases, more than one suspect was arrested during the enquiry. This raises extremely important questions concerning the basis upon which police mis-identify individuals as suspects in the process of investigation, a subject that will be addressed in more detail in Chapter 10.

If, as a result of their investigations, the police believe that there are substantive grounds for suspecting the involvement of an individual in the offence, then it is usual practice, as part of their research, to interview them, or arrest the person with a view to conducting an interview.

Case Construction

If the stage is reached that the police are confident that they have identified the suspect, then they will seek to charge them with the offence and the case construction elements of the process can be developed (see the discussion in the previous chapter). Decisions to charge are made in conjunction with a senior representative of the Crown Prosecution Service who will evaluate the strength of the police case as a whole. If it is considered that there is a reasonable likelihood of the prosecution being successful, then the Crown Prosecution Service should agree to the suspect being charged.

Prior and subsequent to an identified suspect being charged, as with self-solving investigations, the police function becomes concerned with organizing the information they have collected in such a way as to construct an evidenced case narrative. Detectives will look for any further evidence that might support their account and, equally as important, they will try to predict any potential weaknesses in their case. Irving and Dunnighan (1993) argue that it is often the case that at least part of the evidential narrative developed by police will be based upon logical inferences made from the information present. Of central importance in constructing a strong case is establishing evidence that in some way serves to support any such inferences that are being drawn. This is often accomplished through the use of forensic evidence to provide 'hard' proof. Investigators may well follow up some of the unfinished lines of enquiry just as a means of proving to the jury 'that no stone has been left unturned'. This stage is also where the greatest attention was paid to complying with the rules on disclosure of material to the defence.

A further important activity that takes place as part of the case construction is the re-checking of information to confirm aspects of the narrative account and possibly to refute elements of the suspect's account that he or she may be telling police. This approach is illustrated in the following list of actions issued by a major incident room just prior to and after the suspect's arrest:

A86 T/I[93] [name] [address] who [suspect name] says he spent part of the day with.
A87 T/I [name] referred to by [suspect name]...
A94 Enquiries with TV companies re. programmes mentioned by [suspect name] [date]...

A108 Check [suspect name] signing on at Job Centre...
A114 View CCTV tapes check [suspect name's] movements—says went to the Job Centre and Library...
A120 T/I [name] On Saturday after murder [suspect name] knocked on his door and said the police will want to speak to you soon...
A133 Enquiries with [suspect name] family.

The following extract from a different case file records how after the suspect had been charged, two detectives were assigned to re-interview the suspect's girlfriend. This was due to the fact that they needed to check several pieces of information offered by the suspect and also because they had received information from an independent witness, alleging that the girlfriend knew more than she told police in her original statement. The action raised was to 'Re-visit and interview witness [name]'. Subsequently, the officers filed a report in which they recorded the results of the action:

Re-interviewed [witness name] on [date] at her home address. She seemed very frightened and was very reluctant to provide any information. She said that she had suspected [suspect name] was using drugs—but claimed not to know that he was dealing. We questioned her about the period mentioned by [suspect name] and she failed to recall any phone call from him or anyone else, thereby contradicting his version of events.

In a different case, the lines of enquiry in the case construction stage of the investigation were directed towards tracing the people whom the suspect had been in contact with after the crime. As a result of these enquiries, the investigators discovered that the suspect had visited a friend in a different part of the country. From the friend's house they recovered items of clothing with the victim's blood on them and the friend also revealed that the suspect had made incriminating remarks about being involved in the killing.

In constructing the case, police are concerned with the conversion of all the relevant information gathered by the investigation into a form appropriate for use by the legal system and the collection of corroborating evidence. This is an important aspect of the structure of the investigative process because the police investigation is strongly motivated to identify and apprehend the offender as quickly as possible. The quicker that the suspect is arrested, the less opportunity they have to destroy any evidence that may connect them to the crime and also the other evidence that is available is more likely to be of a high quality. There is also a financial incentive for the police to identify and arrest the suspect as quickly as possible, in order to reduce the overall cost of the investigation. Thirdly, it is also possible that there are issues related to the safety of the public that come into play in these cases.

Process Structures

The argument that has been proposed throughout the last two chapters is that the process of investigation is essentially ordered and structured. Murder investigations are oriented around a set sequence of stages of investigative activity, with the subsequent stages conditioned by the work performed in the preceding stages of the enquiry, and expectations about the work that is likely to be required subsequently. This notion of an ordered process is significant in that it identifies that at a meso-level, the investigative work performed is patterned and underpinned by a pragmatically justified logic. The two 'maps' of the passage of murder investigations which analytically deconstruct the sequencing of investigative actions illustrate what I term 'process structures'. They capture the sense that the work performed by detectives is ordered and structured, and that the development and introduction of specific lines of enquiry is not random, but deliberative and purposive. Comparison of the different investigations in the sample shows that they are broadly similar in terms of how they are conducted. This patterning is a reflection of how the police organization responds to the problems encountered in investigative work through the development of established systems, rules, routines, procedures, and conventions. These modes of working encapsulate and are embedded in the organizational experience of the police service in responding to this sort of crime. Furthermore, they act to mediate the requirements of the legal frame, ensuring that in principle the products of an investigation should be compliant with the standards and requirements of the adversarial justice system. At the same time, they are responsive to the more situated problems routinely encountered in dealing with suspicious deaths.

In discussing the investigative process structures, I have, so far, concentrated upon developing them as a linear sequence of actions. However, in reality, the operations of the process structures are more complex. There are important recursive qualities to the process based upon what I term 'iterative looping'. At any point in an investigation, the production of new information can lead to the retrospective reinterpretation and reconfiguration of previously held information and/or knowledge. Indeed, this is a key principle in terms of understanding how the investigative process works. Detectives are continually engaged in a process of reinterpreting and re-framing established knowledge in the light of new information. It is a way of evaluating the strength of the provisional understanding of the crime they have and testing the reliability and validity of any new information that has been forthcoming.

Conclusion

The discussion over the last two chapters illustrates a number of important points about police murder investigations. Most obviously, it documents a basic fact that some murders are more difficult to solve than others. Cases are not easily comparable units and investigative outcomes are to a great extent shaped by the qualities and characteristics of individual incidents. This is implicitly recognized by the police officers who distinguished between the categories of whodunits and self-solvers. Furthermore, and equally importantly, it has been shown that the social functions of the investigative role are not restricted to the simple identification of a suspect. Murder investigations are complex social phenomena, involving multiple networks of action, interaction, and decision-making, which require detailed analysis.

The policing of murder routinely involves a range of investigative techniques and strategies, used in concert, in an attempt to establish whether a crime has occurred, identify the offender, and to construct a case to support a successful prosecution. In the modern adversarial legal environment, cases are constructed through evidential narratives which are produced not simply to demonstrate the offender's involvement, but also to pre-empt and forestall any possible defences that might undermine the prosecution case.

The concept of process structure has been developed to capture the fact that the police's investigative actions are not a random series of unconnected interventions. Murder investigations are social processes that take account of the particular circumstances of the incident and the structured objectives deriving from the social and legal contexts in which police work is structurated. The police organization, at least as part of its social function, exists as a mechanism for the communication of a certain degree of 'knowledgeability' about how and why crimes occur and consequently how they can be best investigated.

10

Murder Investigations
in Extremis

In my discussion of the process structures of self-solving and who-dunit investigations, I attended to the contours of the patterned and ordered nature of the work that is conducted. The two process structures capture the passage of work involved in the vast majority of homicide investigations. There are, though, two further scenarios that warrant consideration if I am to provide a full and comprehensive overview of the range of circumstances encountered and dealt with on murder enquiries. These are the small number of murders that assume a very high public profile and those cases that the police fail to solve.

The first of these scenarios relates to a small minority of cases which, as Rock (1998a) puts it, acquire the status of 'extra-ordinary crimes'. Whodunit investigations will usually receive local media coverage and sometimes national media attention. There are, though, a few incidents that receive extensive and pro-longed coverage from all major media outlets. The murders of Holly Wells and Jessica Chapman, Jill Dando, Sarah Payne, Damilola Taylor, James Bulger, Rachel Nickell, and Stephen Lawrence amongst others are recent examples of this phenomenon in England. These extra-ordinary 'cases célèbres' rapidly acquire political significance for the police, media, and public alike. They are effectively viewed as litmus tests of police investigative competence in dealing with serious crime. The level of media and public interest in such cases, and the consequent demand that the investigation be successful, introduces a set of particularly intense and amplified pressures upon the enquiry team.

The second scenario relates to unsuccessful investigations. Consideration of how and why in some cases the police either fail to identify a suspect or to secure a conviction is obviously an important matter. Related to such concerns is the issue of miscarriages of justice, where suspects have been wrongly convicted. There is now substantial evidence pointing to the fact that in a number of major investigations, police officers have in different ways falsified evidence and subverted the course of justice (Ashworth, 1998). In these cases, it has often been years after the original conviction that the nature and extent of the wrongdoing perpetrated by officers has been proven and the Appeal Court has overturned the original verdict. As yet though, there has been little convincing explanation of why officers should want to take the risk of trying to secure a conviction through a corrupt route. For the most part, the accounts that have been provided have utilized a 'politics of blame' that focuses upon the wholesale corruption of a small minority of officers. This has tended to obfuscate the extent to which mistakes and errors are common to many investigations, including those where a suspect is eventually convicted.

In this penultimate chapter, I will argue for a more sophisticated and nuanced understanding of such occurrences. In looking at cases célèbres, miscarriages of justice, and failed investigations, my intention is to show how these 'problematic' cases and the various 'pathologies' they encapsulate can be understood in relation to the broader framework I have previously developed. I will show how a process I term 'compliance drift' occurs, which assists us in understanding why certain investigations encounter difficulties and, more contentiously, may provide us with a sense of why some officers choose to falsify evidence.

Cases Célèbres

Each year a small proportion of the 700 or so homicides that occur in this country receive some sort of reportage from national media organizations. Of these, maybe two or three will receive prolonged and extensive coverage by all the major news media outlets. The reasons why these cases are selected are varied, but it does seem possible to identify a small number of core factors. Usually the victim is an attractive female or a child, for whom journalists have a photogenic image that can be repeatedly used in an iconic fashion to accompany the story. Relatedly, the victim tends not to have been killed by a close acquaintance, rather the crime bears the hallmarks of a 'stranger murder'. As a result, the suspect is not rapidly identified by police and there is an extensive hunt for the assailant into which the media is enlisted as an investigative resource by the enquiry team. Furthermore, the political economy of contemporary news media organizations is such that they effectively create their own 'webs of significance'. If one organization elects to run a particular story, then this in itself can establish its importance for other journalists working in different organizations. What is significant about cases célèbres is that they tend to be comparatively difficult to solve, they are complex, long-running enquiries, and as a result considerable pressure develops upon the police to 'get a result'. In the cases in my sample, two of the investigations bore all the hallmarks of being cases célèbres and a further one was fairly similar.

Media interest is crucial in the construction of an incident as a case célèbre. Indeed, journalists rapidly become central protagonists in the dynamics of such cases. As suggested above, this interest may be generated by the identity or status of the victim. However, it can also arise as an unintended consequence of the police seeking to co-operate with and co-opt journalists in the conduct of the enquiry. If the police seek to generate public interest in the case by utilizing a high-profile campaign in order to encourage potential witnesses to come forward, there is a potential danger that if the investigation does not make progress, then the media attention that they encouraged may turn against them and journalists may start critically questioning the competence of the SIO and their team. In a number of recent cases, such criticisms of police investigations have involved the media exposing the dissatisfaction of surviving relatives with how the police are handling the enquiry.

As a consequence, police co-operation with journalists has to be carefully managed. When making a presentation about the case, the police carefully select the language they use in order to support their objectives of generating information from the public. This use of language was illustrated in a comment in a statement made by an SIO in a press briefing: 'Whoever did this is obviously extremely dangerous, the fact that the victim seems to have been picked at random is a matter for grave concern. It is important that we find whoever did this and quickly... We're pulling all the stops out on this one.'

The use of dramatic language was a deliberate ploy in this case to secure interest in the story. Similar uses of this discourse of danger manifested were found on a different case in the sample, where the victim had been sexually assaulted before being killed very violently. Two extracts, from two separate press statements that were made by the SIO stressing the risk and danger posed to the public welfare, were particularly demonstrative of the affective significance of language. In the first extract the officer said, 'We are saddened by this brutal killing, but are determined to find the killer and your help is vital to us . . . It is vital that the public be protected from this man, as he is obviously highly dangerous and there is a possibility that he will attack again.' Here the 'pathological' nature of the killer is emphasized, as is the need for the public to assist police in their investigation. Later in the same enquiry, once the offender had been charged, the SIO made a second statement, 'We are grateful for all the help that we have received from the public and in particular from sections of the community where assistance is not usually forthcoming . . . The police and the whole community were horrified by this brutal attack.' This second statement reiterates similar themes to those in the earlier one, thus emphasizing the importance of the work conducted by police and the need for public assistance in these sorts of crime.

The use of a discourse of manifested danger by police in such cases is motivated by pragmatic and instrumental concerns. SIOs are aware that if they are to accrue the potential benefits of widespread media coverage to do with contacting a large number of geographically dispersed potential witnesses quickly and for comparatively little financial cost, then they have to co-operate with the media and frame their appeals in such a way that they meet journalists' institutional criteria for newsworthiness. However, the symbolic content of such image management work should not be neglected. Senior ranks in the police service are acutely aware that effective media appeals are important in the battle for institutional legitimacy at a time when the police role is increasingly ambiguous and contested (Innes, 1999). The Head of CID in the force in which this study was conducted put such concerns in the following way:

The media are an extremely important tool that you should use, but not just to solve the murder, there are other issues such as public safety, deflecting potential criticism. Not covering up 'cock ups' what I mean is perhaps the family are saying the police aren't doing this or that, then you might take a decision to bring the media in to show that you are.

However, the use of a discourse of danger may have more diffuse and unintended effects at a cultural level. The use of dramatic language and the propagation of a climate of fear that is common in such cases may have an important role in escalating public demands for the widening or deepening of the state's crime control apparatus (Cohen, 1985; Garland, 2001).

Some senior officers did appear to be aware of the potential for such effects and urged caution in relation to the content of any public pronouncements that are made by the police in relation to specific cases. A couple of the senior detectives were highly attuned to the fact that they did not want to be seen to be trying to panic the public and they also sought to maintain a sense of proportion about the case and its seriousness in the public eye. One brief example from the fieldwork serves to illustrate such matters. It relates to a case that I did not observe directly, but it took place at the same time as I was conducting ethnographic observation on another investigation. The officer leading the other enquiry had not been an SIO for very long, but due to personnel shortages he had been given command of what turned into a highly complex, very high-profile investigation. At an early stage of the enquiry, he appeared before a national press conference and stated, 'This is the most horrible and sickening case I have ever had to deal with in my career'. This statement may well have been true and it certainly supports the argument that I have been developing that certain murders are invested with a particular expressive content for police and public. But for one of the more experienced SIOs in the force there was a feeling that you have to be careful in making such dramatic comments in a public forum. As he said after we both saw the broadcast,

You shouldn't say things like that, you have to be professional when you're doing things like this and you have to make sure you convey a sense of professionalism. But also when you've seen the things I've seen you wouldn't say that, because you know that it is unlikely to be true for very long. The one thing that I do know after 30 years in this job is that nothing will ever surprise me about what people are capable of doing to each other. Some of the things that I've had to deal with . . . the violence . . . the violence is almost unimaginable.

Although this comment was made in passing, it perfectly captures the attitude of the seasoned homicide investigator and the meaning that this work has for them. Moreover, it demonstrates the need for 'front-management' by both the organization and individual officers when engaged in mediated communication. The caution expressed in this quote was perhaps also informed by experience of how media interest can not only assist an investigation, but also hinder it.

A key motivation behind police co-operation with journalists is to try and control their interest and prevent them from conducting independent enquiries that may prove detrimental to the police investigation. On high-profile cases where there is an obvious public interest, journalists frequently try and get 'exclusives' so that they can lead on a story. The strategies and tactics they use are often problematic for police as the following intimates:

During 'morning prayers' [briefing] the SIO led a discussion concerning some information received from the Family Liaison Officer who has been taking the lead role in looking after the victim's family. He said 'Ok as you know the family are having problems with certain sections of the press who have been "doorstepping" and trying to make contact with them. This has been upsetting for them. We are holding a press conference today in an effort to try and deflect some of the attention. Obviously I don't need to remind you that I don't want anyone else talking to the press.'

On a different investigation, problems were caused for the police by the actions of a journalist working for a tabloid newspaper who offered money to some of the witnesses to tell their story. When the accounts provided by these people were printed in the paper, they contained details that had not been made available to the police.

The involvement of journalists in a case can create other sorts of problems for a murder squad. Particularly on cases célèbres, the intense media interest can create unexpected effects when the police try and exploit it to assist their enquiries. In making media appeals the police are seeking to encourage people to forward information to them that may be of relevance to the investigation. But on high-profile cases, where public sentiments and emotions are strongly evoked, too much information can result from a media appeal. If, when making an appeal, the police either cannot or do not set the parameters of what sort of information they are seeking, then there is a potential that the investigative system will be over-loaded by calls from the public.

This information overload occurred on one case studied where the investigation was the subject of intense media scrutiny. The police appeals resulted in thousands of calls from the public, many of which were totally irrelevant. The trouble was that all the calls had to be answered and the information processed by the major incident room in order for its usefulness (or otherwise) to be divined. The system was overwhelmed in that there was more information flowing into the investigation than it could handle. The media strategy invoked as part of the investigative methodology in this case resulted in it taking a long time for all the material to be worked through and probably the arrest of the suspect was delayed as a result. As will be discussed presently, this approach to responding to an 'information deficit' and the resultant 'information overload' is a feature of some failed investigations.

It was not that the police were unaware of such problems, for as one of the more experienced SIOs interviewed said:

It's a very difficult area the press, they can make or break a murder enquiry. I actually don't think we get it right a lot of the time with the press. We're too keen to push out broad appeals which actually bog the system down. A prime example of this is photofits. I'd like to know how many of them have cleared crimes especially murders . . . I think the number would be very small. The trouble with photofits, e-fits and descriptions is that they might be right, but they are just as likely to be wrong. They create a tremendous amount of enquiries that will take you nowhere. More importantly . . . it's probably going to stop mum or a girlfriend or neighbour from making the phonecall because they think matey was acting suspiciously or came home with blood on his clothes or something and they look at the photofit and they say 'oh it's not him.'

However, when under pressure and 'in the thick of the action' SIOs frequently did put out appeals that effectively impeded the investigation.

Of course there is no guarantee that the needed information will result from a media appeal. On one of the cases studied, which received a reasonable media profile, I observed a situation where an arranged press conference produced very little:

In the MIR after the press conference this morning. The story is going out on the national 1 o'clock news and local news and on the radio. The MIR and the Call Centre have evidently been set up to expect lots of calls. There is a sense of anticipation for the afternoon . . . The story was aired but as yet there has been little response, only a handful of calls, none of which seemed particularly important . . . The SIO in his de-briefing this evening described it as 'the results were a bit disappointing'. They are though set up again for tonight in case there is a better reaction to the story this evening.

The involvement of media and their participation in the case also contributes to the politics of the investigation within the police organization. A high media profile increases the sense within the senior echelons of the force that this is a case which must be solved and as a consequence there is perhaps a tendency for these kinds of cases to receive more resources for a longer period of time than less politically significant enquiries. Situated in the contemporary environment where the political economy of policing is manifestly shaped by ongoing attempts at rationalization, it does seem that public attention and concern is crucial in enabling an investigation to sustain the level of their resources in order to pursue more remote lines of enquiry. There are, then, obvious advantages for an SIO in terms of maintaining (or increasing) resource levels on a difficult investigation, by encouraging a high level of media interest, as one SIO implicitly acknowledged:

Grading is important because on a Grade A normally you'll have no trouble getting resources because the thing is high profile, it's attracting a lot of publicity, it's normally a pretty awful murder and the getting and sustaining of resources is normally fairly straightforward . . . those sorts of issues make it very difficult to pull the plug on that job.

Therefore, there are certainly incentives for an SIO to manipulate the level of publicity for a case by encouraging media interest in it. Such possibilities do, though, raise important ethical questions about the investigative response provided for different cases. It seems that certain investigations involving certain types of victims attract media coverage and as a consequence a high level of investigative response. These cases tend to be provided with lots of investigative resources over an extended period of time in order to try and ensure that the crime is solved. In other cases, though, where the crime is more mundane or the victim is less 'attractive', it is not always clear that the same level of investigative response is made available.

The combination of factors that contributes to an incident becoming a case célèbre also results in a number of problems being encountered by the investigation. Chief amongst these is the increased complexity of the enquiry. The high-profile nature of the investigation often results in large amounts of information being forwarded as a result of media appeals. This is combined with the extra information generated as a result of the additional resources that are made available for 'Grade A' enquiries. Overall, more lines of enquiry tend to be conducted and more information has to be managed and processed by the members of the murder squad. This requires a lot of painstaking and methodical work in order to follow up potential leads, and to identify which ones are worth developing further. Moreover, in terms of the strategic direction of the enquiry, it requires the SIO to set a systematic policy in terms of how all the information is to be organized, prioritized, and worked through. Maintaining the quality of the fairly intensive, detailed work over an extended period when there is often mounting pressure to 'break' the case is often exceedingly difficult. The other reason that an investigation may receive a high level of media attention is if it is felt to be experiencing difficulties or to be failing in some sense.

'Failing' Investigations

Some of the problems associated with extremely high-profile, politically charged investigations are common to those enquiries which are adjudged to be at risk of failing to identify or convict a suspect. In discussing 'failing' investigations, I am referring to two sets of circumstances. There are those investigations that are not successful due to some quality 'extrinsic' to the work of the detectives but related to the circumstances of the offence, which makes it very difficult to investigate successfully. Secondly, there are the enquiries that suffer because of 'intrinsic' errors and mistakes made by investigators.

One investigation studied in this research provides some indication of the nature of the problems experienced by police and their response when confronted by extrinsic difficulties. The torso of a victim was found in a wooded area by a member of the public. The exposure of the torso to the elements had led to an advanced state of deterioration. Upon closer inspection, the police found that the lower arms and head of the victim had been removed. These were never located. The pathologist's report provides more details of the crime:

The deceased was a white male somewhere in his 60s approx. 5'9" – 5'10". Deceased's head, hands and forearms been amputated after death. Number of stab and cutting wounds on the body all of which appear Post-Mortem.

Injuries carried out with a sharp knife. Amputation of the neck vertebrae and of the forearm bones appears to have been performed using a crushing implement. The amputation could be caused in this manner by an axe or implement with crushing jaws such as a bolt cutter.

One can appreciate the problems that confronted the police in this case, in that they could not even identify the victim.

In order to cope with such circumstances, the SIO implemented a combination of routine lines of enquiry. In the policy file, these were recorded as follows:

(1) Identify deceased.
(2) House to house enquiries.
(3) Further sightings of car along [main road] to be established.
(4) Identify clothing from manufacturers and outlets.
(5) Forensic examination of scene and exhibits...
(23) Metropolitan Police to be contacted re. possible gangland killing.
(24) [Local area] Mispers [missing persons] to be checked...
(37) Road check to be carried out in [road name]. All vehicle occupants and pedestrians to be questioned.

Point 23 above is significant in that we can see how, in the absence of any conclusive leads, the police interpret the condition of the body as being indicative of a certain type of crime. However, this original hypothesis was discounted, as a result of research conducted following this line of thought. As the SIO subsequently recorded in his policy file, 'It is my view that this murder was unlikely to be connected with London criminal gangs. The method employed by gangs today is that assassinations take place in busy public houses or similar venues to gain a maximum publicity for the murderer.'

In addition to points 4 and 24 above, a range of more creative and innovative lines of enquiry were set up by the SIO in an attempt to establish the victim's identity. As recorded in the policy file, amongst other things, publicizing the clothes being worn by the victim was used to try and establish a trace:

Sketch to be made of the shirt motif and issued to teams. Photos of the label are to be made and blown up... A priority is to obtain identical clothing to that worn by the deceased. When this obtained full press release including photos to be obtained... National circulation re all details of missing males aged 30+ since [date]....Foot impression of deceased to obtain accurate shoe size... Details of blood/alcohol level, blood group, underpants and shoe size to be released to the press. No mention to be made of hairy mole on right leg.

This last detail was kept back for the purposes of validating any potential identification that might be made. As a result of these enquiries, the force intelligence unit produced a list of over 200 possible names for the victim and 1,457 missing persons were identified who possibly matched the description that the police had available. All of these were worked through and eliminated.

Of particular concern to the identification strategy was investigating why the forearms had been amputated at a higher level than usual. In the case file, the inference drawn from this was that, 'The possibility of the deceased having tattoos or other distinguishing marks could account for the high amputation of arms'.

Overall, for the most part, this investigation was based around an intelligence-oriented mode of operation. The majority of work related to either investigating possible known suspects for the crime, contacting and tasking informants to see if they could be of any assistance, and researching intelligence databases for potential leads.

This investigation also reveals some of the difficulties that can be experienced in terms of attracting media attention to cases which do not fulfil the criteria for newsworthiness. In his policy file, the SIO recorded that, 'Attempts to obtain the assistance of Crimewatch UK was editorially turned down on the basis that the murder was too brutal for public consumption'. Relatedly, the SIO stated that a 'Decision not to mention the possible homosexuality of the deceased had been taken for fear of losing public interest in the murder'. It was not until ten weeks into the investigation that this suspicion was revealed in a press conference. At the same time, police took the unusual step of revealing the identities of suspects for the crime for whom they had been unable to find any direct evidence connecting them to its commission. This was done in a last attempt to generate the needed 'break' for the enquiry.

Officially 'unsolved' murder investigations in Britain are never 'closed'; rather what happens is that investigative effort is simply withdrawn, unless new information is forthcoming which can be used to reactivate the police enquiry. Sometimes, then, as in this case, the police simply exhaust their lines of enquiry and concede defeat. A letter from the SIO to the coroner captured this, 'In short, despite lengthy and in-depth interviews I was unable to ascertain any direct evidence that would link them to the murder... In truth the murder could possibly be connected with [the suspects], but if this is the case I have absolutely no clue as to the identity of the body.'

As discussed previously, though, some problems in major investigations arise as a result of how the work is performed by detectives. 'Intrinsic' problems cause difficulties on investigations where no suspect is identified, where a suspect is identified but the prosecution fails, and on investigations where mistakes are made but the investigation is eventually successful in its objectives. They are also integral to the kinds of issues and difficulties that can be identified in relation to the aforementioned miscarriages of justice. There is, of course, an inherent problem in terms of analysing mistakes and errors and trying to identify their causative impact upon the passage of an investigation. That is, one can never be sure whether or not an alternative line of action would have produced a substantively different result for an enquiry.

To reiterate a comment I made in the previous chapter, cases are not easily comparable and equally solvable. However, it is important that this is not used as a blanket absolution for the police. The presence of a thorough and well-managed investigative strategy, together with carefully conducted investigative actions, does influence whether a crime is solved. As such, whilst acknowledging that some crimes may to all intents and purposes be virtually unsolvable, we do need to be aware that mistakes and errors on the part of police officers may contribute to some investigations experiencing problems and/or failing.

By drawing upon the Macpherson Report (1998), the Byford Report (1982), and the data collected in this study, we can start to develop our understanding of the types of mistakes and errors made in homicide investigations and their causes. The Macpherson Report (1998) into the Metropolitan Police Service's handling of the Stephen Lawrence case strongly suggested that a series of errors by police probably led to established suspects avoiding a conviction for the crime. Some 20 years previously, the Byford Report (1981) into the Yorkshire Ripper investigation argued that problems with the police information management system resulted in a number of early opportunities for the identification of the killer being missed.

In both of these cases, though, the problems uncovered were attributed to the force of extraordinary circumstances.

In contrast, my fieldwork observations suggest that mistakes and errors are fairly common on murder enquiries, although the majority are not sufficiently serious to cause an investigation to fail. Mistakes in processing forensic evidence, failing to identify a suspect, or mistakenly identifying people as suspects featured in a number of cases. One SIO described how

I hear some terribly naïve things being said by people who seem to have accepted at face value things that people have said where quite clearly they're being extremely naïve about it. I've sent thousands of officers back to do things again to cover things they should have dealt with . . . we've had people where they accept the answer and they say they've interviewed someone and fill in the form and let it go . . .

The officer concerned saw this as highly problematic because, 'Solving a murder is frequently about details, it relies on thoroughness and persistence and making sure that you're not taking things at face value'. The high levels of technical complexity relating to the conduct of various domains of enquiry means that to some extent errors have to be expected. This is particularly so for enquiries that are being conducted under high levels of pressure, such as cases célèbres and failing investigations. Therefore, an important element of the investigative process is the ability to retrieve errors and to ensure that they do not completely undermine the integrity of an ongoing investigation.

I have already identified that the information management capacities of the major incident room can be tested if too much information is generated by the lines of enquiry set by the SIO. The resultant 'systemic overload' can slow down the overall ability of the detectives to make progress in the investigation. During the fieldwork conducted on a long-running investigation, this problem was evident, 'Discussed the state of the enquiry with the deputy SIO. During our discussion he said, "we've just got bogged down in paper because people haven't stopped to think . . . they're just ploughing into the system and they've lost sight of what they're there to do".'

In the following discussion, it can be seen how in a high-profile investigation that received significant media interest, the SIO had to acknowledge that the lines of enquiry he set were resulting in information overload. As a consequence, he tried to re-focus and prioritize the work to be done on several occasions. In his policy file, at the start of the enquiry, it was recorded that, 'The number of officers currently working on the enquiry are 30 detective officers, 15 incident room staff, 4 FIU officers and 30 uniform officers on house to house'.

He set the following

High priority lines of enquiry:-

1. Identify make of shoe re. footprint and check FIU index.
2. Establish last movements of victims.
3. Interview all relatives.
4. T/I/E all recent visitors.
5. T/I/E all persons in the vicinity of the scene between [time/date] and [time/date].
6. T/I/E man seen vicinity of scene [time/date] by witness [name].
7. T/I/E owner of clothing found in [name] road...
10. Contact local informants...
12. Whole scene to be forensiced and fingerprinted.
13. [Name] club to be visited with the view of tracing persons who attended on [date].

It can be seen then that there were a number of fairly unfocused lines of enquiry introduced at this point. The following day the SIO issued further instructions to 'Extend the house to house area' and he set up a press conference for the third day of the enquiry to try and generate further information. In addition to this he made provision for 'An operation to be mounted between [time/date] and [time/date] with the objective of interviewing all persons in vehicles and on foot passing through [road name]. Purpose to trace persons who were in the area of the scene at material time.'

All of these lines of enquiry were intended to and did generate a lot of information. The investigation was in fact swamped by incoming information. In recognition of this, the SIO recorded in his policy file: 'Indexers to be increased by 3 officers in view of increased amount of indexing caused by house-to-house forms'. Two days later, though, he had to issue a further instruction that for one whole day of the investigation no more information was to be generated and all squad members were to assist in processing the backlog of material: 'Due to the vast amount of information being received [date] to be given over processing all information to identify new priority lines of enquiry'. After this, there were still concerns about the volume of information that was having to be managed. He stated, 'In view of the number of MO suspects, parameters to be set to determine the order in which they will be T/I/E'd'. Furthermore, it is recorded in the file that, 'Due to the large number of House to house questionnaires received, they are to be reviewed by the whole team—feared that important information may be lost within the system'.

However, the lack of focus to the information generating strategy continued to cause problems, as indicated two days after the previous extract: 'Due to the large number of house-to-house questionnaires and the time being taken to enter them on computer (20 mins.) there is a need to re-prioritise the order for putting them on the computer'.

In this investigation, the SIO implicitly acknowledged that he had made a mistake in introducing too many lines of enquiry with insufficient focus which had resulted in the information management systems becoming saturated and overloaded. More positively, though, he recognized this to be the case and sought to try and address the issues involved.

Too much information introduces 'systemic delays' in processing the information, which may result in officers simply working to get the data on the system, rather than maintaining a critical eye and carefully assessing its value to the investigation. This in turn may lead to officers bypassing the system to avoid the delays that they know are slowing up their work. Other causes of problems are: officers not having knowledge of the technical requirements for a particular aspect of the work; placing inappropriate emphasis on incoming information; or simple pressures of the work resulting in basic errors being made.

Reviews

In an effort to deal with the problems experienced on difficult and failing major investigations, the police service in England and Wales have increasingly utilized a system of review. The principle of review is that through the introduction of an individual with expertise in the conduct of major crime investigations who is external to the original murder squad, the performance of the enquiry can be evaluated and quality assured. Furthermore, it provides a mechanism for checking that no investigative opportunities have been missed.

There are a range of different types of review utilized by police, the most significant of which is the progress review. In the national guidance on review provided by ACPO, it is identified that reviews can be conducted by an outside force. However, this tends to be the exception and is reserved only for high-profile investigations. The majority of reviews were intra-force, conducted by colleagues of the SIO and the other officers of the murder squad. This lack of independence obviously creates problems in terms of the ability to identify systemic flaws in the procedures and routines employed by the organization.

Although in recent years there has been a rapid development in the conduct of reviews, at the time that the fieldwork for this study was being conducted, they remained a comparatively new innovation. And although I did not research them directly, there was a general sense amongst officers that when they happened they were little more than an administrative requirement and had little to contribute to the 'real work' being performed.

Constructing the Wrong Suspect

Investigations under pressure are particularly susceptible to the mis-identification of suspects and the associated problems that this involves. In the previous chapter, it was made clear that the identification and subsequent elimination of several suspects was a feature common to the dynamics of the passage of the investigation in many whodunit enquiries. However, such problems are especially consequential in those investigations that are already under pressure. This is because, in such cases, the pressures upon individual officers may encourage them to interpret any incriminating information against the suspect in accordance with their established hypothesis, whilst ignoring possible alternative interpretations.[94] The problem of mis-identification of suspects is then a complex process, involving both individual and social factors.

One long-running investigation provides a good example of some of the processes at work in terms of how an investigation can come to focus upon a suspect who was later eliminated. The case involved a shooting and through their house-to-house enquiries and other research, the police had established a vague description of several people seen in the area near to the crime, at around the material time. One description of a man wearing a green coat was believed by police to be particularly significant.

By working through the information that they had gathered, they came to interview a man who admitted to having been in the area on the night in question. He said that he had visited a friend that night, and claimed that his friend could confirm this. The description of this man was similar to one of the descriptions of persons seen near the crime scene. As a consequence, when the officers returned the information from their first interview with the suspect to the major incident room, the man in question was subject to a number of background enquiry checks. These revealed that he was a distant relation to the victim. At this point, the police interest in him intensified. A detective sergeant and detective constable were quickly despatched to re-interview the man. The following extract from the sergeant's statement describes what happened next:

... approached the house of [suspect's name] and his father [name] ... We discussed the murder with them. [Suspect's name] had a noticeable stoop in his gait and he appeared nervous in our presence and asked whether a shotgun had been used to kill [victim name]. He said 'was anybody seen?' When I replied 'yes there was a witness who saw somebody' [suspect's name] eyes widened and he looked at the father and appeared worried by this ... In the kitchen I noticed a box of shotgun cartridges ... Also on the back of the chair a Green Barbour Jacket. I also inspected two shotguns. [Suspect's name] was very nervous whilst writing out his statement. On the evening in question he said that he was wearing jeans, jumper and black shoes. He replied 'no' when I asked him if he was wearing a coat ... After some further questioning the father became very abusive. [Suspect's name] refused to give fingerprints and we left the property.... We later returned on observations and at [time] we arrested [suspect's name] and having conducted a search of the property we seized a number of items ...

Following his arrest, the man was subject to intense police research for over one month, during which time he spent some time being held in custody. At the point at which he was identified as a suspect, the investigation had been running for a number of days and although there were a number of enquiries being conducted on various members of the victim's family, there was nothing substantive for the police to go on. When this person came to their attention, there was a definite shift in the police activity. But what is particularly interesting about the extracts provided is the way in which they give an insight into how police officers intensively searching for a suspect can easily produce circumstantial evidence and can construe and configure it in an incriminating fashion. From their own perspective, this serves to justify more intense research of the suspect concerned.

The initial and precursory justification for identifying the man as a suspect was incidental suspicion based upon his being in the locale at the time of the crime, which was subsequently reinforced when it was established that he knew the victim. But the statement of the officer identifies a number of behavioural and material signifiers that were interpreted by the officer as indicative of the man's potential involvement. In particular, the man's reactions were commented upon and it was strongly implied that these 'involuntary' physical responses and the man's seeming inability to 'repress' them should be read as signifiers of guilt. The officer's interpretation of these interactionally based signals was seemingly further influenced by the presence of the guns and the green jacket. The inferences drawn were compounded by the suspect's refusal to provide fingerprints and the father's reaction to the whole scenario.

However, an alternative interpretation of these events can easily be produced. It should be noted that this encounter took place in a rural setting, and both the suspect and his father were poorly educated and were not especially well off. It is unlikely that they had much experience of dealing with authority figures, especially within their own home and in a matter as serious as a murder in the local community. Therefore, what the officer read as being signifiers of the suspect's involvement can be attributed a more innocent cause. Similarly, the possession of a green jacket and shotguns is not unusual in rural communities. After several weeks of being viewed as a suspect, the police's attention switched to another man, when substantive evidence linking him to the crime was found.

Particularly when police are under pressure, but of potential importance in all major investigations, significant consequences can flow from an officer misconstruing a situation and interpreting it in such a way as to wrongly construct a person as a suspect. When an individual fits the police's 'fuzzy' stereotypes about what sort of person tends to be involved in murder, and they can be connected to the crime, there is a tendency for police to unwittingly instigate a recursive 'cycle of suspicion'. Being suspicious of an individual led the police to investigate them, which in turn, because of the way in which the results of such research are interpreted, often results in the amplification of the police's suspicion. The elimination of suspects tends to be based on tightly controlled criteria, and if a suspect cannot be eliminated, then the police's interpretative stance leads them to believe that the evidence against the suspect has been strengthened. It is surprisingly easy when searching for a suspect to establish circumstantial evidence that can be interpreted so as to seemingly implicate a person in a crime.

Compliance Drift

Some murder investigations fail or experience problems because of the deliberate and wilful actions of detectives. In cases where it appears that an identified suspect was apparently 'going to get away with it', it has been documented that police have fabricated evidence of various kinds to secure or support a prosecution. However, although there are now a number of cases where this has been shown to be the case, this research suggests that most problems on major crime investigations are of a different nature. The majority of problems in major crime investigations stem from errors and mistakes made by officers who believe themselves to be acting appropriately and certainly do not intend to cause problems. Interestingly though, the causes of both deliberate and non-deliberate actions may be related.

An explanation of how and why such problems occur can be provided by a concept of compliance drift. Compliance drift refers to the way that when working under pressure on long-running cases deviations from standard practice creep into the work of detectives. There are several causes of compliance drift, but essentially they all result from the perceived need of detectives to maintain the investigative system's efficacy when it is under strain. Compliance drift involves individual officers making adaptive responses in their working practices that circumvent various forms of standard procedure and regulation in order to reduce the pressure being experienced. These adaptations are introduced on the basis that they appear to provide a solution to factors that are inhibiting the effectiveness of the investigation. Because they appear to solve the perceived problem, such innovations can become rapidly accepted and normalized by the work group. The problem, though, is that they can, in the right circumstances, introduce unexpected 'iatrogenic' effects at a later stage of the investigation, causing further, more profound problems to be experienced.

This approach to understanding the causes of errors made on murder enquiries owes much to Diane Vaughan's (1996) analysis of the Challenger Shuttle disaster and in particular her concept of 'the normalisation of deviance'. Through a finely grained and highly detailed 'historical ethnography', Vaughan documents how the NASA technicians and their contractors engaged in a line of action that was not based upon wilful misconduct, but that nevertheless resulted in the flawed decision to risk launching the fated shuttle. She shows how working under extreme pressure, the engineers, scientists, and technicians on the shuttle programme progressively deviated from standard operating procedures and countenanced and justified such deviations until it became normal practice amongst the workers.

On complex, long-running, high pressure investigations, where there is a lot of information to be processed, requiring meticulous attention to detail, officers may cope with the pressures by departing from the standard operating procedures. Such innovations in practice can be caused by the way in which the socio-technical system operates when under pressure, as one SIO noted,

HOLMES may blunt the efforts of good investigators, it can easily become bogged down in information and details and you can quickly reach a situation where you have a whole team of investigators looking at this bit which is ultimately going to be irrelevant to what you are trying to achieve. It doesn't matter how good the investigators are if they are working in that situation.

In such circumstances, detectives may not attend to the details of the information they are engaging with, simply doing the work as fast as they can. Alternatively, their drift from complying with established procedures may be stimulated by a perceived need to circumvent seemingly extraneous requirements and to keep the momentum of the investigation moving. An example of this is provided in the following story recounted by a detective inspector:

I went off and after digging around I got a good lead and I went back to [SIO name] and showed him what I had. I said to him look give me a couple of officers, I knew who I wanted for this not people who were going to mess about, anyway just give me a couple of officers and I reckon we could crack this. But [Office Manager name] was there saying 'oh you can't do that we've got to follow procedure and put it through HOLMES'. I said to him 'Don't be bloody stupid, by the time it's gone through there they'll have cleaned up after themselves and got rid of anything connecting them to the crime. We need to act now if we're going to get them.' To his credit [SIO name] listened to me and anyway we turn up at the address and there's the stuff there in the kitchen cupboard.

In this case, the apparent willingness to circumvent routine procedures contributed to the solving of the crime. More importantly, though, it perhaps signals the extent to which officers 'on the ground' are cognizant of the fact that the bureaucratic procedures associated with the investigative system both can and should be legitimately bypassed in certain circumstances. This understanding creates an important precedent for detectives. It identifies that, in principle, compliance with formal procedure is not absolute, thus allowing them to conceive of the utility of adapting their practices.

An additional cause of compliance drift may be repetition and boredom. This was a real problem for long-running investigations. The SIO on one such case said, 'Where we're sending all the detectives out to T/I owners, it is very difficult to keep their motivation and attention after a week. There's a real danger that they won't recognise it if it's in front of them.' On protracted investigations which as a matter of course involve a lot of unproductive lines of enquiry having to be carried out, it is difficult to sustain the motivation and attention to detail of officers.

It has been identified, then, that a significant cause of compliance drift was pressure upon the murder squad. This pressure is not just found on high-profile cases though. It was also observed on some of the cases which should have been the more routine and standard types of major investigation. The reasons for such pressures were largely related to the organizationally based political economy of murder investigations. As identified in Chapter 4, major crime investigations are extremely resource intensive and can impact upon the ability of a force to deliver other services to the public. As a consequence, SIOs were constantly under pressure to be aware of the costs involved in running the investigation, and to try and run the enquiry within budget. There were, then, manifest pressures upon them to identify suspects as quickly as possible. At least potentially, this could encourage a lack of attention to detail when constructing the case. Certainly, once a suspect was identified, there was immense pressure to discontinue previous lines of enquiry which were now seen as unproductive and costly. This is a risky strategy over the longer term, as to some extent it precludes alternative hypotheses about the crime being considered.

There were additional sources of pressure upon major enquiries, particularly where several investigations were being run concurrently by a force. When major incidents clustered, as they did on several occasions during the research period, it was the case that force resources were stretched. On occasions, the enquiry teams simply had to 'make do' with what was available and there were too few officers on the squad, or officers were working in roles of which they had little experience. Such conditions obviously increase the sense of pressure experienced by all members of the team, and were then another potential cause of compliance drift.

The concept of compliance drift acknowledges the gross instances of detective malfeasance that have been recorded in a number of miscarriages of justice. Such deviations from accepted practice can be explained by a perceived need on the part of these officers to ensure that an identified suspect is convicted, even though the evidence available through standard investigative practices may not support this. Compliance drift is, however, particularly persuasive in accounting for the far greater number of 'normal errors' that are a more routine feature of major crime enquiries. These mistakes, which may not cause any substantive harm for an investigation overall, have been largely ignored. Political and academic attention has been focused upon the more obvious and blatant forms of failure and wrongdoing. In contrast, compliance drift identifies that both types of problem may be connected and that they may share similar causes. Indeed, it is possible that the accepted presence of compliance drift in major investigations, as a normal consequence of how major investigations are resourced and working practices enacted, may establish the preconditions for the rarer, more serious types of deviation. The causes of some of the key problems experienced in conducting major crime enquiries are effectively designed into the police investigative systems.

Compliance drift explains how and why pressures and problems on major crime enquiries are both experienced and responded to at a systemic level. At a more individual and informal level, detectives make use of what I term 'distancing strategies'.

Distancing Strategies

Distancing strategies are the ways in which detectives attempt to manage the stress, emotions, and pressures of working on serious, affectively visceral and potentially disturbing cases. They are cognitive and behavioural techniques that are supported through the values of detective culture, which establish accepted cultural scripts for dealing with pressure and emotions. A characteristic of the distancing strategies used was the recounting of atrocity stories in conjunction with a cynical form of humour. The comment of a middle-ranking officer on a case where the victim had been burnt to death was fairly typical:

He was that badly burned that there were only the soles of his feet and his arse that were still intact. It took ages to try and remove the body, to be honest we should have just got some tin-foil, an envelope and a postage stamp and sent him to the pathologist. It would have saved messing about and just think, we would have saved a load of money for the firm as well.

An alternative distancing strategy can be identified in terms of how detectives sometimes talked about their work as being analogous with a 'game'. Such a language served similar purposes, guarding the individual from the intense emotional pressures stemming from their work. On the whole, detectives appear to be fairly cynical individuals. Nevertheless, when working on a murder enquiry, they did seem to care and did want to ensure that the person responsible was punished. Indeed, such emotional involvement in a case may partly explain the deliberate and purposive forms of compliance drift that have been identified in some of the infamous miscarriages of justice.

As Everett Hughes (1958) identified, one aspect of the role of the professional is the capacity to deal with other people's extraordinary crises. Distancing strategies are ways in which the individuals and groups of people who are plunged into often complex social dramas seek to manage their emotions, actions, and thoughts in situations that could prove to be profoundly unsettling and a cause of deep ontological insecurities. They allow these people to get on and do the work that has to be done, in order that some degree of response to the crisis in question can be manufactured.

In responding to murders, detectives are confronted with scenes that contain the after-effects of extreme brutality, rage, and sometimes, for the want of a better word, evil. Death is a messy business, with blood and other bodily excretions part of the ways and means of homicide. Such products of the crime are frequently amplified by the more base biological processes associated with death. Often, by the time that a corpse is discovered, decomposition has started. And yet the detective cannot recoil or withdraw from such matters. They have to carefully examine the details in a way that deconstructs what has happened so as to piece together an intimate understanding of what occurred.

As a further part of their work, they will have to deal with members of the family of the victim who are experiencing profound loss and whose emotions may be at their rawest. They have to question these people in order to extract information about the deceased. It is likely that the detectives may well view them as suspects and will conduct intimate researches of their life. Furthermore, in dealing with suspects and witnesses, the police may well encounter some very unpleasant people who will attempt to deny their involvement in the crime or to undermine the police's efforts.

The sorts of pressures that stem from the nature of the issue being investigated are further amplified by the working patterns that are followed by the officers on an enquiry. Typically, the officers assigned to an enquiry would be working long days over an extended period of time. They would become intimately familiar with the actors involved in an incident and many seemed to develop a strong emotional attachment to a case and a desire to ensure that the crime is solved. This was especially evident in any case involving children.

At the same time, there are contradictions experienced. There is little doubt that in modern homicide investigations a key consideration is economic management and as one officer put it, 'solving crimes to a budget'. Officers are aware that except for extraordinary cases, financial considerations are a key factor in shaping investigative strategy. At a personal level, then, there is a need to reconcile the tensions that can arise on murder enquiries between the affective investment that individual officers make and the organizational considerations about cost-effectiveness.

What is evident is that the work conducted is very complex, as are the emotions that may be evoked in officers. Distancing strategies are ways of dealing with the various pressures that come to bear upon individuals, roles, and the murder squad as a whole.

Conclusion

All murder investigations are to a greater or lesser extent comparatively high pressure undertakings. Phenomena such as the use of distancing strategies and the development of compliance drift in the conduct of investigative actions are common features of many investigations. Such issues are particularly pronounced in terms of understanding the passage of the minority of extraordinary major crime investigations that are conducted.

In focusing upon these kinds of enquiry, I have sought to show both how and why some investigations are viewed as especially problematic by police officers. Some problems that are experienced are external to the investigation and stem from the circumstances of the crime amongst other factors. But others develop as a result of the ways in which lines of enquiry and investigative actions are carried out by detectives. Significantly, I have sought to stress that although much attention has been focused upon a small number of high-profile miscarriages of justice, this may have obscured the identification of a number of more routine and normal errors in major crime enquiries. I have also shown that the ultimate source of many of these errors is designed into the socio-technical investigative system. As a result of this, an understanding of these errors may contribute to our understandings of why the more deliberate and gross illegal actions are made by a small number of detectives.

Overall then, an examination of investigations *in extremis* develops our understandings of the range of activities and strategies utilized by detectives. At the same time, though, attending to such matters also helps to clarify the core issues involved in more 'normal' and routine investigations.

PART IV
Conclusion

11

Crime Investigation and the Creation of Collective Memory

Criminal homicide represents one of the most serious infractions of our moral and legal codes. For this reason, it is attributed a special symbolic status, and held to warrant a particular form of response from the state. However, the presence of this status, together with the nature of the social reaction that regularly accompanies it, tends to obscure the fact that the definition of an act as murder, manslaughter, or some other form of criminal homicide is the outcome of specific social processes. Acts are labelled and defined as crimes as a result of the information collected, interpreted, and constructed by the police investigation as part of the criminal justice process.

What are often understood and referred to as 'the facts' of a case are manufactured through the investigative work performed by police detectives. Thus, the 'facts' which allow sense to be made of the incident and enable it to be treated as a meaningful occurrence are objectified elements of an authoritative account of what happened that is assembled through the process of investigation. As such, the work performed by investigators can be identified as being concerned with the social construction of meaning. Through their investigative actions, officers manufacture a sense of understanding of the incident, which allows both the police and other socio-legal actors to act as if they know how and why the victim died, and who was responsible. The purpose of this study has been to document and analyse how police detectives accomplish this task. It has been concerned to map out the investigative processes, procedures, and practices that contribute to how a situation becomes defined as a criminal homicide and an individual identified as a killer.

The work that detectives perform in setting out how and why they believe that the victim was killed, together with the wider social reaction to this account, can be conceptualized as being akin to constructing a form of 'collective memory'.[95] In producing a narrative of the incident, in accordance with the epistemology provided by the legal frame, the police investigation effectively establishes how the incident is to be remembered by the wider community. That is, was the event a murder or manslaughter, who was the victim and who the perpetrator, and who did what to whom? Of course the police account may be contested by various actors (Rock, 1998b; May, 2000), but if proven, as it is in the majority of cases of murder, then it is the police's account of what happened that provides the legally and socially sanctioned record of the past.

The emphasis that has been placed in this study upon the constructive agency of detectives in producing an account of a crime is not intended to negate the very real harm that is caused by homicidal acts. Rather, the focus has been upon how public, community, and individual rememberings of such past events are framed by the manufacture of knowledge undertaken by investigators. Detectives assemble an account of the incident from an array of often contested and conflicting information sources. The ways in which the act is defined and explained, and thus the meaning it is attributed, do not inhere within the act itself, but are socially produced. Murder investigations, as part of a wider legal process, are ways in which a society defines and ascribes meaning to a past act.[96] The narrative that police construct is, then, both a product of the individual pieces of information that they have available to provide them with details of particular aspects of the incident, but also a transcendence of them.

Overall, this study has demonstrated that detective work is principally concerned with the manufacture of knowledge through the identification, interpretation, and application of information, and that crime investigation can be conceptualized as a social process. Through concurrently and sequentially ordered investigative actions, organized through lines of enquiry which collectively constitute the investigative process, detectives are seeking out information, assessing its validity and reliability, and trying to establish how it relates to their understanding of the incident. Within this interpretative process, the information work performed by detectives is central to the dynamics and trajectory of the passage of the investigation. Actions are performed in order to collect information that is selectively interpreted so as to form 'leads' and 'clues', which in turn are used to inform subsequent actions and re-configure interpretations of previously held information.

Underpinning the passage of the process structures of murder investigations is the fact that, in manufacturing knowledge about a crime, detectives construct a series of abductive inferences based upon their readings of signs of crime. Objects and actions performed by those people thought potentially connected to the crime are construed as signifiers which if correctly decoded and interpreted will advance the understanding of who did what to whom and why.

This semiotic dimension to crime investigation fundamentally underpins the investigative methodology and the use of particular investigative technologies. As a concept, investigative methodology captures the sense in which detectives draw upon a repertoire of techniques and understandings about human behaviour and fatal violence, to produce information and manufacture knowledge concerning a particular incident. Investigative practices are not performed in ad-hoc ways, but rather are informed by established and familiar patterns which are derived from a conjunction of individual and organizational experience in this area. Broadly speaking, this accounts for why, in the early stages of a homicide enquiry, in the absence of leads to the contrary, investigators will focus upon people known to the victim and those with previous convictions, as possible suspects. The investigative methodology is fundamental in terms of how lines of enquiry are ordered and organized and thereby in terms of structuring of the whole process of investigation.

The investigative methodology used for homicides is different from that employed for some other types of crimes. The nature of this difference reflects the selection of a set of investigative technologies and their introduction at particular stages of the process structures. I have sought to distinguish between those investigative technologies that are employed in the production of information and those utilized in the translation of this information into knowledge. This distinction is important because it reflects two interrelated problematics that are routinely encountered by detectives. First they have to gain access to information about the incident subject to investigation and then they have to evaluate the validity and reliability of this data, in terms of how it contributes to their understanding of the incident. This process of translation is informed by an often unreflected-upon set of common-sense, index-ical, analogical, and legal reasoning styles.

Although individual investigations demonstrate different levels of complexity, reflecting situational factors connected to the incident, on the basis of this research we can identify that there are three key tasks that underpin the passage of investigation in all enquiries. First, a decision has to be made as to whether the incident should be defined as a type of crime and thus warrant further investigation. Secondly, if it is a crime, then the police have to work towards the identification of a suspect. Subsequent to this, the officers need to construct a case for the prosecution that sub-stantively evidences this identification.

The work that the detectives perform is then akin to producing a retrospective definition of the situation that sets out how and why the victim came to be in this state. But in the initial stages of responding to a suspicious death, in the often confused conditions of the scene, deciding upon how the incident should be defined can be problematic. Detectives draw upon a combination of common-sense understandings and expert opinion about death to decide how the incident should be treated. Crime scenes regularly provide a significant amount of information for investigators. In addition to the detailed forensic analysis of the scene, investigators also use the scene and the body of the victim in a reflexive interpretative pro-cess. Individual artefacts at the crime scene are isolated and evalu-ated in terms of what they might indicate as to how, when, or why the crime occurred. At the same time though, the detective also employs a synoptic form of analysis in which they use the infor-mation contained in the crime scene to reconstruct an understand-ing of how the crime is likely to have taken place and why. This can be used to identify the crime as being of a particular type, which in turn can be used to direct subsequent investigative activities. For the detective, the scene and the body of the victim are a set of signifiers which, if correctly interpreted, should reveal traces of the author of the act's identity and promote their understanding of the crime as a whole.

Due to the circumstances in which most criminal homicides occur, the identification of the suspect is often comparatively simple for the police. It is only a minority of incidents that can be classified as whodunits, involving a more protracted search in order to iden-tify a prime suspect. For both self-solvers and whodunits, though, a crucial stage of the investigative process structures is the work connected to developing a case against the identified suspect. It is here that the police seek to provide an evidenced narrative that clearly identifies how the death was caused and the role of the suspect in this.

The conduct of investigative actions is manifestly shaped by the presence of the legal frame. Law and the legal process regulate police work both explicitly and implicitly. They set out definitions as to what constitutes criminal behaviour, provide police with a set of powers for the investigation of crime, and identify what evidence needs to be provided in respect of different illegalities. But it is important to note that the legal frame does not determine investigative actions. Police as knowledgeable actors are able to use the law as a resource in their enquiries and to manoeuvre around and through many of the constraints that are in place. Moreover, it is through the investigative actions of the police that the knowledge for the subsequent stages of the legal process is produced. As such, the law can be conceptualized as a negotiated order in investigative work. It both shapes and is shaped by the lines of enquiry enacted by detectives. It is in this sense that, from the perspective of detectives, the legal frame can be understood as a mode of rationality. It provides a way of understanding certain situations, sets out an epistemology for the production of legal knowledge, and establishes procedures for ascertaining the reliability and credibility of this knowledge. In effect, it provides a way of publicly defining acts as crimes of homicide and for deciding who did what to whom in these fatal interactions.

To an extent, the specifications maintained by the legal frame are mediated by aspects of the police organization. Through the development of socio-technical systems, forms of administrative control, procedures, routines, and conventions, the organization seeks to ensure that both the investigative process and the products that result from it are in accord with the requirements of law. It is these elements maintained by the organization that do much to order the work conducted.

Manufacturing knowledge about a crime and its participants is fraught with difficulties for detectives. They are aware that the members of the public whom they encounter in a number of different roles will, for a variety of reasons, provide them with misinformation and disinformation. On a number of occasions, it was observed that detectives were misled by information provided to them, which thereby inhibited the progress of the enquiry. But even when they are not misled, they are often making decisions based upon contested, contingent, and frequently ambiguous information. Such experiences provide a persuasive explanation for the presence of an intense suspicion and cynicism that can often be found in the 'police personality' of detectives. This is further amplified by a resignation to the fact that even if you catch this killer, tomorrow, the day after, or maybe the week after, there's going to be another case, another victim, and another murderer. There is, then, a degree of pessimism shared by those who must deal with the effects of extreme violence on a regular basis, who, faced with the grim and bloody realities of a body on the floor, must pick through the pieces to reconstruct the last moments of the deceased in an attempt to identify who is responsible for ending their life.

As this summary intimates, an understanding of murder investigations has to take proper account of the dialectical interplay that exists between action and context. The actions, interactions, and interpretations performed by detectives are embedded within and conditioned by the particular context in which they are situated. At the same time, though, these actions mediate the contextual conditions and contribute to their constitution. This is due to the fact that organizations frame the actions of their members, who in turn recursively constitute the organization. But at the same time, organizational action is itself framed by relationships with other organizations and social institutions. As such, at a more general sociological level, the study has drawn attention to the fact that, whilst context moulds and constrains social action, permutations of action and experience are always available as a result of the ways in which the situated social actor interprets, and subsequently responds to, their setting through selecting particular lines of action.

In drawing attention to the ordered and structured nature of the process of investigating homicides, I have not meant to imply that all homicide investigations are exactly the same. It is evident that they are not. The situational qualities of the incident concerned will obviously shape and influence the passage of the work performed by detectives. However, what this analysis has shown is that the investigative response of the police is built around: a particular investigative methodology; the deployment of a bureaucratic division of labour enacted through a socio-technical system; the use of a combination of investigative technologies and practices; and a set of understandings about the nature of homicide and its causes. The discussion of this combination of factors has sought to show how they respectively contribute to the conduct of a set of concurrent and sequential lines of enquiry, which collectively comprise one of the two investigative process structures. However, I have also sought to show how these same factors are implicated in those investigations that experience problems. In effect, my argument has been that, although the majority of homicide investigations are successful in solving the crimes, under certain circumstances the routinely enacted procedures, understandings, and systems can contribute to the failure of an investigation.

Murder investigations encounter a range of difficulties which may contribute to them being viewed as problematic cases or cause a form of failure to occur. In cases where a prime suspect either could not be identified, or sufficient evidence could not be collated to support a prosecution, detectives frequently held the view that they knew who did it, but they simply couldn't get the evidence. However, this research has shown that investigations experience problems and failures not just because of an informational or evidential deficit. Too much information flowing into the investigative system can hinder progress and ultimately lead to the vital clue or lead being missed. As such, the causes of investigative failure may effectively be designed into the system, rather than being simply attributable to the wilful corruption or ineptitude of a small number of officers. The tendency to focus upon corruption that has followed in the wake of a number of miscarriages of justice has served to obscure the fact that mistakes and errors are fairly commonplace on major crime investigations. The concept of compliance drift seeks to capture how and why different forms of mistake occur. Importantly, though, I have demonstrated that the propensity for compliance drift can be located in how the bureaucratic system is made to work on occasions by detectives, which establishes an influential precedent for them in terms of how they view and understand the system that co-ordinates and directs their work. In turn, this may create some of the preconditions which enable the more blatant contraventions of procedure and law found in the miscarriages of justice.

Over recent years the problems that have been experienced in a number of major crime investigations have been crucial in articulating the concerns of various sections of the public about policing. Indeed, these failures and problems, underpinned by broader structural social processes (cf. Garland, 2001), have been central to the increasingly ambiguous status that the institution of policing has come to have for many people. The ability of this small number of murder investigations to elicit such concern is not based solely upon the failures that they encapsulate. Rather it is a refraction of the symbolic status that detective work and murder investigations have traditionally been attributed in the police mythology.

Communicative Policing

Successful crime investigations provide the materials for the construction of a collective memory of the incident concerned. In relation to murder, the circumstances of the offence or the characteristics of the victim sometimes provides the basis for the establishment of an especially potent public memory. A small number of high-profile murder investigations have seemingly entered the cultural frame, and been particularly influential in shaping the contours of public and political debates about crime and the criminal justice system.

For a long time now, the policing of murder has been symbolically constructed as the apotheosis of the police mission. It is a crime of a serious and dramatic nature, where the need for police intervention on behalf of the public is evident. For police officers and police culture, whodunit murders in particular fulfil a prototypical vision of 'crime-fighting' and detective work, dealing with 'real villains', 'Murder in particular offers an opportunity for detectives to confront "evil", the worst kind of crime . . . for murder incites demands for action that coincide with the unambiguous implementation of police power in response to society's wrath' (Hobbs, 1988: 206). This can be contrasted with the everyday routines of police work where the provision of order out of social conflict is beset by ambiguities, complexities, and negotiation. Communities are diverse and factional, sharing divergent interests and wishes that are often incompatible, as a consequence of which the fabricated social order is only ever provisional. The investigation of murder is far less ambiguous. The murderer is symbolically posed as a manifest danger to the collective order in both a physical and metaphysical sense.

It was notable, during the fieldwork, that the stories that detectives told as a means of illustrating the key facets of the detective craft regularly concerned more serious types of crime (Innes, 2002). They are examples of what Clifford Geertz (1973) termed 'stories they tell themselves about themselves', implicated in the figurative reproduction of some of the core precedents of the occupational culture (Shearing and Ericson, 1991).

Likewise, for members of the public and the wider culture, the deliberate killing of an individual is an act involving serious unequivocal harm where the specialist skills and powers of the police can and should be put to work. Therefore, in these cases the police can recursively construct their role as being a moral and in a sense 'sacred' one, where they are acting as the protectors of the social order.

Although all murders are important in symbolically representing a number of our core cultural values, it is the small number of whodunit cases, and even more pronouncedly the cases célèbres, that appear to perform an especially significant role at the symbolic level. It is these statistically rare types of crime, often committed by strangers to the victim, who may well be drawn from a sociodemographic group not usually associated with criminal victimization and where the police often struggle to identify the offender, that almost paradoxically become a central symbolic focus of policing. For whilst the 'bobby on the beat' iconography of the English police system continues to resonate in terms of generating an implicit degree of support for the police, it is the moral drama associated with a small number of particularly serious violent cases that often comes to constitute particularly influential collective memories. As such, we can identify that murder investigations have an important communicative role, wherein they are enacted as 'symbolizations' of police work. The crime of murder remains comparatively rare in England and Wales, and yet it is established as a quintessentially denotative symbol of the police function and police role in society. For police and public alike, the investigation of murder has contributed to the preservation of an evocative, symbolically loaded collective memory of the nature and role of policing in society.

This shift to a consideration of the symbolic construction of murder investigations sensitizes us to the fact that such aspects of police work, in terms of the ways in which they are represented, are dramaturgical communications that both express and give rise to important cultural sensibilities. Murder investigations are thoroughly implicated in the politics of legitimacy of the police organization. And although media participation in covering the work of murder investigations can be encouraged on instrumental grounds, it is also exploited at an ideological level. Mediated representations of murder investigations are important in terms of legitimating the police function to both police officers and public alike, at a time when there is an increased sense of ambiguity about the conduct of police work.[97]

In part, this ambiguity is a consequence of the highly publicized miscarriages of justice. But it also reflects the politics of criminal justice over the past two decades, where it is serious violent crimes that continue to garner publicity, but high volume property crimes that have been the principal focus of political attention. At the same time, as with other public services, policing has been increasingly governed by an economic imagery of rationalization, despite rises in the fear and insecurity that people express about crime (Garland, 2001). In spite of this complex of pressures, which appears at times to be pulling policing in different directions, the continued willingness of police forces to direct large amounts of resources to single murders in an attempt to solve them is indicative of the status that these crimes retain.

The iconic mythology of murder investigation provides the opportunity for a symbolic representation that abstracts from the complex reality of police work, clarifying the roles of the participants. It encodes important values through selective representation and arranges the polyphony of potential meanings and the complexities associated with the police role into a single communicable form. The mythology of policing reifies detective work, action, and crime-fighting amongst police officers and publics, and is a way in which the fundamental ironies and uncertainties that inhere in the police function can be reconciled and resolved, at least for the duration of an investigation.

Almost paradoxically, though, it is the very status attributed to murder investigation that has contributed to its role in undermining public confidence in the police. It is because of the symbolic status of murder investigations that when investigations publicly fail or miscarriages of justice occur, public concern about the efficacy of police tactics and the police service as a whole is so profound.

The Order of Death

The symbolic construction of police murder investigations in our society and culture is inflected by the sense in which it is a method via which we collectively seek to understand how and why particular types of unexpected and unnatural deaths occur. In this sense, then, it can be conceptualized as an example of how our culture invokes particular ceremonial and ritual responses to the existential problem posed by death (Ricoeur, 1967). Ultimately, death signals the limits of our control over, and knowledge about, ourselves. Nevertheless, although it remains a profound existential problematic, our society has increasingly developed technologies that allow us to ascertain and identify 'the causes' of death. The forensic dissection of deaths caused by human agency encapsulated in the murder investigation reflects this desire to explain and rationalize, in order to alleviate the ontological insecurity that such events can provoke.

As part of this deconstructive orientation, those individuals who are responsible for causing the death of another are held to represent a specific danger to the collective security of society. They have disrupted the social and to a degree the natural order, and as such must be apprehended and punished. The power that is attached to death, and those who wilfully cause it, reflects the status of the killer as a figure who exposes the fragility of human existence and order. Particularly in respect of the more 'pathological' murders, we can observe that established traditional moral conceptions concerning notions of 'good' and 'evil' continue to be called upon, in order to try and manufacture a meaningful response to such events.

Indeed, it is arguably the case that as society becomes increasingly tolerant of certain lesser forms of deviance (Newburn, 1992), as a corollary to such movements it is becoming less tolerant of violence and more serious forms of crime (Young, 1999). Given such a situation, it may be that the response by the police and other state agencies to more serious crime types becomes increasingly important to the reproduction of their public legitimacy.

However, the degree of 'social repulsion' extended against the deviant transgressor is not constant; it is determined according to the adjudged reprehensibility attached to the particular act (Black, 1993). Just as the seriousness of different types of crime is stratified in society in accordance with certain key values, so too are homicides defined in terms of their seriousness, both in popular consciousness and legal discourse.

Two key variables determine the stratification of patterns of public opinion on homicide, relational distance and the concept of dangerousness. As we have seen in the police classifications of murder, killings involving strangers are more often held to be more serious and demanding of a higher investment of resources to solve them, than is the case for homicides where those involved were known to each other. These trends are particularly explicit on those occasions where there is a 'pure' victim, for it is in such cases that moral roles and the attribution of blame are particularly well defined.

An individual who kills deliberately and volitionally, and thus wilfully transgresses society's 'sacred' legal and moral codes, is identified as more dangerous and evil than the person who kills in the midst of a highly emotive and emotional confrontation. Certain murderers then become established as *de facto* 'folk devils', whose acts elicit particular degrees of concern. Their identity is redefined by the act that they have committed, they are labelled as a murderer, and within both police and cultural discourses there may be a tendency to portray them as evil incarnate. As someone who has deliberately caused the death of another, there is a certain symbolic danger and maleficent power attached to the figure of the killer. They are the embodiment of evil, the forbidden, and the immoral. Thus in providing a response to and protection from the actions of the murderer, the police are potentially cast as 'folk heroes' and the legitimacy of their role in society symbolically enacted and produced.

Policing Murder as a Cultural Agent

In the process of contributing to the ideological legitimation of the social institution of policing, the investigation of murder also performs an important symbolic role in terms of how our culture defines and reacts to otherwise inchoate and nebulous concerns, such as the nature of deviance, control, and order.

The process of criminal justice and the imposition of punishment by the state has never been about the attainment of purely instrumental objectives. Strategies of punishment and social control have an important expressive or symbolic role. In the words of David

Garland (1990), they are 'cultural agents', framing and influencing the values, beliefs, and sensibilities that underpin our moral orders. From Foucault's (1977) eighteenth-century 'theatres of punishment', to the wigs and robes of the magistracy and the uniform of the police constable, the social control strategies of the state have been replete with iconography, ritual ceremony, and symbolism. The effecting of control is not merely about intervention in respect of certain prohibited behaviours. Control enacts meanings in a culture and indicates the appropriate way of thinking and feeling about such issues.

Collective experience is organized through a complex, culturally relevant, reflexive network of signs and symbols that function to frame existential properties and 'objectify' or 'make concrete' abstract conceptual qualities (Needham, 1979). Cultures are produced and reproduced by the interactions and meanings that participants construct, and the collective memories that they hold in common. Thus, in the process of being produced, culture frames existence. Cultures organize and clarify the meaning of events in the world and in the midst of doing so they establish modes of thinking appropriate to being able to 'go on' with everyday life. But within the context of human societies, it is obvious that not all the problems of day-to-day existence are of equal concern and value. There are certain key problems relating to the existential experience of the human condition which cultures are enacted to either solve or at least palliate for their members. Issues of life and death, security and danger, and deviance and punishment are all key ontological concerns within contemporary life and they are all embedded within representations of murder investigations. As such, the ways in which murder and the police response to it are constructed within contemporary cultural formations reflects the fact that such representations are one way in which particularly troublesome aspects of the human condition can be rendered orderly, understandable, and manageable.

The dominant cultural discourse on murder investigations makes use of a sense of reality that is framed in such a way as to enable the momentary integration of state, law, and morality, together with the reification of the police institution. Thus, in addition to their very pragmatic rationales, murder investigations help to communicate a number of deeply embedded social meanings. They denote and help us to conceive of abstract qualities such as good and evil, normal and pathological, order and disorder. Such considerations are of particular concern to a late-modern democratic culture which is marked by its social and moral heterogeneity and pluralism. Murder investigations are enacted to demarcate the boundaries of the sacred and profane.

Investigating murder is primarily sense-making work. At a pragmatic, instrumental level, in attempting to identify and catch killers, detectives are looking to collect and interpret information in order to establish how and why the victim died. This aspect of their work involves the construction of a narrative account of the event that is central in defining public understandings of what happened and thus how it is to be collectively remembered. At the same time, and at a more abstract and diffuse level, the investigative work brings to the fore and symbolically portrays notions of good and evil, sacred and profane, and control and chaos. In addition, then, to the material, practical accomplishments of policing, there is an important symbolic dimension that feeds directly into the maintenance and reproduction of the moral, social, and cultural order. It is in relation to the policing of murder that such symbolic meanings become particularly well defined.

APPENDIX A
Methodology

Investigating Murder is a qualitative study of how the police respond to incidents of criminal homicide, and the practices, processes, and problems that influence their investigations. The data for the study were collected through ethnographic fieldwork on five murder enquiries in progress, qualitative content analysis of 20 complete case files, supplemented by a review of the police case summaries for an additional 50 investigations. Further data were collected through a series of formal and informal interviews, together with an analysis of police policy documents. This use of mixed methods was informed by the principles of 'within method' and 'between method' triangulation (Denzin, 1970).

Setting

The research was conducted in a police force in southern England between January 1995 and August 1997. The force area was composed of five major urban conurbations, a number of medium- and small-sized towns and a widespread number of smaller rural communities. This area was divided into nine Basic Command Units which were largely coterminous with the local authority areas. At the time of the fieldwork, the recorded crime rate for all crime was below the national average and the force's detection rate was fractionally above the national average. Seventy-seven per cent of all recorded violent crime was detected, compared with the national average of under 73%.

In the postwar period there had on average been 16 murders per year in the area studied, although as with the national trends for homicide, this figure had been rising slightly over the last 30 years. Between 1988 and 1997 the homicide rate for the area stood at 1.3 per 100,000 population. The police had been extremely successful in solving the vast majority of these cases, although it is worth mentioning that towards the end of the fieldwork period and subsequent to the research finishing, there have been several murders that have remained unsolved. Overall, between 1988 and 1997 the force recorded 94% of all murders as detected. In terms of the numbers of homicides recorded and the performance of the force in detecting them, the area in which the research was conducted seems to be fairly representative of the situation nationally.

Access

An initial approach to the police organization where the study was conducted was made in January 1993, via a personal contact. Initial negotiations as to the terms and conditions of access commenced shortly afterwards. The outcome of these negotiations was that the police organization agreed to provide access, but a condition of access was that anonymity should be maintained in respect of the organization, its officers, and all cases featured in any presentations of material connected with the study. This agreement has been adhered to throughout the study.

Murder investigations necessarily and obviously involve extremely sensitive police data and therefore considerable ethical issues for research. These ethical issues were manifested both in terms of how the data were collected and how they have been presented. In respect of this latter concern, material from cases is presented in a way that is sufficient to substantiate the analytic interpretations made by the author, but also in such a manner, it is hoped, as to avoid readers being able to identify individual cases. Thus only a selection of the data collected can be presented within the book, although the analytic conclusions are drawn from the wider data-set.

The intention when the project was initially being formulated was to do a comparative study in two police organizations. Once access was obtained in the first police organization, an approach was made to several other police forces in an attempt to secure similar conditions. The success with the first organization was not replicated and none of the other organizations approached was willing to grant access. As a result, the focus of the study was slightly adjusted to compensate for these difficulties. This merely serves to emphasize the significance of the extensive degree of co-operation that was provided to me in conducting this study, into what is a particularly sensitive area of police work.

Data Collection

The methodology for the study was based upon a structured yet adaptable multi-method approach. A brief documentary review of 75 cases was conducted, where salient details of the incidents and the police response were noted, including the circumstances of the crime, the setting, the *modus operandi* employed, the socio-biographic details of victims and offenders, and how the police solved the case (if at all). This information was used to identify a sample of 20 cases, which were subjected to more detailed study through examination of the complete case files maintained by police on the HOLMES computer system. The data from the analysis of case files were supplemented by formal and informal interviews with officers who had been involved in each of the 20 cases. These interviews also addressed other related issues. In addition, ethnographic observation was conducted on five enquiries in progress.

Fieldwork

The ethnographic fieldwork for the study was divided between two settings. In both settings, the role assumed was that of an observer as participant (Burgess, 1984). This was due to the fact that the study was based in a 'closed setting' (Lofland and Lofland, 1995). In total, approximately five months was spent 'in the field'. The periods of observational work were split up over the two-year period to avoid any potential for over-identifying with the police role, which might affect the validity of the material collected (Hammersley and Atkinson, 1983; Punch, 1979). In terms of the fieldwork, the usual provisions about collecting material in the field were adhered to. Whilst in the presence of those I was studying, note-taking and any activity that overtly reflected my researcher status was as far as possible avoided. Field notes were written up when appropriate opportunities occurred. Fieldwork was conducted on enquiries in progress and at police headquarters.

Observations of the five enquiries in progress varied between one day on one case and 28 days on another. Wherever possible I tried to work similar hours to the detectives being observed. During this element of the fieldwork, I tried to observe all of the different roles and types of work that were being conducted. A number of problems to do with conducting observations of highly sensitive work were experienced. Overall, though, the ethnographic research served to produce a lot of important and highly detailed 'rich' data (Lofland and Lofland, 1995) and 'thick description' (Geertz, 1973) for the study.

Further ethnographic data were collected from a three-month period spent working in the HOLMES office at police headquarters. Ostensibly, I was there to review the 20 case files, but whilst there I was able to observe the detectives who specialized in using the HOLMES system.

The officers concerned performed a specialist function within the division of investigative labour and two of these officers, selected through a rolling shift system, would attend every major crime investigation for the duration of the enquiry. Because of this, the detectives in this office had acquired a great deal of knowledge about murder, its investigation, and in particular the range of cases that had occurred in the area under study. As I was researching the case files, I was able to ask them questions about various points and they were able to provide me with thicker descriptive data that explained some of the decisions taken and the problems that had been involved with particular cases.

As they came and went between the various assignments, aspects of the cases would be discussed with their colleagues and this general talk was useful to me in understanding how detectives conceptualize murder and the problems of the investigative process. The fact that I was with these officers over a longer period of time than was possible for those on enquiries allowed me to collect a range of information relating to their work and outlook which supplemented the other areas of observation.

In terms of the nature of my relationship to the subject and people being researched, I think it appropriate to conceptualize the project in terms of a process. By this I mean that I was not wholly what Davis (1973) terms a 'martian' or a 'convert'; rather I travelled between these two role-identities as the project progressed. I started as an outsider, learning the subjective meanings, procedures, and nature of crime investigation and becoming increasingly familiar with them and their use in the situated social worlds maintained by detectives. Gradually, though, as I became increasingly familiar with the subject of study, my status and orientation became more similar to that of a convert, immersed within the routines and currents of the social world being studied. Once the fieldwork was completed, though, my sense of 'distance' returned to a degree, which was useful in terms of trying to detect analytic patterns within the data I had collected.

Interviews

Linked to the use of ethnographic methods were the data collected through interviews with detectives of varying ranks. About 20 one-hour formal interviews were conducted on a range of topics relating to homicide investigations. In addition, a far larger number of unstructured interviews or what Burgess (1984) terms 'interviews as conversations' were conducted as part of the fieldwork.

The two approaches yielded slightly different types of data that in effect complement each other. The informal interview style was selected as a technique because of a number of considerations relevant to the particular setting of the research. The area being researched was particularly sensitive and on a number of occasions involved material that was *sub judice*. As a result, it was not appropriate to try and get officers to discuss such matters 'on the record'. I have little doubt that they would have refused anyway. The presence of a tape recorder, making any comments attributable, would have precluded some of the frank and open discussions about sensitive material and issues that were enjoyed by the researcher.

Therefore the majority of interviews were of the semi-structured or unstructured variety, conducted within the situated routines of the subjects' working environment. This included work that was in the office, 'out and about' on enquiries, and in an assortment of licensed premises. The conducting of these types of interviews was integrated with the observation of detectives. These interviews were part of the observer as participant role, in which conversations were directed by the researcher asking questions of those being observed, as observational material was also being collected. The questions raised would deal with particular issues that had arisen and were of interest to the project, and often formed part of conversations that were more broadly based. Where appropriate, notes of these conversations were written up at the first available opportunity.

An important aspect of the practicalities of this approach was that a balance had to be struck between asking questions and observing. Asking too many questions might have disturbed the routine of subjects. The fact that the interviews were often conducted in the working environs of the detectives meant that it was often the case that a number of officers would become involved in the conversations. On a number of occasions, the conversations were between the researcher and a number of officers. This proved to be a very useful strategy. By subtly directing the topics covered, I was able to obtain some interesting data about how detectives viewed their tasks. Having three or more officers reflect upon their work and debating aspects of it was highly illuminating in relation to how detectives as knowledgeable actors construct their social world.

Case Files

The final major source of data in the study is the information obtained from analysis of police case files, which were analysed through 'ethnographic content analysis' (Altheide, 1996). As was discussed previously, the period spent collecting information from 20 case files took three months and also afforded the opportunity for the collection of a large amount of observational data. I should, though, briefly mention how the data from the case files were collected and analysed.

The investigative process is ends-oriented, the object being to produce a case that supports (it is hoped) a successful prosecution. The case file maintained by the police does not just detail the results of the investigation, but rather it records complete details of the process of investigation. It shows how all the lines of enquiry were developed by detectives, all the pieces of information that were collected by police, all the actions performed by officers, and the directions issued by the Senior Investigating Officer. As such, it proved to be a very useful resource for research purposes.

The observational data were important in understanding the situated complexities associated with the work performed by the police, as well as the officers' subjective understandings of their work. The records maintained in the case files were, however, ideal for obtaining a comprehension of the overall structure of the investigative process.

It is important not to be quixotic about such sources. Case files are very much constructed 'texts' and were examined accordingly. Throughout the analysis, a keen awareness that the case files were deliberately and manifestly constructed objects was retained. They were produced with a particular purpose in mind, relating to the investigative function in an adversarial legal context. Nevertheless, they proved to be a useful source of information. They detailed what the product of the police investigative activity is and provided a record of the manufacturing process.

Data Triangulation

The combined method approach was selected to overcome the problems of relying on just one research instrument. But having utilized several methods within the research strategy, it is important to detail how they are combined and used at the data analysis stage of the research. On all cases in which observational data were collected, the case file was also studied, interviews were conducted with detectives involved in the case, and the case summary analysed. This allowed for cross-referencing between those cases which I studied in depth and those which received less extensive coverage, to ensure that they were broadly representative of the fundamental patterns and trends. Similarly, on the 20 cases where the files were examined, interviews were conducted with officers involved in them to establish thicker descriptive data.

Through the use of a multi-instrument methodology, I have been able to cross-reference the different sources to produce a more complete story of the realities of police murder investigations. The individual weaknesses associated respectively with particular techniques have been overcome and the data they have produced have served to complement the findings as a whole.

The qualitative data were analysed in accordance with the procedures of analytic induction, whereby concepts and theories are the outcome of repeated testing for 'fit' against the data. Where appropriate, as for example in Chapter 2, descriptive statistics are provided to map out relevant patterns and trends.

Tracking Analysis

An important element of the methodological analysis of the investigative process is based upon the development of what I have termed diachronic and synchronic tracking. This approach was devised in order to overcome some of the problems encountered in capturing the processual nature of the concurrent activities of the detectives involved in a particular investigation. This was resolved by an analysis of the case files. But in order to perform this element of the analysis, a degree of methodological innovation was required, focusing upon the inter-relation of information and actions.

Tracking analysis provides one way of following the development of information based upon material held in large, complex qualitative data-sets and constructing a useful analysis of it. Thus, it provides a way of researching and analysing forms of work that focus upon the generation, communication, or management of information. The concept of 'tracking discourse' is featured in David Altheide's (1996) discussion of qualitative media content analysis, but he does little to develop it. In order to make the concept of tracking applicable to the study of investigative processes, a considerable amount of development of these basic ideas was performed.

In effect, the analysis of the case files through the principles of tracking allowed for an analytic framework to be constructed that sets out the most significant patterns of action, interaction, and interpretation relevant to the activities of detectives. The data derived from more traditional forms of ethnographic observation were fitted into this framework to supplement and augment it, and to provide a greater degree of explanation as to what was really going on.

Diachronic tracking represents a particular way of capturing the dynamics and trajectory of a social process where information and action are mutually productive. In this study, it is used to evaluate the relationship between the actions of detectives and the production of information over the course of an investigation. It shows how the focus and objectives of action shift as the information needs of the actors develop and adapt in response to other developments. The diachronic tracking analysis was based upon coding the data about the actions performed by detectives contained in the case files according to what information they were intended to generate. The progress of the investigations was then divided into small temporal stages and the various coded actions plotted. The resulting graphs demonstrate how over the course of an investigation the focus of police activity, in terms of the information it seeks to generate, shifts and develops. The results of this analysis were central to identifying the key stages in the sequential process of investigation.

In contrast, synchronic tracking analysis focuses upon the 'morphological properties' of information and the ways in which its meaning and status alters as an investigation progresses. For the purposes of this study, the synchronic analysis is concerned with situating individual units of information in context, in order to map out how detectives establish a network of interpretative relations between pieces of information.

This analysis was constructed by identifying the key points of evidence within the police case and then 'tracking' back to see how these evidential points were established through particular interpretations and combining pieces of information and knowledge. The analysis presented is somewhat simplified when compared with the complexities of the actual case files.

The strategies of diachronic and synchronic tracking are seemingly useful methodological techniques appropriate for the analysis of complex qualitative data-sets. In their respective emphases upon time and space, they are complementary techniques for mapping out the contours of information and its relationship to specific forms of action and interpretation.

In sum, the methods used in this study are united by an orientation based around a process of progressive focusing upon key issues, together with the principles of analytic induction. This approach was designed to try and ensure that the validity of the results presented in the study is high and that a holistic picture is constructed which accurately details the reality of police homicide investigations.

APPENDIX B
Case Details for the Continuum

Self-Solvers

Case 1

Case 1 is close to the 'ideal type' self-solver. The incident involved a husband killing his wife. The police case was built around the fact that the suspect was arrested shortly after the crime and confessed to the murder. In addition, there were substantial amounts of forensic evidence and a reliable 'indirect witness' to support the police case.

Case 2

The victim was a young child who was killed by her mother's boyfriend. The suspect was identified due to the fact that the boyfriend was the only person in the house when the child died. There was also forensic evidence available and the man had previous convictions for violence.

Case 3

In the third case in the continuum, the victim died in a fight between two groups of young men outside a public house. There were several witnesses who made statements to the police to identify the killer as well as forensic evidence. Under interview, the suspect made self-incriminating statements.

Case 4

Case 4 was a fairly typical male status confrontation and the police investigation was assisted by a number of indirect witnesses, forensic evidence, and the suspect's confession.

Case 5

The suspect was a middle-aged woman who fled the scene of the crime, but confessed to a friend, who in turn phoned the police. There was substantial forensic evidence and a number of indirect witnesses.

Case 6

This case involved a male killing his female partner. The suspect was identified through this relationship and because he was the last one seen in the company of the victim. The investigation struggled to establish forensic evidence to support the charge.

Case 7

The male suspect was identified because he was a friend of the victim. Once he had been identified, the police enquiries found forensic evidence and a number of indirect witnesses to link the suspect to the crime.

Case 8

There was a direct witness to the killings and a number of indirect witnesses but the investigators encountered difficulties in establishing forensic evidence to support the witnesses' evidence.

Case 9

The two suspects were identified through having the physical opportunity to commit the crime and there was also substantial forensic evidence. They fled the area and the enquiry team expended a lot of effort in locating them. Once arrested, one of the two suspects admitted their involvement under interview and implicated the other in the crime.

Case 10

The suspect was identified through being seen in the company of the victim prior to the estimated time of death. Once identified, the enquiry established forensic evidence and indirect witnesses.

Hybrids

Case 11

The suspect was identified through his attempts to involve himself in the enquiry. There was also good forensic evidence and a number of indirect witnesses. The police background checks revealed previous convictions.

Case 12

The victim was a young female who was killed by a family member. There were no witnesses and the forensic evidence was only revealed after detailed testing. The enquiry took some time to identify the family member as a suspect.

Whodunits

Case 13

The victim was killed by a third party, hired by his wife to kill him. This was a very complex investigation that was eventually solved through a combination of factors.

Case 14

In this case, because the police collected a lot of forensic evidence at the scene, as soon as the suspect was identified the case was effectively solved. However, for a number of reasons it took them a long time actually to identify the individual.

Case 15

This case was a typical 'stranger murder'. There were various pieces of forensic evidence recovered from the scene, but as with case 14, actually identifying the individual was problematic. Once identified, though, the forensic evidence linked the suspect to the crime. He had also taken property from the victims' house and a number of important indirect witnesses were established.

Case 16

Another 'stranger murder' where there were no witnesses. The prosecution case rested upon forensic material recovered at the scene and circumstantial evidence.

Case 17

The victim was a female murdered in her home. Once the suspect was identified, there was forensic evidence to link the suspect to the crime.

Case 18

Case 18 was a shooting of a male victim and was unsolved.

Case 19

The victim was a middle-aged man who was beaten to death in his own home. Long-term unsolved.

Case 20

Torso of victim found in a remote location. Long-term unsolved.

Notes

1. The terms murder and criminal homicide are often popularly confused as detailed in Chapter 3. The focus of this book should properly be termed 'homicide investigations', but throughout the text I tend to refer to 'murder investigations', as a reflection of the fact that this was the preferred terminology of the police officers studied.
2. A more detailed description of the research process is provided in Appendix A.
3. In particular, the study is informed by a variant of symbolic interactionist sociology.
4. Aspects of this approach to understanding the links between meaning and acting are variously described in Rock (1979), Goffman (1983), and Blumer (1969).
5. See Goffman (1959) and Burke (1962) on dramaturgical analysis.
6. This also supports Sanders's (1977) finding that in routine detective work physical evidence is most often used to substantiate allegations against an individual arrived at by other means.
7. Including interview techniques, statement taking, forensic evidence, and the use of informants.
8. For a general discussion of the importance of symbolic power, see Bourdieu (1990). In relation to the police role, see Manning (1997) and Loader (1997).
9. See Havard (1960) for a discussion of the forms of response prior to the introduction of the 'new' police in 1829.
10. As I will discuss presently, it is a change that is exacerbated by the intervention of media interest in such incidents.
11. The adoption of this analytic stance obviously requires one to avoid, at least momentarily, consideration of the moral sensibilities associated with unlawful killings. This is not easy, nor is it intended to play down the very real distress that people feel in relation to this subject. Indeed, it is precisely the moral indignation and the deeply felt sensations that such crimes elicit that makes murder particularly interesting as a topic of social research (see Rock, 1998*a*). However, there is little doubt that discussions of murder and homicide are often rendered particularly susceptible to value-laden, subjective judgements, as a result of what Professor Glanville-Williams (1958) deemed to be the emotionally confusing and logically irrelevant fact of death. For the purposes of sociological analysis though, one must try to distance oneself from the

accepted social conventions with which one has been socialized through the discourses of law and culture.

12. The anthropological literature provides several examples of societies organized around alternative forms of private response to 'unlawful' death (Douglas, 1966; Ricoeur, 1967; Needham, 1979).

13. For a discussion of the legal definitions of all homicide offences, see Chapter 3, and Smith and Hogan (1992) and Ashworth (1993). On the relationships between the different offence definitions, see Ashworth and Mitchell (2000), Box (1983), Hawkins (1992), Hutter (1997), and Punch (1996).

14. See Morris and Blom-Cooper (1964) and Rock (1998b) for similar arguments.

15. Figures based upon *Criminal Statistics England and Wales 1997*, table 4.1.

16. Lane (1997) identifies a number of problems in conducting comparative historical research on murder, and I feel that the issues he identifies are equally valid for cross-national comparisons. The principal problems are: changes in legal definitions of murder result in fluctuations in which behaviours are defined and thus counted as homicides; changes in the legal status of citizens may affect which incidents the state agencies record as homicides; developments in record keeping and population monitoring by the state may increase the awareness of levels of unnatural deaths; and developments in law enforcement and medico-legal science have probably increased the potential to detect murder (see Havard, 1960).

17. Based upon figures for 1988–97 (*Criminal Statistics England and Wales 1997*, table 4.4).

18. *FBI Uniform Crime Reports.*

19. Based on *Criminal Statistics England and Wales 1997*, table 4.4.

20. *Criminal Statistics England and Wales 1997*, table 4.4.

21. *Criminal Statistics England and Wales 1997*, table 4.5.

22. Leyton (1995) draws upon Elias's 'civilizing process' in an attempt to explain why given similar levels of economic and social development there should be such a wide disparity in the homicide rates for England and the USA.

23. *FBI Uniform Crime Reports 1996.*

24. Based on figures for the years 1988–97 inclusive, *Criminal Statistics England and Wales 1997*, table 4.3.

25. Based on Home Office data for 1988–97, *Criminal Statistics England and Wales 1997*, table 4.8.

26. *Criminal Statistics England and Wales 1997*, table 4.8.

27. This may in part be attributable to the abolition of the death penalty.

28. Based upon *Criminal Statistics England and Wales 1997*, table 4.2.

29. The two males and one female who died in these incidents are included in the analysis due to the fact that the decision to record the incident as 'no-crime' was only arrived at as a result of the police investigation.

30. In a similar way, it appears that in the wake of the Stephen Lawrence Enquiry the term 'racially motivated homicide' is entering police parlance, as a reflection of the particular problems and political sensitivities that such cases are felt to pose for the police.

31. These structures of moral feeling are reflected in the bureaucratic organization of the investigative efforts, as will be discussed in Chapter 4.

32. See Daly and Wilson (1988) and Polk (1994).

33. This formulation draws upon Dewey (1933).

34. See Rock (1993).

35. Evidence can be either direct or circumstantial. Direct evidence is that which, if believed, directly establishes a fact at issue. Circumstantial evidence is evidence of fact(s) from which a fact(s) in issue may be inferred.

36. In this aspect of their work, detectives are aided by the specialist skills of a forensic pathologist, whose role has become increasingly important due to advances in forensic medicine (Havard, 1960). It is now common practice for the defence to conduct an additional autopsy examination of the victim. This occurred on several cases in this study. On one case a total of eight autopsies were performed on the two victims.

37. It is worth mentioning at this point that there are a number of examples of cases where it is alleged that the police's initial investigation wrongly failed to identify an incident as a homicide, only for this to be demonstrated at a later stage.

38. A more detailed discussion of the use of signifiers of intent is provided in Chapter 7.

39. It is probably worth adding a minor caveat at this point. Motive is not the same as intent. To secure a charge of murder it is not necessary for the prosecution to establish the motive for the assault, although they must demonstrate intent on the part of the offender. None the less, from the police point of view, it is held to be useful to be able to suggest a motive as this is seen as important in terms of persuading the jury of the overall validity of the police case.

40. P indicates police officer and S indicates suspect.

41. The extent to which police are able to deceive suspects is becoming increasingly tightly controlled by law. None the less, there remain a variety of techniques which allow for subtle deceptions on the part of the police.

42. It is, of course, not unknown for the police to launch a murder investigation where only parts of a corpse have been found, or where a person has gone missing in highly suspicious circumstances. However, the majority of enquiries are launched as a result of a body being found.

43. Unlike the major metropolitan forces, the police force studied did not retain a specialist 'murder squad'.

44. Some of these problems are addressed through the recent introduction of the next generation HOLMES 2.

45. The force studied did not have a separate role of 'Indexer' as used by some other forces.

46. This integration of the analytical function within the MIR is a relatively recent development and it is not present in the systems employed by all police forces.

47. In this chapter, I will merely detail the nature of the different types of information. The techniques by which they are produced will be the key focus of Chapter 6.

48. In several of the miscarriages of justice referred to previously, it was problems in the forensic interpretations of evidence that led to the convictions being overturned.

49. The importance of publicly provided information in solving all types of crimes was discussed previously in Chapter 1. The findings of this study support the general claims made by Greenwood et al. (1977) and Ericson (1993), amongst others, that a significant proportion of crimes are ostensibly solved for the police by members of the public.

50. Of course, further problems can be created by the fact that not everyone who confesses to a crime will actually have been involved in it. The psychological phenomenon of 'false confessions' is discussed in Gudjonssen and MacKeith (1988).

51. Fielding (1995) found that a similar view of police–community contacts was widely held by officers involved in other aspects of policing.

52. A discussion of the methodological procedures and rationale underpinning tracking analysis is provided in Appendix A.

53. As with other forms of audit trail, to construct this one, I started with the key outputs of the investigation (on the left of the figure) and traced back how they were arrived at.

54. See Goffman (1959).

55. This is a version of cognitive interviewing familiar to social scientists, wherein particular 'mnemonic techniques' are employed to aid the recovery of information from witnesses and victims.

56. Present: R—researcher; DS—detective sergeant; DC—detective constable.

57. In the interview are the suspect, their legal representative who does not comment in the passages reproduced, and two police interviewers, P1 and P2.

58. When arrested the suspect was found in possession of a small amount of cannabis resin.

59. A more detailed discussion of the role of media in major crime investigations is provided in Chapter 10 and also in Innes (1999) and Feist (1999).

60. See Latour and Woolgar (1990) for an extended discussion of representation in science.

61. The importance of time in investigative work was noted by Sanders (1977).

62. See Lyman and Scott (1970).

63. The narrative was in fact more detailed, but some elements have been excluded in order that the victim cannot be identified.

64. In the literature, variations of these questions are widely used. See e.g. Swanson *et al.* (1996); Palmiotto (1994); Brian-Morgan (1990).

65. For a discussion of such concerns, see Maines (1993); Plummer (1995); and Denzin (1996).

66. See Goffman (1963) on the existential properties of bearing a stigma.

67. This concept of career has been utilized by a number of authors. See Goffman (1961); Rock (1973); and Hutter (1997).

68. This term is borrowed from Shibutani (1970).

69. My use of the term abduction draws explicitly on the work of Peirce (1955, 1998). See also Eco (1983) and Shank (2001).

70. My approach to what is essentially an 'interpretative semiotics' is informed variously by the work of Manning (1988, 1992, 1996), Hodge and Kress (1988), Eco (1976, 1983), and Sebeok and Umiker-Sebeok (1983).

71. Pseudonym.

72. It is according to Shank (2001) 'a logic towards meaning'. See also Eco (1983).

73. This discussion develops Knorr-Cetina's (1980) work on scientists' reasoning.

74. See Giddens (1984).

75. Of course, this does not preclude a 'stranger' being identified as a suspect at an early stage through some means. What is being mapped out are the general trends involved.

76. Similar classifications are reported by Sanders (1977) where the detectives differentiated between 'walk-throughs' and 'whodunits'. David Simon (1991), in his study of detectives in Baltimore, reports that cases were divided between 'dunkers' and 'whodunits'.

77. This is a specialist forensic technique involving the use of lasers to identify fingerprint marks.
78. This is a pseudonym.
79. The suspect makes an interesting slip into the present tense here.
80. It was confirmed that he had done this. In situations such as these, it is established police practice to obtain a copy of the 999 telephone call for evidential purposes and it is also a means of checking exactly what was said in the call.
81. Indicates deceased person.
82. Instruction to 'take statement'.
83. This supports the comments made in Chapter 2 regarding the importance of male 'sexual propriety' attitudes over female partners as a motivation for homicide.
84. This notion of discreditable identities is drawn from Goffman (1963).
85. The time scale on the left of the page charts the time elapsed between significant events in the investigation.
86. This point supports the argument put forward in Chapter 7 in respect of the importance of the temporal frames in organizing investigative activities.
87. An in-depth discussion of such issues is provided in Geberth (1995).
88. See Goffman (1952).
89. Conversely though, as I have mentioned elsewhere in this book, on several investigations the police only identified a family member as a suspect at a comparatively late stage, after initially discounting the involvement of a member of the family.
90. The notion of the suspect profile has in recent years been most usually associated with the techniques of psychological profiling. Police officers also produce similar profiles but these tend to be more tacitly and experientially based compared with those produced through the application of 'scientific' psychological principles.
91. See McConville et al.'s (1991) discussion for similar trends in respect of 'less serious' types of crime investigation work.
92. Websdale (1999) provides evidence that a significant proportion of male killers have previous convictions for various criminal offences. The fieldwork data from my study confirm that certainly one way in which the police would regularly identify potential suspects was if a person was known to the victim and had previous convictions.
93. Denotes 'trace and interview'.
94. A sociological grounding for this understanding of interpretation is provided by Garfinkel's (1967) discussion of the 'documentary method of interpretation'.
95. My use of the concept of 'collective memory' in this fashion draws on the work of Halbwachs (1992), blended with Mead's (1932) theory of

the past. My reading of both authors suggests that although drawing upon different epistemological traditions, they are seeking to tackle a similar problem. Halbwachs's account is probably more convincing on the consequences of constructing the past, whereas Mead's account is better at capturing the agentive processes of symbolic construction. Therefore a synthesis of the two is both necessary and desirable.

96. This deliberately echoes Mead's (1932) dictum that pasts are always symbolically reconstructed and that people act and then figure out what they did. But whereas Mead was concerned with acting individuals, I have transposed this idea to a collective, societal level.

97. Of course, this doesn't mean that all media coverage of murder investigations is supportive of the police. Rather, what I am discussing here are the over-arching trends present.

References

Ainsworth, P. (1995) *Psychology and Policing in a Changing World*. Chichester: Wiley.

Altheide, D. (1996) *Qualitative Media Analysis*. Thousand Oaks, Calif.: Sage.

Ashworth, A. (1993) *Principles of Criminal Law*. Oxford: Clarendon Press.

—— (1998) *The Criminal Process: An Evaluative Study*. Oxford: Clarendon Press.

—— and B. Mitchell (2000) *Rethinking English Homicide Law*. Oxford: Clarendon Press.

Audit Commission (1993) *Helping with Enquiries: Tackling Crime Effectively*. London: HMSO.

Banton, M. (1964) *The Policeman in the Community*. London: Tavistock.

Becker, H. (1963) *Outsiders: Studies in the Sociology of Deviance*. London: Free Press of Glencoe.

Bennet, L., and M. Feldman (1981) *Reconstructing Reality in the Courtroom: Justice and Judgement in American Culture*. New Brunswick, NJ: Rutgers University Press.

Bittner, E. (1970) *The Functions of the Police in Modern Society*. Chevy Chase, Md.: National Institute of Mental Health.

Black, D. (1976) *The Behaviour of Law*. New York: Academic Press.

—— (1993) *The Social Structure of Right and Wrong*. New York: Academic Press.

Block, R., and C. Block (1992) 'Homicide Syndromes and Vulnerability: Violence in Chicago's Community Areas over 25 Years', *Studies on Crime and Crime Presentation*, 1: 61–85.

Blumer, H. (1969) *Symbolic Interactionism*. Berkeley: University of California Press.

Bottomley, A., and C. Coleman (1982) *Understanding Crime Rates*. London: Gower.

Bourdieu, P. (1990) *The Logic of Practice*. Cambridge: Polity Press.

Bowling, B. (1999) 'The Rise and Fall in New York Murder: Zero Tolerance or Crack's Decline', *The British Journal of Criminology*, 39/4: 531–54.

Box, S. (1983) *Power, Crime and Mystification*. London: Routledge.

Brian-Morgan, J. (1990) *The Police Function and the Investigation of Crime*. London: Gower.

Burgess, R. (1984) *In the Field*. London: George Allen & Unwin.

Burke, K. (1962) *A Grammar of Motives*. Berkeley, Calif.: University of California Press.

Burrows, J., and R. Tarling (1987) 'The Investigation of Crime in England', *The British Journal of Criminology*, 27/3: 229–51.

Byford, L. (1981) 'The Yorkshire Ripper Case: Review of the Police Investigation of the Case', unpublished.

Chan, J. (1997) *Changing Police Culture*. Cambridge: Cambridge University Press.

Chatterton, M. (1976) 'Police in Social Control', in J. King (ed.), *Control Without Custody*. Cambridge: Institute of Criminology.

Cicourel, A. (1968) *The Social Organization of Juvenile Justice*. New York: John Wiley & Sons.

Cohen, S. (1980) *Folk Devils and Moral Panics*, 2nd edn., 1st pub. 1972. London: Palladin.

——(1985) *Visions of Social Control*. Cambridge: Polity Press.

Cole, S. (2001) *Suspect Identities: A History of Fingerprinting and Criminal Identification*. Cambridge, Mass.: Harvard University Press.

Couch, C. (1996) *Information Technologies and Social Orders*. New York: Aldine de Gruyter.

Criminal Statistics England and Wales 1995. London: HMSO.

Criminal Statistics England and Wales 1997. London: HMSO.

Daly, M., and M. Wilson (1988) *Homicide*. New York: Aldine de Gruyter.

Davis, F. (1973) 'The Martian and the Convert: Ontological Polarities in Social Research', *Urban Life*, 3/3: 333–43.

Denzin, N. (1970) *Sociological Methods: A Sourcebook*. Chicago: Aldine de Gruyter.

——(1996) *Interpretative Ethnography*. Thousand Oaks, Calif.: Sage.

Dewey, J. (1933) *How We Think*. London: D. C. Heath.

Dixon, D. (1997) *Law in Policing: Legal Regulation and Police Practices*. Oxford: Clarendon Press.

Doney, R. (1990) 'The Aftermath of the Yorkshire Ripper: The Response of the United Kingdom Police Service', in S. Egger (ed.), *Serial Murder: An Elusive Phenomenon*. Westport, Conn.: Praeger.

Douglas, J. (1967) *The Social Meanings of Suicide*. Princeton: Princeton University Press.

——(1971) *American Social Order*. New York: The Free Press.

Douglas, M. (1966) *Purity and Danger*. London: Routledge & Kegan Paul.

Duster, T. (1971) *The Legislation of Morality*. New York: Free Press.

Eco, U. (1976) *A Theory of Semiotics*. Bloomington, Ind.: Indiana University Press.

——(1983) 'Horns, Hooves, Insteps: Some Hypotheses on Three Types of Induction', in U. Eco and T. Sebeok (eds.), *The Sign of Three*. Bloomington, Ind.: Indiana University Press.

Egger, S. (1990) 'Serial Murder: A Synthesis of Literature and Research', in S. Egger (ed.), *Serial Murder: An Elusive Phenomenon*. Westport, Conn.: Praeger.

English, J., and R. Card (1996) *Butterworths Police Law*, 5th edn. London: Butterworths.

Ericson, R. (1993) *Making Crime: A Study of Detective Work*, 2nd edn. Toronto: Toronto University Press.

—— J. Baranek, and J. Chan (1987) *Visualizing Deviance*. Milton Keynes: Open University Press.

—— and S. Haggarty (1997) *Policing the Risk Society*. Oxford: Clarendon Press.

Feist, A. (1999) *The Effective Use of the Media in Serious Crime Investigations*. London: Home Office.

Fielding, N. (1988) *Joining Forces*. London: Routledge.

—— (1991) *The Police and Social Conflict*. London: Athlone Press.

—— (1995) *Community Policing*. Oxford: Clarendon Press.

Foucault, M. (1977) *Discipline and Punish*. London: Penguin.

Garfinkel, H. (1967) *Studies in Ethnomethodology*. Cambridge: Polity Press.

Garland, D. (1985) *Punishment and Welfare*. Aldershot: Gower.

—— (1990) *Punishment and Modern Society*. Oxford: Clarendon Press.

—— (2001) *The Culture of Control*. Oxford: Oxford University Press.

Geberth, V. (1995) *Practical Homicide Investigation*. New York: CBC Press.

Geertz, C. (1973) *The Interpretation of Cultures*. New York: Basic Books.

Giddens, A. (1984) *The Constitution of Society*. Cambridge: Polity Press.

—— (1991) *Modernity and Self Identity*. Cambridge: Polity Press.

—— (1993) *The New Rules of Sociological Method*, 2nd edn. Cambridge: Polity Press.

Goffman, E. (1952) 'On Cooling the Mark Out: Some Aspects of Adaptations to Failure', *Psychiatry*, 15: 451–61.

—— (1959) *The Presentation of Self in Everyday Life*. London: Penguin.

—— (1961) *Asylums*. London: Penguin.

—— (1963) *Stigma: Notes on the Management of Spoiled Identity*. London: Penguin.

—— (1969) *Strategic Interaction*. Philadelphia: University of Pennsylvania Press.

—— (1974) *Frame Analysis*. Boston, Mass.: Northeastern University Press.

—— (1981) *Forms of Talk*. Philadelphia: University of Pennsylvania Press.

—— (1983) 'The Interaction Order', *The American Sociological Review*, 48: 1–17.

Greenwood, P., J. Chaiken, and J. Petersilia (1977) *The Criminal Investigation Process*. Lexington, Mass.: D. C. Heath.

Gudjonssen, G. (1992) *The Psychology of Interrogations, Confessions and Testimony*. Chichester: Wiley.

——and J. MacKeith (1988) 'Retracted Confessions: Legal, Psychological and Psychiatric Aspects', *Medical Science Law*, 28/3: 187–94.

Gusfield, J. (1981) *The Culture of Public Problems*. Chicago: Chicago University Press.

Halbwachs, M. (1992) *On Collective Memory*, 1st pub. 1941. Chicago: University of Chicago Press.

Hall, S., C. Critchley, T. Jefferson, J. Clarke, and B. Roberts (1978) *Policing the Crisis*. Basingstoke: Macmillan Press Ltd.

Hammersley, M., and P. Atkinson (1983) *Ethnography: Principles in Practice*. London: Tavistock Publications.

Havard, J. (1960) *The Detection of Secret Homicide*. Basingstoke: Macmillan & Co. Ltd.

Hawkins, K. (1983) 'Bargain and Bluff: Compliance Strategy and Deterrence in the Enforcement of Regulation', *Law and Policy Quarterly*, 5: 35–73.

——(1984) *Environment and Enforcement*. Oxford: Clarendon Press.

——(1992) *The Uses of Discretion*. Oxford: Oxford University Press.

Heidensohn, F. (1985) *Women and Crime*. Basingstoke: Macmillan Publishers Ltd.

——(1992) *Women in Control*. Oxford: Clarendon Press.

Her Majesty's Inspectorate of Constabulary (HMIC) (2000) *Policing London, Winning Consent*. London: HMSO.

Herbert, S. (1996) 'Morality in Law Enforcement: Chasing "Bad Guys" with the Los Angeles Police Department', *Law and Society Review*, 30/4: 799–818.

——(1997) *Policing Space*. Minnesota: University of Minnesota Press.

Hobbs, D. (1988) *Doing the Business*. Oxford: Oxford University Press.

Hodge, R., and G. Kress (1988) *Social Semiotics*. New York: Cornell University Press.

Holdaway, S. (1983) *Inside the British Police*. Oxford: Blackwell.

Holmes, R., and S. Holmes (1996) *Profiling Violent Crimes: An Investigative Tool*, 2nd edn. Thousand Oaks, Calif.: Sage.

Hughes, E. (1958) *The Sociological Eye*. New Brunswick, NJ: Transaction Publishers.

Hunt, A. (1993) *Explorations in Law and Society*. London: Routledge.

Hutter, B. (1988) *The Reasonable Arm of the Law?* Oxford: Clarendon Press.

——(1997) *Compliance: Regulation and Environment*. Oxford: Clarendon Press.

Ianni, E., and R. Ianni (1983) 'Street Cops and Management Cops: The Two Cultures of Policing', in M. Punch (ed.), *Control in the Police Organization*. Cambridge, Mass.: MIT Press.

Innes, M. (1999) 'The Media as an Investigative Resource in Murder Enquiries', *The British Journal of Criminology*, 39/2: 269–86.

——(2000) 'Professionalising the Police Informant: The British Experience', *Policing and Society*, 9: 357–83.

——(2002) 'Organisational Communication and the Symbolic Construction of Police Murder Investigations', *British Journal of Sociology*, 53/1: 67–87.

Irving, B., and C. Dunnighan (1993) *Human Factors in the Quality Control of CID Investigations*, Royal Commission on Criminal Justice Research Study No. 21. London: HMSO.

James, W. (1975) *Pragmatism*, 1st pub. 1907. Cambridge, Mass.: Harvard University Press.

Jefferson, T. (1997) 'Masculinities and Crime', in M. Maguire, R. Morgan, and R. Reiner (eds.), *The Oxford Handbook of Criminology*, 2nd edn. Oxford: Oxford University Press.

Jenkins, P. (1992) *Using Murder: The Social Construction of Serial Homicide*. New York: Aldine de Gruyter.

Josephson, J., and S. Josephson (1996) *Abductive Inference: Computation, Philosophy, Technology*. Cambridge: Cambridge University Press.

Katz, J. (1988) *The Seductions of Crime*. New York: Basic Books.

Kind, S. (1987) *The Scientific Investigation of Crime*. London: Forensic Science Service.

Klockars, C. (1985) *The Idea of Police*. Beverly Hills, Calif.: Sage.

Knorr-Cetina, K. (1980) *The Manufacture of Knowledge*. Oxford: Pergamon Press.

——(1999) *Epistemic Cultures*. Cambridge, Mass.: Harvard University Press.

Knox, S. (1998) *Murder: A Tale of Modern American Life*. London: Duke University Press.

Lane, R. (1997) *Murder in America*. Chicago: Ohio State University Press.

Latour, B. (1985) *Science in Action*. Milton Keynes: Open University Press.

——and S. Woolgar (1990) *Representation in Scientific Practice*. Cambridge, Mass.: MIT Press.

Leo, R. (1996) 'Miranda's Revenge: Police Interrogation as a Confidence Game', *Law and Society Review*, 30/2: 259–88.

Levi, M. (1997) 'Violent Crime', in M. Maguire, R. Morgan, and R. Reiner (eds.), *The Oxford Handbook of Criminology*, 2nd edn. Oxford: Oxford University Press.

Leyton, E. (1995) *Men of Blood: Murder in Modern England*. London: Constable.

Lloyd-Bostock, S. (1992) 'The Psychology of Routine Discretion: Accident Screening by British Factory Inspectors', *Law and Policy*, 14/1.

Loader, I. (1997) 'Policing and the Social: Questions of Symbolic Power', *The British Journal of Sociology*, 48/1: 1–18.

Lofland, J., and L. Lofland (1995) *Analyzing Social Settings*. Belmont, Calif.: Wadsworth.

Luckenbill, D. (1977) 'Criminal Homicide as a Situated Transaction', *Social Problems*, 25: 176–86.

Lyman, S., and M. Scott (1970) *A Sociology of the Absurd*. New York: Appleton Century-Crofts.

Lynch, M. (1994) *Scientific Practice and Ordinary Action*. Cambridge: Cambridge University Press.

McBarnet, D. (1979) 'Arrest: The Legal Context of Policing', in S. Holdaway (ed.), *The British Police*. London: Edward Arnold.

——(1981) *Conviction*. London: Macmillan.

McConville, M., A. Sanders, and R. Leng (1991) *The Case for the Prosecution*. London: Routledge.

Mackay, D. (1969) *Information, Mechanism and Meaning*. Cambridge, Mass.: MIT Press.

Macpherson, W. (1999) *Report of an Inquiry into the Investigation of the Murder of Stephen Lawrence*. London: HMSO.

Maguire, M., and C. Norris (1992) *The Conduct and Supervision of Criminal Investigations*, Royal Commission on Criminal Justice Research Study No. 5. London: HMSO.

Maines, D. (1977) 'Social Organization and Social Structure in Symbolic Interactionist Thought', *Annual Review of Sociology*, 3: 235–59.

——(1993) 'Narrative's Moment and Sociology's Phenomena: Toward a Narrative Sociology', *Sociological Quarterly*, 34: 17–38.

——(2001) *The Faultlines of Consciousness*. New York: Aldine de Gruyter.

Manning, P. (1980) *The Narc's Game*. Cambridge, Mass.: MIT Press.

——(1988) *Symbolic Communication*. Cambridge, Mass.: MIT Press.

——(1992) *Organizational Communication*. New York: Aldine de Gruyter.

——(1996) *Semiotics and Fieldwork*. London: Sage.

——(1997) *Police Work: The Social Organization of Policing*, 2nd edn. Prospect Heights, Ill.: Waveland Press.

——(2001) 'Technology's Ways: Information Technology, Crime Analysis and the Rationalizing of Policing', *Criminal Justice*, 1/1: 83–103.

Marx, G. (1988) *Undercover: Police Surveillance in America*. Berkeley: University of California Press.

Matza, D. (1969) *Becoming Deviant*. Englewood Cliffs, NJ: Prentice Hall.

May, H. (2000) 'Who Did What to Whom? Victimization and Culpability in the Social Construction of Murder', *British Journal of Sociology*, 50/3: 488–506.

Mead, G. H. (1932) *The Philosophy of the Present*. Chicago: University of Chicago Press.

——(1934) *Mind, Self and Society from the Standpoint of a Social Behaviourist*. Chicago: University of Chicago Press.

Miller, W. (1979) 'London's Police Tradition in a Changing Society', in S. Holdaway (ed.), *The British Police*. London: Edward Arnold.

Mills, C. Wright (1959) *The Sociological Imagination*. Oxford: Oxford University Press.

Mitchell, B. (1990) *Murder and Penal Policy*. Basingstoke: Macmillan.

Monkkonnen, E. (2001) *Murder in New York City*. Berkeley: University of California Press.

Morris, T., and L. Blom-Cooper (1964) *A Calendar of Murder: Criminal Homicide in England since 1957*. London: Michael Joseph.

Needham, R. (1979) *Symbolic Classification*. Santa Monica, Calif.: Goodyear Publishing Co.

Newburn, T. (1992) *Permission and Regulation*. London: Routledge.

Palmiotto, M. (1994) *Criminal Investigation*. Chicago: Nelson Hall.

Peirce, C. S. (1955) *Philosophical Writings of Peirce*. New York: Dover Publications.

——(1998) *Charles S. Peirce: The Essential Writings*, ed. E. Moore. New York: Prometheus Books.

Plummer, K. (1995) *Telling Sexual Stories*. London: Routledge.

Polk, K. (1994) *When Men Kill*. Cambridge: Cambridge University Press.

Prothero, M. (1929) *The History of the Criminal Investigation Department at Scotland Yard*. London: Herbert Jenkins Ltd.

Punch, M. (1979) *Policing the Inner City*. London: Macmillan.

——(1985) *Conduct Unbecoming*. London: Tavistock.

——(1996) *Dirty Business: Exploring Corporate Misconduct*. London: Sage.

Rachlin, H. (1995) *The Making of a Detective*. New York: W. W. Norton & Co.

Reiner, R. (1991) *Chief Constables*. Oxford: Oxford University Press.

——(1992) *The Politics of the Police*, 2nd edn. Hemel Hempstead: Harvester Wheatsheaf.

——(1994) 'The Dialectics of Dixon: The Changing Image of the TV Cop', in M. Stephens and S. Becker (eds.), *Police Force, Police Service*. Basingstoke: Macmillan.

Ricoeur, P. (1967) *The Symbolism of Evil*. Boston: Beacon Press.

Riley, K., P. Lattimore, J. Leiter, and J. Trudeau (1997) *A Study of Homicide in Eight US Cities*. Washington: National Institute of Justice.

Robertson, B., and R. Vignaux (1995) *Interpreting Evidence: Evaluating Forensic Science in the Courtroom*. Chichester: John Wiley.

Rock, P. (1973) *Making People Pay*. London: Routledge & Kegan Paul.

Rock, P. (1979) *The Making of Symbolic Interactionism*. London: Macmillan.

—— (1993) *The Social World of an English Crown Court*. Oxford: Clarendon Press.

—— (1998*a*) *After Homicide: Practical and Political Responses to Bereavement*. Oxford: Clarendon Press.

—— (1998*b*) 'Murderers, Victims and Survivors: The Social Construction of Deviance', *The British Journal of Criminology*, 38/2: 185–200.

Sanders, A. (1997) 'From Suspect to Trial', in M. Maguire, R. Morgan, and R. Reiner (eds.), *The Oxford Handbook of Criminology*, 2nd edn. Oxford: Oxford University Press.

Sanders, W. (1977) *Detective Work*. New York: Free Press.

Sebeok, T., and J. Umiker-Sebeok (1983) 'You Know My Method: A Juxtaposition of Charles S. Peirce and Sherlock Holmes', in U. Eco and T. Sebeok (eds.), *The Sign of Three*. Bloomington, Ind.: Indiana University Press.

Schlesinger, P., and H. Tumber (1994) *Reporting Crime: The Media Politics of Criminal Justice*. Oxford: Clarendon Press.

Shank, G. (2001) 'It's Logic in Practice, My Dear Watson', *Forum: Qualitative Social Research*, 2/1, http://qualitative-research.net/fqs-texte/1-01/1-01shank-e.ht.

Shearing, C., and R. Ericson (1991) 'Culture as Figurative Action', *The British Journal of Sociology*, 42/4: 481–506.

Shibutani, T. (1970) 'Personified Adversaries', in T. Shibutani (ed.), *Human Nature and Collective Behaviour: Papers in Honour of Herbert Blumer*. Englewood Cliffs, NJ: Prentice Hall.

Silverman, D. (1993) *Interpreting Qualitative Data*. London: Sage.

Simon, D. (1991) *Homicide: A Year on the Killing Streets*. London: Coronet Books.

Skolnick, J. (1994) *Justice Without Trial*, 3rd edn. New York: Wiley.

Smith, D., and J. Gray (1983) *Police and People in London, vol. iv. The Police in Action*. London: Policy Studies Institute.

Smith, J., and B. Hogan (1992) *Criminal Law*, 7th edn. London: Butterworths.

Smith, N., and C. Flanagan (2000) *The Effective Detective*. London: HMSO.

Sparks, R. (1992) *Television and the Drama of Crime*. Buckingham: Open University Press.

Steer, D. (1980) *Uncovering Crime*, Royal Commission on Criminal Procedure Research Study No. 7. London: HMSO.

Stockdale, J. (1993) *Management and Supervision of Police Interviews*, Police Research Group, Police Research Series Paper 5. London: Home Office.

Sudnow, D. (1965) 'Normal Crimes: Sociological Features of the Penal Code in a Public Defenders Office', *Social Problems*, 12: 203–19.

Swanson, C., N. Chamelin, and L. Territo (1996) *Criminal Investigation*, 6th edn. New York: McGraw-Hill.

Sykes, G., and D. Matza (1957) 'Techniques of Neutralization: A Theory of Delinquency', *American Sociological Review*, 22: 664–70.

Tamanaha, B. (1997) *Realistic Socio-Legal Studies*. Oxford: Clarendon Press.

Van Maanen, J. (1978) 'The Asshole', in P. K. Manning and J. Van Maanen (eds.), *Policing: A View From the Street*. Santa Monica, Calif.: Goodyear.

Vaughan, D. (1996) *The Challenger Launch Decision*. Chicago: University of Chicago Press.

Waddington, P. (1994) *Liberty and Order: Public Order Policing in a Capital City*. London: UCL Press.

Websdale, N. (1999) *Understanding Domestic Homicide*. Boston: Northeastern University Press.

Weick, K. (1995) *Sense-Making in Organizations*. Thousand Oaks, Calif.: Sage.

Williams, G. (1958) *The Sanctity of Life and the Criminal Law*. London: Faber & Faber.

Williams, R. (2001) 'An Improvised Practice: Report to Durham Constabulary', unpublished.

Willmer, M. (1970) *Crime and Information Theory*. Edinburgh: University of Edinburgh Press.

Wilson, J. Q. (1968) *Varieties of Police Behaviour*. Cambridge, Mass.: Harvard University Press.

Wolfgang, M. (1958) *Patterns in Criminal Homicide*. Philadelphia: University of Pennsylvania Press.

Young, J. (1999) *The Exclusive Society*. London: Sage.

Young, M. (1991) *An Inside Job: Policing and Police Culture in Britain*. Oxford: Oxford University Press.

Zander, M. (1979) 'The Investigation of Crime: A Study of Cases Tried at the Old Bailey', *Criminal Law Review*, 203–19.

Index